THE HISTORY OF
THE ROYAL GEOGRAPHICAL SOCIETY 1830-1980

To the Farthest Ends of the Earth

IAN CAMERON

Forewords by David Attenborough and John Hunt

MACDONALD

Macdonald and Jane's · London and Sydney

First published in 1980 in Great Britain by
Macdonald General Books
Macdonald and Jane's Publishers Limited
Paulton House
8 Shepherdess Walk
London N1 7LW

ISBN 0 354 04478 8

Filmset in 'Monophoto' Baskerville by
Servis Filmsetting Limited, Manchester
Printed and Bound in Great Britain by
Hazell, Watson and Viney Limited, Aylesbury

The Society has sent explorers and scientists to almost every country on earth. The diversity of its expeditions is reflected in the first few illustrations:—

The Society's expeditions have added enormously to our knowledge and understanding of the world we live in.

FRONT END-PAPERS:
Elephant on the Shire River being fired at from Livingstone's launch the Ma Robert.
HALF TITLE:
The mist wreathed foothills of Gunung Mulu, photographed during the Society's recent expedition to the rain forests of Sarawak (© Royal Geographical Society Expedition to Mulu).
FRONTISPIECE:
Native boats on a tributary of the River Amazon.

BACK AND END PAPERS:
Endpapers: family of Nomadic Penan in the Gunung Mulu National Park, Sarawak (© Alan Hutchinson).

"We shall go
Always a little further: it may be
    Beyond that last blue mountain barred with snow,
Across that angry or that glimmering sea."

Hassan: James Elroy Flecker

Shiwakte: one of the highest peaks of the Chinese Pamirs, first photographed by Clarmont P. Skrine in 1926

Contents

Acknowledgements

I should like to thank the Royal Geographical Society for their help.

A formal "thank you" for the use of their library, archives and map room. Without access to these the book could not have been written.

Also a personal "thank you" for all their kindness, patience and encouragement while I have been working on the book. From the President to the lady who makes the tea in the kitchen, almost everyone at the Society has made me feel not only a colleague but a friend. My special thanks are due to the President, Lord Hunt; to the Director, John Hemming; and to the Keeper of the Map Room, George Hardy. Also to the librarian, George Dugdale and his assistants, and to the archivist, Christine Kelly. To Dorothy Middleton for help with the chapter on Africa; to Margaret Shinnie for help with the history of the *Journal*; to Professor Mead for advice on the educational work of the Society; to Maryanne Chandor for all her help; to Nigel Winser and Shane Wesley-Smith for help relating to the Society's expedition to Mulu; to Jane Gordon and Deborah Boys – it seems almost unfair that any one person should have *two* such efficient and charming assistants. And last but very far from least to Rosemary Reed, for work "beyond the call of duty" in locating and identifying almost all the illustrations in the book – well over 300 of them – out of the Society's enormous collection of pictures and photographs.

In the text quotations from the Society's records and publications are made by permission of the R.G.S. Quotations from *Cooper's Creek* and *The White Nile* by Alan Moorehead and from *Man and the Conquest of the Poles* by Paul-Emile Victor are by permission of Laurence Pollinger Ltd. and Hamish Hamilton Ltd. Quotations from *High Adventure* by Sir Edmund Hillary are by permission of Hodder and Stoughton. The quotation from *Mount Everest: Formation, Population and Exploration* by Toni Hagen, Günter-Oskar Dyhrenfurth, Christof von Fürer-Haimendorf and Erwin Schneider is by permission of the Oxford University Press. The quotation from *A History of Polar Exploration* by David Mountfield is by permission of The Hamlyn Publishing Group Ltd. Quotations from *Everest: the Challenge* by Sir Francis Younghusband are by permission of Thomas Nelson and Sons Ltd. The quotation from *Abode of Snow* by Kenneth Mason is by permission of Granada Publishing Ltd. And the quotation from Prof. H. P. Moon's book *Henry Walter Bates* is by permission of the Leicestershire Museums Art Galleries and Records Service.

All illustrations are reproduced by permission of the Royal Geographical Society with the exceptions listed below. Every effort has been made to ensure that the copyright of the pictures, where applicable, is here acknowledged.

The illustrations on pages 46 and 47, Eyre and his Aborigine guide on page 49, Sturt leaving Adelaide on page 52, the photograph of Darwin on page 55, the illustrations on pages 62 and 63, and Gregory's camp site on page 65 are reproduced by courtesy of the Australian Information Service, London. The portrait of Charles Sturt on page, 52, that of Samuel Baker on page 90, and of Charles George Gordon on page 105 are reproduced by permission of the National Portrait Gallery. The illustrations on pages 112 and 113 are from a copy of the *Illustrated London News* in the private collection of Felix Brenner. The photographs on page 116, and that of rough sledging over Polar ice on page 272 © Wally Herbert/Robert Harding Associates. Pressure ridges on page 133, white out on page 134, Shackleton's hut and interiors on page 151, Scott's hut and stables on page 154 and the Hercules aircraft in the Antarctic on page 272: Jeremy Sutton-Pratt: photographs taken during the 1976–77 New Zealand Antarctic Research Programme. The illustrations on pages 171, 172, 173, and 174 are reproduced by kind permission of Captain John Noel. The illustrations on page 208, the entrance hall and reading room, and the photograph of John Hemming on page 257 are reproduced courtesy of Homer Sykes. Phases in the spoliation of a rain forest (cutting down and burning trees, and irrigating a ranch) on page 211, illustrations on pages 214, 218, 219, 220, 222 and 223; Douglas Botting. The plane landing on page 220, the driving in of cattle on page 211, the inset on 213, and the illustration on page 216 are reproduced courtesy of Alan Hutchinson. The illustration on page 212–13 is reproduced by kind permission of R. F. Montgomery. The illustrations on pages 225, 226, 228, 229, 230, 231 and 232 were taken on the Royal Geographical Society Expedition to Musandam, photographer Norman Falcon. The illustrations on pages 233, 234, 236, 238, 239, 240, 242, 243, 244, 245, 246, 247, 248, 249 and 251 are reproduced by courtesy of the Royal Geographical Society and members of the R.G.S. Mulu (Sarawak) Expedition. The photograph of Eric Shipton on page 270 is reproduced by permission of Bassano and Van Dyk. The illustration on page 279 is reproduced by courtesy of the Royal Geographical Society and Keith Shackleton.

The maps of North Polar Regions and South Polar Regions were drawn from *The International Reference Atlas* by J. G. Bartholomew Ltd., published by George Newnes Ltd., 1918. That of Australia is from *A New General Atlas of the World* by John Doner, published by Henry Teesdale & Co., 1834. The maps and decorative vignettes for N.W. Passage and Africa are from *The Royal Illustrated Atlas of Modern Geography* by Dr. Norton Shaw, honorary secretary of the Royal Geographical Society, published by A. Fullarton & Co., 1864.

Foreword

During the 150 years of our history, the Royal Geographical Society has reflected characteristics of our island's race passed down from an earlier tradition. That tradition was founded, in part, upon the forces of circumstance; but in greater part it stemmed from a spirit of quest, a curiosity to discover what lay beyond the seas, an urge to reach out towards the ends of the earth. This period of history embraced the rise and demise of our Empire; or rather transformed it into a commonwealth of nations whose links were forged under the seal of the Pax Britannica.

This book describes a period of British exploration which reached its peak in the second half of the nineteenth century, when the Empire also achieved fulfilment. But in the aftermath of that Golden Age our explorers have continued to extend, in less spectacular ways, our knowledge of the Earth. I think it appropriate that the part played by our Society in this continuing task of discovery, recorded as it was at the earlier landmark of 50 and 100 years by two distinguished Fellows, should at this point in time have been appraised, and the facts made available to a wider public by an independent witness. Ian Cameron has done a fine job in telling the story of the RGS in a style which everyone can enjoy.

THE LORD HUNT OF LLANFAIR WATERDINE, K.G., C.B.E., D.S.O.

Foreword

Explorers are not, perhaps, the most promising people with whom to build a Society. Indeed, some might say that explorers become explorers precisely because they have a streak of unsociability and a need to remove themselves at regular intervals as far as possible from their fellow men. Yet explorers also need a meeting place in which to compare notes and find rivals, a library and map room in which to deposit their findings, even an audience to applaud their exploits, and a hundred and fifty years ago, a small group of them set about founding an institution which would provide such things, as well as pursue the more scientific and altruistic aims which appear in its formal list of objectives. But the very nature of the men and women who were to join the new Royal Geographical Society ensured that within its meetings and its journals, there would be dramas and debates, famous quarrels and doughty rivalries. Indeed, the history of the R.G.S. is full of excitements – the arguments about the sources of the great rivers of Africa, the race to reach the Poles, the repeated assaults on Mount Everest.

The Society has only occupied its present headquarters since 1913, but even so, the personalities of its pioneering members are easy to discover there. The building itself looks like the luxurious country home of a wealthy Edwardian family, sitting snugly facing Kensington Gardens, close by those great Victorian temples to art, science and the acquisition of knowledge, the Victoria and Albert and the Natural History Museums. But inside it, you find exotic relics brought back from what were once, and in many cases still are, the wildest corners of the globe – the chair in which the dying Livingstone was carried on his last wanderings in central Africa and a section of the tree trunk beneath which he was buried; the diary kept by Lord Hunt during the ascent of Everest; the sledge that carried Mawson across the Antarctic; and the magnificent pictures painted by Baines of the newly-discovered Victoria Falls. Its walls are hung with panels listing the expeditions that the Society has supported and the names of the men and women to whom it has awarded its coveted medals. As well as the household names like Scott and Livingstone, there are those of many other great travellers who unaccountably have never received the fame that was their due – Schomburgk who explored Guyana, Barth who crossed the western Sahara, and Eyre, Leichardt, Gregory and Stuart who travelled through country as demanding as the Antarctic, who tackled geographical mysteries as baffling as any in Africa, and who opened up the interior of Australia.

The men on those lists are the great heroes of exploration, and then rank so throughout the world. But, as is the way with heroes, they themselves, by their own labours, brought an end to the heroic age. The blanks on the maps were slowly filled by the information they discovered. More travellers followed in their wake meticulously observing, measuring, surveying, sketching and collecing. The Society's journals chronicled their findings, its map room collated their surveys. As geographical knowledge grew, so the Royal Geographical Society changed. Today, no substantial part of the land surface of the earth remains unmapped. But now the shape of a landscape is known, the need is to discover exactly what animals and plants live on it, what rocks it is made of and what are the processes that are continuing to shape it. That work requires the skills of a multitude of specialists and so the Society has been sending out a new kind of expedition made up of a large group of scientists, sometimes operating in relays, who make a sustained investigation, lasting may be several years, of a little-known region. So the second one hundred and fifty years of the Society's history will certainly be very different from the first. But the stimulus that sends its members on arduous journeys to remote places will surely remain the same; and the Society, thankfully, will continue to serve them.

DAVID ATTENBOROUGH, C.B.E.

Introduction

WHEN THE ROYAL GEOGRAPHICAL SOCIETY WAS FOUNDED IN THE SUMMER OF 1830, large areas of the world were still unmapped, and geography was a subject which aroused little enthusiasm either among the public or among academics. How different the situation is today, when there are no longer blank spaces on the map, when almost every area on earth has been scientifically studied, and geography is one of the most common and popular subjects at schools and universities throughout the world.

No institution has done more to bring about this change than the Royal Geographical Society, whose story, it has been claimed with some truth, is "Nothing less than the history of nineteenth- and twentieth-century British exploration".

Our theme, therefore, is an epic one: how the last of the blank spaces on the map came to be filled in. How Franklin discovered a North West Passage – and paid for his discovery with his life; how Speke unravelled the two-thousand-year-old mystery of the sources of the Nile; how Peary won fame at the North Pole, and Scott immortality at the South; how Hillary and Tenzing became the first men to set foot on the summit of the world. The archives of the Society throw fresh light on these great feats of exploration.

But all this, you may say, is in the past. What of the future? Surely now that there are no more virgin shores to chart nor unclimbed mountain ranges to triangulate, the Society has become an anachronism?

The truth is just the opposite. . . . Geography is a progressive science, and in recent years its emphasis has shifted from discovery to investigation, to the compilation and dissemination of knowledge, which the Society has always been particularly interested in and particularly good at. Such work may lack the glamour of hauling sledges to the Pole, but at a time when man is interested as never before in the world he lives in, it is very much in keeping with the needs and spirit of the age. It would therefore be true to say that on its hundred-and-fiftieth anniversary the Society can look back on a stirring past with pride, and forward to a useful future with confidence.

1. The Founding of The Society

IT WAS MIDSUMMER, BUT THE APPROACHES TO THE SOUTH SHETLAND ISLANDS WERE still choked with ice, and His Majesty's sloop *Chanticleer* was hard-pressed to make a landing.

"5th January 1829," Lieutenant Kendall wrote in his diary, "the partial clearing of the fog brought to view the desolate lands of Shetland. The first descried was a mountainous island, the westernmost of the group, called Smith's Island; and a more dreary aspect of rugged barrenness I never beheld. It rises abruptly from the water's edge, and towers to a height of between six and seven thousand feet, and might readily be mistaken for a mighty iceberg, but for a few patches where the sides, too perpendicular to retain snow, allow the blackness of the rock to show through. Icebergs in great numbers were strewed in every direction, no fewer than eighty-one being counted at one time. A heavy tide-rip was running; and the height of the land – which we had approached too closely in consequence of the fog – becalmed the sails, which flapped uselessly against the masts, so that the ship was driven to and fro at the mercy of the currents."

After charting, with some difficulty, the coast of Smith's Island, the *Chanticleer* managed to land a group of seamen in the flooded crater of nearby Deception Island. Once ashore, Kendall "set out to survey the island with four men, sleeping at night on the cindery beach with no other covering than a canvas tent. . . . Before leaving," he wrote, "we buried a register thermometer, so that any future visitor might become acquainted with the extreme ranges of this inhospitable climate."

Kendall's diary was not a specially remarkable document. It did, however, typify the increasingly scientific attitude with which explorers began to regard their calling in the years immediately after the Napoleonic Wars – an earlier expedition would never have thought of leaving behind a thermometer. Perhaps because it reflected so exactly this new attitude, Kendall's diary was one of the first papers to be read and published by the newly-founded Geographical Society of London.

This Society, founded in 1830, began life in the guise of an exclusive club. Yet within thirty years it was leading the world – as it has continued to lead it since – not only in exploration but also in geographical research. To understand how this came about, we need to know something both of the scientific atmosphere in which the Society was conceived, and of the exclusive climate of the London in which it was nurtured.

Nothing is wholly new under the sun; and the so-called "new" approach to geography in fact had its roots firmly in the past – as long ago as 500 B.C. the Greeks defined geography as γεω γραφία (the description or study of the earth) and compiled lists of

(On facing page)
The Antarctic islands sighted by Kendall are among the most desolate in the world. An American sealer coined the classic description of them: "when Mother Nature fashion'd these methinks She must have been drinking!"

15

*Sir John Barrow
(1764–1848), one of the
seven founding fathers of the
Society whose portraits
follow. For forty years
Secretary to the Admiralty,
he master-minded the search
for a North West Passage*

*Robert Brown
(1773–1858). Described by
Humboldt as "facile
Botanicorum Princeps",
his appointment to the
Society's committee was
evidence of the new scientific
approach to geography*

botanical specimens, while no-one could doubt the commitment to science of an eighteenth-century explorer such as Cook. It would, however, be fair to say that in the early nineteenth century men like Humboldt and Ritter did bring about a change in the concept of what geography was about. Before them, its essence had been descriptive narrative. After them, its essence was detailed investigation in a number of specialized disciplines – botany, for example, or hydrography, geology or geomorphology. The men who helped to found the Society were very conscious of this increasingly scientific attitude. Three of them – Murchison, Smyth and Brown – were among the leading authorities in the world in their particular discipline; and their influence ensured a serious and forward-thinking outlook in what might otherwise have become no more than just another fashionable club.

Regency London provided the right climate in which such a progressively-minded Society could flourish.

In 1815, at the end of more than twenty years of conflict, the aristocratic hierarchy in England who had controlled the prosecution of the war found itself at the head of a stable and increasingly prosperous society. This hierarchy may have been exclusive, but its ideas were far-ranging – men like Bentham, the radical jurist, and Wilberforce, the opponent of slavery, could hardly be accused of fearing innovation. It would therefore be fair to say that although the climate of Regency London was aristocratic it was not unsympathetic to what Woodwood describes as "the increasing pace of change, that great stir and movement which was taking place in every sphere of society". One of the most effective ways of bringing about change was by the formation of clubs or societies dedicated to a particular cause. These had long been a feature of the British way of life, and before the Royal Geographical Society was conceived there had been several organizations in London whose interest in geography was peripheral. Three of these can claim to be the RGS's ancestors: the Royal Society (founded in 1665), the African Association (founded in 1788) and the Raleigh Travellers' Club (founded in 1826). It was among the members of the last named that the idea of forming a new Society, dedicated exclusively to the promotion of geography, was first put forward.

The Raleigh Club was a dining club. It had no more than forty members, all distinguished travellers, the idea being that at fortnightly dinners each member in turn should present a meal consisting of specialities from whatever part of the world he had been travelling in – their first dinner, for example, consisted of reindeer from Spitsbergen, rye-cake from North Cape, and crystallized berries from Lapland, washed down by jars of Swedish brandy.

On 24th May, 1830 it was submitted to a well-attended meeting "that a Society is needed whose sole object shall be the promotion of that most important and entertaining branch of knowledge – geography: and that a useful Society might therefore be formed, under the name of the *Geographical Society of London*".

This motion was carried without dissent, and the members then proceeded to draw up a list of the new Society's objectives: objectives which have been adhered to so faithfully for a hundred and fifty years that they might still today be regarded as the Society's creed.

"1. To collect, digest and print . . . new interesting facts and discoveries.

2. To accumulate a library of the best books on geography, and a complete collection of maps and charts from the earlier period to the present time.

3. To procure specimens of such instruments as are useful to the compendious stock of a traveller.

4. To prepare instructions for such as are setting out on their travels . . . pointing out the researches most essential to make, phenomena to be observed etc. [in order] to obtain such information as may tend to the extension of geographical knowledge.

And it is hoped that the Society may ultimately be enabled from its funds to render pecuniary assistance to such travellers as may require it, in order to facilitate the attainment of some particular object of research.

5. To correspond with similar Societies in different parts of the world, with foreign individuals engaged in geographical pursuits, and with British residents in the remote settlements of the Empire.

6. To open communication with all those philosophical and literary societies with which geography is connected; for as [we] all are fellow-labourers in different departments of the same vineyard, our united efforts cannot fail mutually to assist each other."

The affairs of the new Society were entrusted to a committee of six, all members of the Raleigh Club. These six determined the path on which the RGS set forth and was subsequently to follow, so it is of more than passing interest to see what manner of men they were.

The Chairman, Sir John Barrow, got his first job at the age of fourteen in a Liverpool iron foundry; here he displayed the two qualities which were later to take him to the top of his profession, an immense aptitude for hard work and a lively sense of adventure – as evidence of the latter he was the first passenger in England to make a balloon flight with the Italian pioneer Lunardi, and at the age of fifteen was crewing aboard an Arctic whaler. Later he served with distinction on diplomatic missions to China and on the embassy staff in the Cape of Good Hope. He returned to England in 1803 and was appointed Permanent Secretary to the Admiralty, a position he held for close on forty years. His place within the hierarchy at the Admiralty made him a valuable ally for the Society, and he has been nicely described as "the warmest and most powerful friend to geographical science".

The only man on the committee who never aspired to a title was Robert Brown, the son of an Episcopalian minister. Brown qualified as a doctor, but his heart belonged to the plants which from an early age he collected, studied and classified with an almost obsessive singleness of mind. His discovery of a new type of moss led to his appointment as the botanist on Flinders's expedition to Australia. It was a case of the right man being in the right place at the right time; and during the first circumnavigation of the continent Brown classified its *flora* with such skill that Humboldt awarded him the nickname "*facile Botanicorum Princeps*". Once back in England, this shy, kindly and unassuming man was appointed for life as Keeper of Botany to the British Museum.

A very different character was John Cam Hobhouse, who later succeeded to his father's title as Lord Broughton. Hobhouse held important positions in the government, first as Secretary for Ireland, then as President of the Board of Control. His reputation as a geographer, however, rests on a single and not very substantial work, *A Journey Through Albania*; and about all his contemporaries have to say of him is that he was a "typical English country gentleman, fond of sport". One suspects that his election may have been due to his title.

The same could possibly be true of Sir Bartholomew Frere. We know little about Sir Bartholomew except that he was educated at Harrow and Cambridge, and was "a well-read geographer and scholar, to which accomplishments were added the finest qualities of the heart, a playful wit and the most engaging manners". It is perhaps a little hard on him that his biographers have damned him with such faint praise!

A committee member of more substance was the Hon. Mountstuart Elphinstone, who served for the greater part of his life in the East India Company and had a distinguished career both as diplomat and scholar. He led a successful mission to Afghanistan, became Governor of Bombay, and on retiring to England devoted the rest of his life to his monumental work *A History of Moghul Rule in India*. He brought to the affairs of the Society a considerable knowledge of the East and an aura of literary distinction.

Lord Broughton (1786–1869). Statesman, liberal pamphleteer and travelling companion of Lord Byron

Bartholomew (Bartle) Frere (1778–1851). Diplomat and long-serving member of the Society's committee

The Hon. Mountstuart Elphinstone (1779–1859). Diplomat, scholar and one of the leading authorities of his day on India

Sir Roderick Impey Murchison (1792–1871). "The father of British geology." Friend and supporter of Livingstone, he devoted his life to the advance of geographical knowledge

(On the facing page) Waterloo Place, with the Duke of York's Column and Carlton House Terrace, 1831: site of the Society's first home

Watercolour by Robert Schomburgk: "Trading post at the mouth of the Cayuni River, Gayana, 1836"

The youngest member of the committee was Sir Roderick Murchison, only thirty-eight at the time of his election. For many years Murchison led a conventional life, first as a soldier eager for action and then as a sporting squire – he was, we are told, "one of the greatest fox-hunters in the north of England". Then, largely through the influence of his wife, he became interested in geology. It wasn't in his nature to do things by halves; he sold his hunters, took what we would now describe as a crash course in chemistry at the Royal Institution in Albemarle Street, and devoted the rest of his life to the study of fossils and rocks. It was he more than any other man whose researches led to the classification of the oldest-known fossiliferous rocks and he has been aptly described as the father of Palaeozoic geology.

The committee's first step was to invite another member of the Raleigh Club, Admiral William Smyth, to join them. "When Smyth hoves in sight," wrote a contemporary, "he always has a joke at the mast-head." There was, however, a great deal more to the Admiral than a penchant for humour. He was a brilliant hydrographer – one of the co-founders, with Maury, of the science of oceanography – and in the years to come he was to show more common sense than most of his colleagues in helping to rescue the Society from the shoals of insolvency.

With Smyth a member of the committee and Barrow its chairman, it is hardly surprising that its early meetings were held in the Admiralty; and we can picture the founder-members sitting down that summer in the Permanent Secretary's offices to debate the Society's constitution, the enrolment of new members and the perennial problems of premises, patronage and finance. They did a good job. Within eight weeks of its conception the new Society had a draft constitution, 460 members, and King William IV, "the sailor king", as its patron; and it wasn't long before it began to channel its energies into the two tasks which have occupied it from that day to this: the encouragement of certain specific expeditions and the dissemination of all types of geographical knowledge.

If one looks at the expeditions aided by the Society (Appendix Three) one is struck first by their number and diversity, and second by those that are *not* there. There is, for example, no mention of what was probably the greatest voyage of the nineteenth century (Ross's penetration of the Antarctic), very little about the famous treks across the Australian deserts, and hardly a mention of the arduous journeys which opened up South America; and the fact is that the Society wasn't directly involved with many great feats of exploration. It was, however, nearly always indirectly involved: offering advice behind the scenes, using its influence to secure government patronage, using its association with the Navy to obtain ships and crews, oiling the diplomatic wheels by which every expedition has to be set in motion, and above all (when the explorers had done their work) by publishing their results. This is not to imply that the expeditions which the Society did support were infrequent or unimportant. On the contrary: its efforts in this respect were herculean. In the first few years of its life, for example, it helped to send Back to Northern Canada, Schomburgk to Guiana, Alexander to Southern Africa and Ainsworth to Kurdistan – a programme of exploration which taxed its financial resources beyond the limit of prudence.

Perhaps the most fruitful of these expeditions was Schomburgk's.

Robert Hermann Schomburgk was born in Saxony in 1804, son of a Protestant minister. He first came to the notice of the RGS when his paper *Remarks on Anegada* was read at a meeting in the summer of 1832. Anegada is the most northerly of the Virgin Islands and Schomburgk's survey of it was prompted in the first place by the fact that it had been the scene of more than fifty shipwrecks since the turn of the century. It was, however, more than shoals which Schomburgk charted. His work turned out to be so well-informed and comprehensive that the Society commissioned him to explore the virgin interior of British Guiana on the South American mainland, paying special

attention to the *flora* and to obtaining astronomical fixes which it was hoped would complement the work of Humboldt on the Orinoco. Schomburgk spent five arduous but rewarding years in Guiana, and as Markham tells us "sent home most interesting accounts of the physical aspects of the region, its vegetation and scenery . . . he [also] made Humboldt's work more complete, constructed excellent maps, and brought back large and valuable collections [of plants]". His expeditions are typical of many hundreds which, in years to come, the Society was to support: meticulous, unspectacular, leading to no dramatic discovery or conclusion, but adding another well-documented fragment to man's knowledge of his planet.

The exploits of Alexander and Ainsworth were not so meritorious.

Captain James Alexander, an officer of the 42nd Highlanders, agreed to lead an expedition which it was hoped would push inland along one of the rivers that flow into Delagoa Bay on the east coast of Africa; for this he was given £1,000 (£500 by the Government and £500 by the Society). He got as far as Cape Town, but then embarked on a glorified hunting safari through the interior of what is now Cape Province and Namibia. He did a certain amount of genuine exploring and managed to push as far north as Walvis Bay – no mean feat through the barren hinterland of the Namib. Walvis Bay, however, is on the west coast of Africa, not the east! And Alexander left in his wake a trail of slaughtered animals and debts for ammunition which he expected the Society to settle.

William Henry Smyth (1788–1865). Naval officer and hydrographer who piloted the Society out of the shoals of insolvency

Ainsworth's expedition was equally disputatious. William Ainsworth was an accomplished naturalist and writer, known to the Society both as an authority on the *flora* of the Euphrates valley and as editor of the Edinburgh *Journal of Natural and Geographical Science*. He was also a pillar of the Church; and in 1837 he put forward the idea of taking an expedition to Kurdistan to contact the Nestorian Christians who lived in the mountainous region along the borders of Turkey, Iran and Iraq. For this he was given £500 by the Society for the Propagation of Christian Knowledge and £500 by the RGS. One of Ainsworth's first steps was to appoint as co-leader a Mr. Rassam of Mosul (not to be confused with the Hormuzd Rassam who later assisted Layard). All we are told of Mr. Rassam is that he "had a face like an Assyrian sculpture"; but reading between the lines it is obvious that neither he nor Ainsworth was overblessed with tact. They fell foul of both Turkish and Armenian officials, ran up a staggering accumulation of debts, and then expected their sponsors to bail them out. In the end the Society found itself obliged to contribute nearly £2,000 towards an expedition whose results, though interesting, failed to come up to expectations.

While admiring the young Society for its enterprise and enthusiasm in supporting these projects, one can not help thinking that a more businesslike approach might have served it better. For by the end of the decade it was bankrupt.

One aspect of its work, however, prospered from the start and continued through the good years and the bad with undiminished vigour: this was its publication and dissemination of knowledge.

It may sound unexciting: listening to reports presented often not by the explorers themselves but by members of the RGS committee. But what reports they were! Pick up any one of the Society's nineteenth-century *Journals*, and you will find a cornucopia of information: a treasure trove, in which some remote corner of the earth is spotlit and for the first time examined by the beam of scientific appraisal. It is like holding up a jewel to the light: the brighter the beam – that is to say the more intelligent the appraiser – the more many-splendoured the jewel is seen to be.

(On the facing page) Two views of HMS Enterprise, *captain Richard Collinson, trapped by ice during the search for Sir John Franklin. Painted by Lieutenant J. B. Anderson, R.N.*

Today the media dispense information with such facility that it is hard for us to realize how little people who lived in the mid-nineteenth century knew of their planet. At a time when the masses were largely illiterate and had hardly any access to information except by word of mouth, what *could* they know of South Sea islands, the desolation of the

Ice pinnacles on the Remu Glacier, East Karakoram: photographed by De Filippi's expedition, 1915

tundra or the emptiness of the desert? It would be idle to pretend that they learned of these things direct from the *Journal*. But the *Journal* was the fountain-head, the source from which information subsequently filtered down, via word of mouth, via libraries, via other journals and societies, via books, magic lantern lectures, photographs, newspapers and finally via schools, to a public who the more information they were given the more they wanted.

And how wide the coverage of the *Journal* was, both geographically and scientifically. Take the first volume for example – by no means a special issue and less than a quarter the size of many subsequent editions. To mention only half its contents, it has papers on Western Australia, the South Shetland Islands, Panama, the Black Sea, Morocco, the Straits of Magellan, the coast of Arakan, the River Niger, the Bering Strait, East Greenland and the Cocos Islands. And the information contained in these papers is not only of interest but often of the greatest importance. In the paper on Australia, for example, we find judgments such as: "A pastoral life will probably prove more profitable than an agricultural one. In particular the hills, though rugged, are capable of becoming very good sheep pasture." (Sheep were to be the mainstay of Australia's economy for more than a hundred years.) While on the factual and scientific level the Australian paper includes translations of over 200 Aboriginal words and descriptions of over 200 animals and plants.

If we read the paper on Panama we find:

"The quantity of rain is prodigious. In the wet season it descends in torrents frequently accompanied by storms of thunder and lightning of the most terrific description, the whole province becomes intersected by rivers or quebrada which are impossible to pass, while roads become the beds of streams. . . . The dampness and unhealthiness of the climate [of Porto Bello], combined with the heat, so enervates the constitution that the first attack of an epidemic is generally fatal; and though medical men of eminence have occasionally been induced to settle here, they have seldom found their medicines and learning sufficient to guard even themselves against the effects of the climate. The city has thus acquired the title *La Sepultura de los Europeanos.*"

If Ferdinand de Lesseps had known these facts, he would not so seriously have underestimated the difficulties of building a canal through the isthmus. On the more technical level the Panama paper contains a classified list of nearly a hundred species of indigenous wood, four specimens of each type being deposited with the Society.

As for Kendall's report from the South Shetland Islands, it seems, with its descriptions of flooded craters, icebergs and tide-rips, to epitomize all the romance that is conjured up by the word "exploration". Papers such as these were read with increasing frequency throughout the latter two-thirds of the century; and the most valuable work of the Society has probably been the encouragement, advice, assistance and publicity given to the great multitude of little-known expeditions which over the years have added more strands to the ever-expanding web of our geographical knowledge.

Yet having said this, it is the big dramatic expeditions which lodge in the mind. And as though instinctively acknowledging this, the Society has tended at different times in its history to concentrate its efforts on certain great themes of exploration. In its early years, for example, its main preoccupation was the search for a North West Passage, with ship after ship being sent out in the wake first of Ross and then of Franklin. Towards the middle of the century it concentrated its attention on Africa in general and the search for the sources of the Nile in particular. At the end of the century it devoted itself principally to the Antarctic, while in the 1920s and '30s its main preoccupation was the ascent of Everest.

These great feats of exploration can often be seen in a new light when viewed through the eyes of the Society which inaugurated and brought them to a successful conclusion.

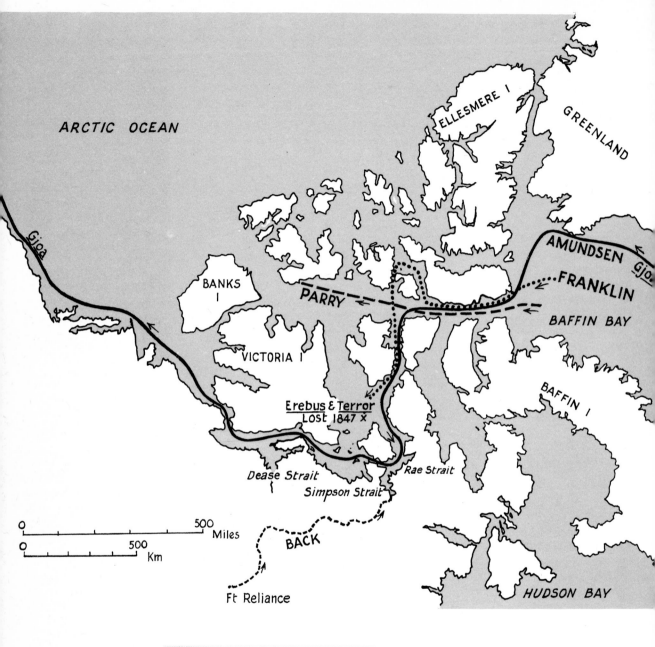

ARCTIC OCEAN

ELLESMERE I

GREENLAND

Gjoa

AMUNDSEN Gjoa

BANKS I

PARRY

FRANKLIN

BAFFIN BAY

VICTORIA I

Erebus & Terror
Lost 1847 x

BAFFIN I

Dease Strait

Rae Strait

Simpson Strait

500 Miles

500 Km

BACK

Ft Reliance

HUDSON BAY

*Contemporary illustrations
of the search for John
Franklin*

2. The Search for a North West Passage

I
T WAS A BATTLE BETWEEN MAN AT HIS MOST PERSISTENT AND NATURE AT her most unyielding.

The Canadian Arctic, where for four hundred years explorers searched for a North West Passage which they hoped would link the Atlantic Ocean to the Pacific, is an ice-bound wilderness the size of Europe: three million square miles of desolation. The land lies locked in permafrost, frozen to a depth of two thousand feet and colandered with lakes – more lakes than in all the rest of the world put together. The sea lies under a pall of ice which looks static but is, in fact, in constant though sluggish motion, driven this way and that by current, wind and tide until it piles up along shores and channels in high, disintegrating drifts. Only for a very few days in a very few places does the ice in this Arctic Ocean melt sufficiently in late summer to allow the passage of a ship.

By 1815 explorers had done little more than discover a route by which the Arctic Ocean could be approached. Then within the span of forty years, in a magnificent spate of treks and voyages, the secrets of the North Canadian coastline were unravelled and the passage in all its tortuous complexity revealed.

Snow cottages of the Boothians, Felix Harbour, from a painting by Sir John Ross: "originally my own sketches, but offered to the public as a faithful illustration, being aware that I do not possess such talent in the art as could embellish it"

25

The search for a North West Passage lasted hundreds of years and cost thousands of lives; it led to privation and suffering, endurance and heroism on a scale without parallel in the history of exploration. It is a dramatic story. Yet it all began soberly enough in the last decade of the fifteenth century as a commercial venture, an effort to find a short-cut via the shores of North America and across the Pacific to the recently discovered spice islands. This was logical; for if a passage for ships had indeed existed among the Arctic sealanes, it would have lopped nearly 5,000 miles off the voyage between London and the trade emporia of the east. What is perhaps not so logical is that the search should have continued long after all hope of finding a commercially viable passage had disappeared, that seamen in general and British seamen in particular should have battered so persistently at a door so patently closed.

The early explorers who sailed in search of this passage had little idea what an impossible task they were taking on. For they underestimated the size of the earth; and even when they came to accept that a whole new continent lay between the Atlantic Ocean and the Spice Islands they were seeking, they misjudged the size of this continent, and thought that a passage must exist either through it or round it. Perhaps the wish was father to the thought; but the concept had its roots also in the old Greek idea of a balanced or symmetrical globe; so that just as cartographers for centuries marked on their maps a Great Continent in the south to balance the landmass of Eurasia in the north, so they marked on their charts a sea passage to the north of America to balance the passage via Cape Horn and the Straits of Magellan which they knew existed to the south.

Dreams die hard. And this, I suggest, is the basic reason why the search for a passage was continued, century after century, with such dogged persistence. Certainly the later expeditions which were supported so assiduously by the Society cannot be understood unless we know something of their precursors.

The first explorer deliberately to seek a North West Passage was John Cabot. In 1497 he discovered Newfoundland, noted the abundance of cod in the sea and timber on the land, and returned to England, convinced that he had "discovered off the coast of Asia an island lying close to Cipango" (the mythical country where all the spices in the world were believed to be grown). King Henry was impressed. He gave Cabot command of five ships and sent him back the following year to explore more thoroughly. But of the five ships only one, near-foundering, returned; the others were never heard of again. It was an augury.

A few years later Labrador was added to the map, then Cape Cod, then the estuary of the Saint Lawrence. The Saint Lawrence indeed was thought for many years to be the mouth of the longed-for passage. Jacques Cartier spent several winters there, convinced that he had found, to quote his own words "the entrance to a great seaway leading direct to Cathay". And a hundred years after Cartier's first landing, another great French explorer, Jean Nicolet, spent half a lifetime among the Indian tribes of the Saint Lawrence carrying wherever he went a robe of Chinese damask, which he was convinced he would one day need to wear when he came to the borders of Cathay.

While the French were carving out an empire in the magnificent country around Montreal and Quebec, the British were forced into less attractive territory in the north. In 1576 Martin Frobisher discovered the desolate coast of Baffin Island. Here he came across what he felt certain was the mouth of the passage – "a great gulf, dividing as it were two mainlands or continents asunder". He sailed into it for 150 miles, never realizing that it was no more than an inlet (Frobisher Bay). He went ashore, kidnapped an unfortunate Eskimo, dug up some pyrites which he thought was gold, and returned to England, where he was hailed as "Lord High Admiral of all the seas and waters that lead to Cathay". He was followed a few years later by John Davis, a more attractive character, who instead of kidnapping the Eskimos played the lute to them. Davis

Portage des Paresseux: May 4th, 1833 by Captain Back, R.N.

penetrated still farther to the north. Hugging the coast of Greenland, in the shadow of mountains and glaciers of spectacular beauty, he reached the 72nd parallel, probably the closest in those days that a European had ever been to the Pole. Between them these two explorers pioneered the one possible approach-route, Davis Strait, by which a passage could be attempted.

Then for almost a hundred years exploration followed a false trail into a *cul-de-sac*.

In 1610 Henry Hudson sailed from England in the diminutive barque *Discovery*, convinced that he would "sight the lands of spice before next Candlemas". It was, however, no palm-covered islands he struggled through to: only that ice-choked graveyard of explorers' dreams now known as Hudson Bay. His voyage was a dark compound of treachery and tragedy. Twenty-two men set out; only eight returned; these eight were certainly guilty of mutiny and almost certainly of murder. And the tragedy of Hudson's expedition didn't end with his death. For the entrance to the bay that he discovered lies well to the south of the entrance to Davis's strait; and inevitably, in the years to come, explorers were to spend a great deal of time probing this wrong route in the south instead of the right route in the north. Seamen like Foxe and James suffered unbelievable hardships trying to force their way through the ice-filled reaches of Hudson's land-locked estuary; they saw their ships founder, their crews die of cold, starvation and exposure; and at the end of it all they were as far as ever from their goal.

After this series of disasters it is hardly surprising that there was a lull in the search for a passage, nor that, when the search was resumed, it was resumed by land.

The words North West Passage have for most of us a connotation with the sea; they conjure up visions of ice on the rigging and ships frozen in for the Arctic winter. Yet it could be argued that most of the more significant expeditions which led to the discovery of a passage were made by land – Hearne's trek to the mouth of the Coppermine for example, Mackenzie's to the mouth of the great river that bears his name, Back's descent of the Great Fish River, Franklin's horrifying perambulations round the Great Bear and Great Slave Lakes, Rae's survey of the coast of Coronation and Queen Maud Gulf. These great land journeys had one thing in common; they were backed, either directly or indirectly, by the Hudson's Bay Company. This Company, founded in 1670, had a virtual monopoly of the highly profitable fur trade of the North West Territories; it has been claimed with some truth that its story is nothing less than the story of opening up the Canadian north; and certainly, throughout the eighteenth and nineteenth centuries its factors and trappers were in a class by themselves when it came to Arctic travel. They knew the land. They could have told the Admiralty that for all practical purposes a passage didn't exist.

The Admiralty indeed were coming to this conclusion themselves. In the 1760s they sent several ships to explore the Pacific coast of Canada, but with meagre results. Then in the 1770s they sent the man who was arguably the greatest seaman the world has ever known, James Cook, with instructions to try to locate the Pacific entrance to a passage. Approaching the Bering Strait in mid-August, Cook found his way blocked by an unbroken barrier of ice, ten feet high and drifting steadily south. He had come in a bad year. He had no option but to give up. And the Admiralty gave up too. For half a century there was another period of inactivity.

Falls of Kakabikka: May 22nd, 1833 by Captain Back, R.N.

The dream, however, wasn't dead: only quiescent. After the Napoleonic Wars it sprang once again to life.

There were several reasons for this post-war revival of interest in a passage. A large number of men had suddenly been released from the Services who had acquired a taste for adventure, improvements in the technique of travel meant that vast new territories were for the first time within the reach of ordinary people, and there was a new scientific spirit abroad; so even though it was now realized that a passage would not be commercially viable, convincing arguments could be put forward for finding it. The

Sir William Edward Parry (1790–1855) was one of the most successful British Arctic explorers. He pioneered the technique of allowing his ships to become frozen-in for the Arctic winter, and discovered the approaches, via Lancaster Sound, to the North West Passage

immediate cause, however, was something more concrete: a letter written in the autumn of 1817 by Captain William Scoresby to the Royal Society.

William Scoresby was both whaler and scientist, a man who not only knew the Arctic at first hand but also was a graduate in chemistry and physics, and had invented useful scientific instruments. His opinion was worth listening to. And when he told the Royal Society that "between 74°N and 80°N the Greenland Sea is now unexpectedly free of ice", the Society acted swiftly. Within three weeks of receiving Scoresby's letter the prime minister had authorized two major expeditions: the first to attempt the Pole via Spitsbergen, the second to attempt the North West Passage via Davis Strait. It was the start of forty years of bitter confrontation.

In this confrontation the newly-formed Royal Geographical Society was soon playing a major role.

In the decade before the Society was founded no fewer than seven expeditions set out in search of a passage; three had far-reaching results.

In 1819 Commander Edward Parry took the *Hecla* and *Gripper* not only north up the Davis Strait but west along Lancaster Sound and into the hitherto unpenetrated reaches of the Melville Sea; here he deliberately allowed his vessels to become frozen in. This was one of the greatest voyages ever made; for in one season Parry penetrated more than half-way to the Pacific, accurately charted a thousand miles of unknown coast, and proved that a ship's company could survive the Arctic winter frozen into the ice. All this he achieved without losing a single member of his crew.

In 1820 and again in 1825 the Royal Navy sent Lieutenant John Franklin to the North West Territories with orders to push through to the Arctic Ocean by land. It is hard to know what to make of these two land expeditions. On the credit side they charted almost a thousand miles of near-inaccessible shoreline, putting, as it were, a roof on the map of Canada. On the debit side they ended in murder, cannibalism, unbelievable suffering, and several deaths from starvation and exposure. One is torn between a very real admiration for Franklin's courage and endurance, and the uneasy feeling that if he had dealt more tactfully with the Eskimos and listened more carefully to the advice of Company factors, the cost of his discoveries might have been less tragic.

The third important expedition was that of Captain John Ross, who in 1829 explored the Gulf of Boothia. Ross didn't have much luck as an explorer. In 1819 he had seen what he thought was a range of mountains (the mythical Crokers) across the end of Lancaster Sound; next year, by sailing clean through the Sound, Parry proved him mistaken. Now, a decade later, leading a privately-sponsored expedition, Ross searched for a passage in exactly the right place. He would, he decided, stand west along Lancaster Sound, and at the end of the Sound turn south into one of the inlets which led towards the mainland; once he reached the mainland he intended to follow it westward, close inshore, until he came to that part of the coast which had been charted by Franklin. This was the route by which a passage was eventually made. But the unlucky Ross turned south about a hundred miles too soon. At the end of Lancaster Sound he headed not into Peel Inlet but into Prince Regent Inlet, a *cul-de-sac* which led only to the ice-choked Gulf of Boothia. Here he disappeared.

It is at this point that the Society comes into the picture.

Ross's expedition had been sponsored not by the Admiralty but by Felix Booth, a philanthropic gin distiller, and when, after a couple of years, Ross failed to return, the Admiralty declared itself disinclined to launch a rescue operation – partly, one suspects, because Ross and Barrow cordially disliked one another. However, various schemes for going to Ross's aid were put forward by private individuals, including one by Dr. Richardson, a tough and experienced Arctic campaigner who had served with Franklin. Richardson's scheme was championed by the Royal Geographical Society. An entry in the Society's *Journal* for 1832 reads:

"Two expeditions have been planned during the present season. One, a trading expedition up the Quorra; the other a land expedition across the territories of the Hudson's Bay Company and along the supposed course of the Great Fish River to the shores of the Arctic. The primary object of this expedition is to ascertain the fate of Captain Ross, and subordinate to this to extend our knowledge of the Arctic shores. . . . The Hudson's Bay Company have consented to provide boats and provisions gratuitously, and Captain Back, one of Franklin's companions, has volunteered to lead the expedition . . . men of all descriptions must wish well to this undertaking, for though humanity is its leading motive, science must gain from it."

Sir John Ross (1777–1856). Able, contentious and unlucky, he spent the greater part of his naval career in search of the North West Passage

Back's expedition turned out to be one of the most important to be sponsored by the young Society. For not only did it trace the course, from source to mouth, of one of the greatest Canadian rivers, it discovered that part of the Arctic coastline which holds the key to a North West Passage; while as a bonus Back's account of his expedition is now recognized as one of the classics of Arctic travel, written with humour and discernment and illustrated with skill.

Back and his second-in-command, Dr. Richard King, spent their first winter at Fort Reliance, on the shore of the Great Slave Lake, probably the bleakest and most isolated of the Company's trading posts. "The temperature," wrote Back, "was 60° minus. Ink and paint froze. . . . When I was washing my face within three feet of our fire, my hair became clotted with ice before I had time to dry it." In the early summer they learned that Ross had managed to break free unaided into Lancaster Sound. This enabled them to concentrate on exploration; and in the middle of June, with eleven specially recruited *voyageurs* and a specially strengthened boat, they set out to explore Thlew-ee-choh (the Great Fish River), which the Indians had warned them was not only impassable but haunted by evil spirits.

The Indians' warning was well-founded; for the Great Fish River turned out to be an appalling succession of rapids and waterfalls interspersed with ice-bound shallows. Here is Back's entry for 22nd July, 1834.

"Bending to the left and in a contracted channel the water glided smoothly but irresistibly towards two stupendous gneiss rocks rising from five to eight hundred feet on either bank. Our first care was to secure the boat in a small curve near which the river disappeared in its descent, sending up showers of spray. We found it was not one fall, as the hollow roar had led us to believe, but a succession of falls and cascades in horrible confusion, through which the river foamed and boiled with deadly fury. . . . At one point the walls were raised into an arch, through which huge masses of ice were tossed into splintered fragments flung high into the air. A more terrific sight could not be conceived. . . . The boat was emptied of her cargo, but even then was too heavy to be carried more than a few yards. So whatever the consequence there was no alternative but to try the falls.

"Every precaution that experience could advise was adopted; double lines to the bow and stern were held on shore by the most careful of the men, and McKay and Sinclair took their stations at each end of the boat with poles, to keep her from dashing against the rocks. It was no common attempt, and excited in me the most lively concern for their safety. Repeatedly did the strength of the current hurl the boat within an inch of destruction, and as often did these able and intrepid men ward off the threatened danger. Still, amongst the many descents, she did not escape without some severe blows, in one of which the remaining keel plate was ripped away. But cool, collected and prompt to obey the signs they made to one another – their voices of course were inaudible – the gallant fellows finally succeeded in guiding her down in safety to below the last fall. . . . I gave the men a good glass of grog, with praises which

*Sir George Back
(1796–1878). Naval officer,
explorer, writer and artist.
Taught himself the Eskimo
language "the better to study
these most interesting
people". Below are two of
his studies: Esquimaux
Man, and Esquimaux
Woman*

they had well earned; and all being weary with exertion we camped for the night. "At 3.30 a.m. next morning, we began carrying down the pemmican and stores...."

A few days later they met a party of Eskimo hunters. It was an anxious moment; for the Indians had warned them that the Eskimos invariably killed anyone who ventured into their territory. Back, however, went forward to meet them alone, holding out his hands and crying *"tima"* (peace); and to everyone's relief his gestures were reciprocated. After friendship had been cemented by the gift of fish-hooks and beads, Back, who had taught himself Eskimo on a previous expedition to the Mackenzie, spent the rest of the evening questioning the hunters, who told him he was within a day's journey of the Great Salt Sea.

Next afternoon, though hampered by a mixture of rain and fog, the expedition pushed on to the shores of the Arctic Ocean. "A massive promontory [Victoria Headland] which has a coast-like appearance may," their leader wrote, "be considered as the mouth of the Thlew-ee-choh, which, after a violent and tortuous course of five hundred and thirty miles, running through an iron-ribbed country without a single tree on its banks, pours its waters in the Polar Sea in latitude 67° 11′ N, longitude 94° 30′ W."

On reaching salt water Back had hoped to sail west, hugging the shore, till he reached that part of the coast which had been surveyed by Franklin. But he arrived in a bad year, and a couple of weeks too early. He found his way blocked by ice. King urged him to head not west but north, where the pack appeared to be split by promising leads; and had the expedition followed this advice they would almost certainly have emerged into Peel Sound and have unravelled the secret of the passage. Back, however, was worried by the weather and the health of his men. "Rain fell incessantly," he wrote, "and each morning disclosed a dense white fog and the grievous spectacle of ice still closely-packed against the shore. The want of warm food excited my apprehension for the health of the crew, especially McKenzie who had become so swollen and bloated he could scarcely walk." On 14th August Back gave up, and headed for home up the river he had so laboriously descended.

On his return to England he found himself under vitriolic criticism from his second-in-command, Dr. King, who accused him of not keeping sufficiently strict discipline, of being on too familiar terms with his men, of associating too freely with Eskimos and Indians, and of lack of initiative. These charges, however, did more harm to King than to Back, and were, a decade later, to rebound in no uncertain manner on the head of the dogmatic and abrasive doctor.

Although neither Ross's voyage nor Back's trek had been a spectacular success, between them they narrowed the area in which a passage might still be looked for; and the Royal Geographical Society was soon petitioning the government to renew the search. "Recent discoveries," wrote the Society's secretary, "have revived public curiosity regarding the geography of the Arctic shores of America, and the Council has examined various plans submitted for further investigation. Communications were received from the President of the Society, Sir John Barrow, Sir John Franklin, Dr. Richardson, Captain Beaufort and Sir John Ross, and these were laid before His Majesty's Government by a deputation who expressed the earnest desire of the Society to see one or more of the plans carried into effect."

In this sort of situation the Society was in its element: giving semi-technical advice, lubricating the cogs of departmental involvement, and exerting pressure in influential circles. Unfortunately on this occasion the government and the Society between them sponsored the wrong plan. Instead of concentrating their efforts in the north and examining the exits from Barrow Strait, they routed their next expedition to the south, to Hudson Bay, instructing Back to sail the *Terror* to Wager River, then haul his boats and stores overland to the mouth of the Thlew-ee-choh. Inevitably the *Terror* became yet another in that forlorn succession of vessels whose progress ground to a halt in Hudson's ice-blocked *cul-de-sac*; and Back's second expedition is memorable less for the discoveries he made, than for the prose and paintings in which he so graphically describes them. Extracts from his *Brief Narrative of the Voyage of HMS Terror*, which he read to the Society a few days after returning to England, give a good idea of the hardships which those who searched for a passage had to face.

"Since the expedition from which I have just returned originated with the Society, I feel it incumbent on me to offer [you] an outline of the principle events which occurred. This will consist of brief extracts from my daily journal. . . . June 23rd, 1836 we took our departure and steered across the Atlantic – the weather stormy. July 29th, fell in with our first ice, and the following day saw the coast of Labrador. August 1st, passed through Hudson's Straits, and a few days later saw some of the Company's ships apparently beset with ice. By keeping close to land we got ahead of them, but on the following day were ourselves hampered. The ice was compact, and covered the horizon towards Hudson's Bay, but to the north it presented a more favourable appearance; I had therefore no hesitation in proceeding in that direction, and we got a run of 40 miles. Two days of westerly wind would now have enabled us to reach our goal; but easterly winds prevailed, and packed the ice in such a manner that we became hemmed in. By dint of boring we worked our way towards Southampton Island. Here on Sept. 20th we were seriously nipped by the ice. . . . From this date the ship was no longer under our guidance, but being closely beset, was carried to and fro according to wind and tide. . . . Sept. 27th a rush of ice from the east lifted the ship's stern seven feet and a half out of the water. . . . In the beginning of November, temperature 17° minus, the ship was housed in, and arrangements made for meeting the rigour of winter; snow walls were raised round the hull, and in this manner we drifted to and fro off the high land of Cape Comfort – at times so close to the rocks as to excite alarm. . . . On Christmas day the first symptoms of scurvy showed themselves. At one time twenty-five of the crew were suffering from this dreadful disease, but only three persons died. . . . At the beginning of January, during a calm night, our floe of ice split with a fearful crash – and this was the commencement of a series of shocks which nothing but the great strength of the mass of timber and iron fortifying the ship could have withstood: as it was the vessel strained in every direction.

"Feb. 18. Early in the morning – thermometer at 33° below zero – a disruption of the floe took place, and great waves of ice thirty feet high started rolling towards the ship. The decks were separated, the beams raised off the shelf-pieces, lashings and spars came tumbling down, iron bolts were drawn, and the whole frame of the ship trembled so violently as to throw men down. Yet this was not our worst disaster. On 15th March, while drifting off a headland since appropriately named 'Terror Point', a tremendous rush of ice took the ship astern, and, although buried to the flukes of the anchor in a dock of ice, such was the pressure that she was thrown over to starboard, her sternpost was carried away, and her stern lifted clean out of the water. The same night, a second rush of ice tore up the remnants of our floe, and forced up the ship so that while her forefoot was quite out of water, her sunken stern was threatened by an overhanging wall of ice full thirty feet high. This advanced on us with a fearful grinding and crashing, until, as it touched the quarter of the ship, it providentially stopped. Water poured in, the ship creaked and groaned. Provisions were got on deck, the boats were lowered, and every preparation was made for the worst extremity, as in the darkness and silence of the night, we awaited the coming of another shock, which must surely have been the last. Heaven, however, ordained it otherwise, and in this novel cradle of the ice we drifted for some time without further injury. The temperature 53° below zero, so that both mercury and brandy were frozen. . . ."

"Salt Plains, Slave River by Captain Back, R.N."

Nor was this the end of their adventures. On other occasions the *Terror* was driven ashore; she lost her rudder, her spare rudder and her inner and outer sternpost; she had her keel twisted out of alignment; eventually she became frozen fast to an iceberg, which, as her crew tried to saw it away, was lifted high out of the water, taking the unfortunate vessel with it. No wonder that when the ice eventually broke up, two pumps had to be kept continually at work to prevent the *Terror* from foundering. Back coaxed her half-sinking out of Hudson Bay and across the Atlantic, and beached her on the first shelving strip of shore that he came to – Lough Swilly in Northern Ireland.

Back, to quote his own words, was "very much shaken" by his experiences; the hardships he had suffered and the strain and anxiety of command so affected his health, both mental and physical, that he never put to sea again. Though not perhaps in the first rank of explorers, he emerges as an attractive and entertaining character, who described the Canadian Arctic in which he spent so much of his life with affection and understanding.

The next decade, 1837–47, saw a succession of journeys made by land: journeys which in fact did more to delineate the passage than many of the better-known and more spectacular voyages. These treks, most of them made by dog-hauled sledge, were sponsored and encouraged by both the Society and the Hudson's Bay Company, and were carried out by Company factors, men like Simpson and Dease, Isbester and Rae, who managed between them to survey all those parts of Canada's Arctic coastline which had not yet been reached by sea.

The most arduous journeys were those made jointly by Thomas Simpson and Peter Dease. Simpson was an able but unattractive character, forever quarrelling with and denigrating his companions – "Dease," he wrote, "is an indolent, illiterate soul. Mine alone is the victory." (The truth, however, is just the opposite; for it was the self-effacing Dease who was in command of their expeditions, and it was Dease's experience and Dease's ability in handling *voyageurs* and Eskimos that contributed most to their success.) In 1837–8 the two men charted three hundred miles of coast to the west of the Mackenzie delta. In 1838–9 they charted 150 miles of coast to the east of the Coppermine, and in 1839–40 they carried out surveys which supplemented Back's around the mouth of the Great Fish River, although unfortunately on this last occasion they missed Rae Strait, that narrow strip of water between King William Island and the mainland which in fact is the key to the passage; for the strait was frozen over at the time of their visit and indistinguishable from the land. An extract from Dease's diary, read to the Society in 1841, evokes not only the desolation of the Arctic shoreline but also its beauty. "We suffered much from lack of fuel and warm food, and as the cold weather set in our prospects grew more cheerless. On the 29th August there began a snow-storm that lasted seven days. After this fierce outbreak we coasted N.W. for 20 miles, and shortly before sunset stood out due N. for Victoria Land. I have never seen anything more brilliant than the phosphoric gleam of the waves when darkness set in; the boats seemed to cleave before them a flood of molten silver, and the spray, dashed from their bows before the fresh breeze, fell back like showers of diamonds into the deep. It was a bitterly cold night; and when we at last made land, cliffs, faced with eternal ice, obliged us to run on for a couple of leagues before we could take the shore with safety." For these exhausting and important surveys the Society awarded Simpson (one rather wishes it had been Dease!) its Founder's Medal.

Of even greater significance were the expeditions of Dr. John Rae, who in a series of remarkable journeys surveyed the Arctic coastline from Boothia Peninsula in the east to Victoria Island in the west. And here, in the area midway between the Atlantic Ocean and the Pacific, he stumbled almost by accident across the one tortuous route by which a passage could be accomplished: by squeezing first through Rae Strait (between King William Island and the mainland), and then through Coronation Gulf (between

Two ways of sledging: the Scandinavian way, using lightweight sledges hauled by dogs, and the British way, using heavy sledges hauled by men. Dog-drawn sledges were used successfully during the search for a North West passage by Hudson's Bay Company factors such as John Rae. Unhappily British polar explorers failed to grasp the significance of the factors' success, and continued for fifty years to pin their faith in man-hauled sledging

Victoria Island and the mainland). If one asks why Rae isn't better known, one reason may be that he made it sound too easy. For when it came to travelling in the Arctic he was a professional in the company of amateurs, and in terrain where Back gave up and Franklin lost his entire ships' companies, Rae sledged happily for up to thirty miles a day and lived equally happily off the land. His report, read to the Society in the autumn of 1851, is almost unique in the literature of early Arctic travel in that it stresses not the emptiness of the tundra, but its comparative abundance. Rae was also the first man to produce tangible evidence, obtained at first hand, that a passage really did exist.

"Left Fort Confidence," he told the Society, "accompanied by 4 men with 3 sledges drawn by dogs, this being the best way of travel. . . . Had a most friendly interchange with the Esquimaux; the men were cleanly dressed and fat, having an abundance of seal's flesh. . . . Many deer were seen, but as we had provisions in plenty no attempt was made to approach them; also many partridges (*Tetrao mutus*); these birds are large and fat and made fine eating. . . . At Cape Kendall ten geese were shot, and double that number might have been got had we required them. . . . Our principal food was geese, partridges and lemmings. The latter being fat and large were very fine when roasted between two stones. The little animals were migrating northward, and were so numerous that our dogs, as they trotted on, killed as many as supported them without

John Rae (1813–93), a doctor as well as an explorer, was one of the few men resourceful enough to learn how to cope with Arctic conditions successfully

any other food. . . . Set off a short time before noon, and as we trusted to killing both deer and geese on our way, we carried with us provisions for only four days. . . . Twenty-one deer had been shot on the coast, and many more could have been killed had I permitted it."

He makes it sound a different world to the wilderness in which so many of his contemporaries died of starvation and exposure.

And the discoveries he made were nearly as astonishing as the manner in which he made them. On 8th August, 1850, cast up on the southern shore of Victoria Island, he found the trunk of a pine tree, some eighteen feet in length. From the condition of the wood and from his knowledge of local tides and forests, Rae deduced that the pine must have come from the west, "that it must have been carried down to the sea by some river to the west of the Coppermine." A few weeks later, also on the southern shore of Victoria Island, he found two very different pieces of wood, a small flag-staff and an oak stanchion, clearly the remnants of a ship, and these, he deduced, must have come from the east. "From the circumstances of the flood-tide coming along the east shore of Victoria [Island]," he wrote, "there can be no doubt but that there is a water-channel dividing Victoria from Somerset, and through this channel I believe these pieces of wood must have been carried, along with the immense quantities of ice which the northeasterly winds and the flood-tide have driven down here."

Victoria Island, in other words, was a meeting-point, a point where the west-flowing current from the Atlantic met the east-flowing current from the Pacific. And if there was indeed such a confluence of ocean currents, it stood to reason that there must be a passage. Rae, in other words, had solved – at least in theory – the problem that had been taxing geographers and seamen for three hundred and fifty years.

It was a great achievement. Yet Rae was not in fact the first man ever to stand at this meeting-point of the oceans. Others had been there before him, not only Eskimos, but men from Europe, men whose skeletons were soon to bear silent witness to their discovery. . . .

When Rae was to achieve so much by land, it was unfortunate that the idea of forcing a way by sea through the North West Passage should have persisted. The architect of this last great assault was Sir John Barrow, now nearing his eightieth year but still at the Admiralty, still "aflame with enthusiasm" and more mindful than ever of the strategic importance of a passage in view of the growing power of Imperial Russia. Barrow enlisted the help of the Royal Society and the Royal Geographical Society, and both organizations lobbied the Government with such persistence that, against the advice of experts who advocated another search by land, it gave way. The President of the Society, Sir Roderick Murchison, sets out very clearly in his 1845 address both the background of this new expedition and its objectives:

"The search for a North West Passage through the Polar Sea has [long] occupied the attention of the British government. . . . This passage is now almost narrowed to one definite route. With the confident hope of accomplishing this [route] Sir John Barrow recently submitted a plan to the Admiralty, with a request that it might be laid before the Royal Society, by whom a resolution was passed in its favour. The plan was then referred to those best acquainted with the subject – Sir John Franklin, Sir Edward Parry, Sir James Ross and Lt.-Col. Sabine – all of whom approved it. The project was finally sent to the head of Her Majesty's Government and being approved, measures were forthwith taken to carry it into execution. Two ships, the *Erebus* and *Terror*, were placed under the command of Sir J. Franklin, and these have just sailed for the service in question."

Murchison goes on to describe the ships – "both specially strengthened and supplied

Sir John Franklin (1786–1847) whose disappearance in the Canadian Arctic led to what was probably the most protracted, far-ranging and physically-demanding search in the history of exploration

The crew of Back's second Arctic expedition (1836–37) dragging boats and provisions away from HMS Terror as their ship is crushed by ice. Drawn by G. Chambers, coloured by Joseph Wilson

with a small steam engine to work a screw"; the commanders – "thoroughly experienced in seas encumbered with ice"; and the men "able, intelligent and well versed in taking magnetic observations". Finally he describes the route they expected to take.

"We all know that Sir Edward Parry entered Lancaster Sound, passed through it and Barrow's Strait, and proceeded as far west as Melville Island, which he found surrounded by ice. Since then Lancaster Sound has frequently been traversed and found free from ice, and has almost yearly been entered by ships employed in the whale fishery. This route leads in a direct line to Behring's Strait, and is therefore apparently the proper and only maritime route to be pursued . . . although there is an opening which issues from the northern side of Barrow's Strait called Wellington Inlet which in appearance is little inferior to Lancaster Sound and may lead into an open sea. . . . I have the fullest confidence that everything possible will be done for the promotion of science and for the honour of Britain; and proud we geographers will be if our gallant Vice-President shall return after achieving such an exploit."

It is clear from this over-optimistic resumé that even after 350 years of failure, the difficulty of the passage was still gravely underestimated, and that Franklin left England without the prerequisites of success – either the knowledge of exactly where to find an ice-free channel, or the ability to live (like Rae) off the Arctic.

On 14th July, 1845, two months out of London, the *Erebus* and *Terror* fell in with a whaler not far from the entrance to Lancaster Sound. The whaling skipper noted in his log that their crew were "in fine spirits, and confident they would finish their work in good time". This was the last occasion on which they were seen alive – except perhaps by a family of Eskimos, who three years later may have watched helplessly as they struggled down one of the bleakest shorelines in the world, dying one by one of exposure and exhaustion.

Franklin's disappearance and the resulting search for him is one of the epic stories of exploration. The search went on for twelve years. It was carried out by the British

Government, the United States Government, the Royal Navy, the Hudson's Bay Company, and a multitude of private well-wishers. It involved scores of ships and thousands of seamen. It added enormously to man's knowledge of the Canadian Arctic. And it led eventually to the discovery of a North West Passage – although it was to be many years before this passage was finally negotiated.

As time passed and nothing was heard of the *Erebus* and *Terror*, the pages of the Society's *Journal* reflect the shift from optimism to uncertainty, from uncertainty to apprehension, and finally from apprehension to the realization that Franklin and his ships' companies must have voyaged beyond the shores of the Arctic and into that "undiscover'd country from whose bourn no traveller returns". In 1846 the President simply told the Society in his annual address: "The last information received from the expedition stated them to be off the coast of Greenland, and well. . . . All we can do is cordially to wish them every success." It is in the 1847 address that we find the first hint of uncertainty. "We still continue without accounts of Sir John Franklin and his adventurous companions, but as his ships were fully stored and provisioned for three years, we may still hope that success will eventually crown their arduous efforts. We may also rely on the Government's adopting every practicable means of furnishing supplies to such points of the coast as they might approach if prevented by insuperable obstacles from completing their passage to Behring's Straits." It is easy, with the knowledge of hindsight, to condemn the government for not taking this hint, to say that they ought, at the first suspicion that things had gone wrong, to have sent relief. But other explorers – Ross and Parry, for example – had spent several winters in the Arctic, and had survived. There was also the problem of where to send a relief expedition; for the area to be searched was the size of Europe, and the experts couldn't agree among themselves where Franklin was most likely to be found. Only one of them, as it happened, had the right idea – the abrasive and abusive Dr. King, who years earlier had got into the bad books of both the Society and the Navy by his criticism first of Back and then of Barrow. King insisted, with more vehemence than tact, that the area to send relief to was the mouth of the Thlew-ee-choh (now known as the Back River): that Franklin, finding his way to the north and the west blocked by ice, must have retreated south via Peel Sound in the direction of the mainland. He was right. But no-one would listen to him. He had made himself so unpopular with the powers that be and in particular with the Admiralty, that his opinion was now dismissed as that of a crank.

It was in fact 1848 before the various relief expeditions got under way. The Society's President, William Hamilton, gave details in his address.

"It is with regret that I have to repeat the statement of my predecessor that we are still without information of Sir John Franklin. [However] it is gratifying to know that the Government, sharing the anxiety of the public, have adopted the most judicious measures. No less than three expeditions have been undertaken for their relief. Commander Moore, in the *Plover*, has been ordered to proceed through Behring's Straits in search of the missing ships, and is already well advanced towards that point. Sir John Richardson, with Dr. Rae, is by this time threading his way through the American rapids on his route to the far McKenzie River, from which he will proceed along the coast in search of his friend and former captain. And thirdly Sir James Ross and Captain Bird, in the *Enterprise* and *Investigator*, will shortly be on their old ground in the neighbourhood of Lancaster Sound, ready to act as circumstances may require. Thus it will be seen that nothing has been omitted on the part of the Government which justice could require or humanity suggest."

These expeditions were well-found and well led; but they met with no success. The *Plover* took more than a year to penetrate the Bering Strait; and when she did at last fight her way through to the Arctic Ocean, her commander reported the swell "enough to overwhelm the boats. As for the ice, I can only compare it to floating rocks which would

(On the facing page)
North shore of the Great Slave Lake, August 13th, 1833, by Captain Back R.N.

Critical position of HMS Investigator *on the north coast of Baring Island, August 20th, 1851, by Lieutenant Creswell, R.N.*

(Overleaf)
Barren Lands: morning, August 24th, 1833, by Captain Back, R.N.

go through a boat like a sheet of paper." The *Plover* gave up. Rae and Richardson meanwhile searched 800 miles of the Arctic coast, from the Mackenzie delta to Victoria Island. They questioned hundreds of Eskimos, but none of them had seen or heard of the *Erebus* and *Terror*. At the same time Ross in the east was making superhuman efforts to break through the ice at the end of Barrow Strait. He fired his guns at regular intervals, discharged rockets each night, every day dropped a cask containing a message, caught foxes and put copper collars round their necks stamped with the position of his ship and then turned them loose; but all to no avail. It was as though the *Erebus* and *Terror* had vanished off the face of the earth.

The President's address in the spring of 1849 reflects the growing fear that things had gone tragically wrong. "It is with feelings of regret, now not unmingled with apprehension, that I have to state that no information has been received during the past year respecting Sir John Franklin." Hamilton went on to tell the Society how the search had been taken up by both the United States and the Russian Governments; how further naval and privately-sponsored expeditions were on their way to the Arctic; and how Lady Franklin had offered £2,000 and the Government £10,000 to the first person to bring news of the missing vessels. In the middle of this anxiety and speculation, the architect of Franklin's and of so many other Arctic voyages died peacefully in his sleep. "It is with regret," Hamilton told the Society, "that we have this year to lament the loss of the late Sir John Barrow. . . . He will long be remembered firstly for the important share he took in the formation of this Society, and secondly for the unwearied energy with which he encouraged Voyages of Discovery, especially those with a view to finding a North West Passage." Doubtless Barrow would have been accorded a much more eulogistic obituary if Franklin had returned in triumph.

In 1850 there was, the Society was told by its new President, "still a ray of hope glimmering through the uncertainty which hangs over the fate of Sir John Franklin". But even that hope was fading. By now twelve vessels were searching for the *Erebus* and *Terror*, eight from the east, and four from the west; there were also at least three expeditions under way by land. Yet for all Dr. King's impassioned pleading, no-one thought it worthwhile to send a search party to the mouth of the Great Fish River.

During the next few years a great deal was learned about the ice-coated archipelago which lies scattered across the northern face of Canada – just how much we can see by comparing a map drawn before the Franklin search with a map drawn after. Commanders became frozen fast in the ice: Collinson for two winters, McClintock for three, McClure for an unbelievable four. Ships were abandoned, capsized, crushed to death, blasted free with explosives. There were rare cases of mutiny, incompetence and court martial, and many more cases of courage, fortitude and fine seamanship; there were amazing feats of endurance – Rae, for example, sledging 5,380 miles in eight months; there were almost incredible coincidences – the crews of the *Resolution* and the *Investigator* converging by chance from opposite sides of the world onto the same ice-bound harbour in Melville Island. But at the end of it all no-one had the slightest idea what could have happened to Franklin.

The comments of the President at the annual meetings of the Society speak for themselves. 1851: "It is a severe disappointment not to be able to congratulate the Society on the rescue of Sir John Franklin. But the mysterious uncertainty remains unbroken." 1852: "Alas that seven years should have elapsed without tidings; but all honour to those who still cling to hope." 1853: "God grant that some at least of our absent mariners may still be in existence." 1854: "The veil is still unlifted which hangs over this sad mystery of the north." It was not until 1855 that a president had the unenviable task of reading Franklin's obituary. For something definite – and tragic – had at last been discovered.

The first hint of what had happened came – Dr. King said predictably – not from one

(On the facing page)
Sledge party leaving HMS Investigator *in Mercy Bay, April 1853, by Lieutenant Creswell, R..N.*

Sledging over hummocky ice, April 1853, by Lieutenant Creswell, R..N.

of the much-publicized naval expeditions, but from a routine sledging journey carried out by a Company factor. The ubiquitous John Rae was surveying the coast of Boothia, when he met an Eskimo who told him that four years earlier white men had been seen struggling south down the coast of King William Island not far from the mouth of the Great Fish River; and to support his story the Eskimo showed Rae a silver plate inscribed "Sir John Franklin". It was too late that year to sledge to King William Island; so Rae returned with his news to York factory on Hudson Bay. As soon as possible the Company sent a team led by James Anderson to investigate by land, and Lady Franklin sent a team led by Captain Leopold McClintock to investigate by sea. Not far from the mouth of the Great Fish River the search parties found first tent-poles, oars and axes, then skeletons, then a cairn containing the last messages ever written by men from the *Erebus* and *Terror*.

From these it has been possible to piece together the story of Franklin's last and tragic voyage. . . .

To start with all seems to have gone well, and though Franklin must have been disappointed to find Melville Sound choked with ice, he can't have been particularly surprised. Finding that he couldn't advance to the west he turned north, and, in accordance with his orders, stood into Wellington Channel. But here too he found his way blocked; and here, round about the 77th parallel, he spent his first winter, the winter of 1845–6. Next summer he must have tried again to break through to the north or the west, but without success; the only open water lay to the south, in Peel Sound; so south he went. But by the time he had negotiated the Sound, winter ice was again closing in; so Franklin headed for the north-west coast of King William Island where he clearly intended to winter. If only he had headed instead for the north-east coast! Then he would have found and almost certainly have sailed through the passage. He didn't, however, realize that a strait, soon to be known as Rae Strait, divided King William Island from the mainland; and so by a few degrees and a few miles the *Erebus* and *Terror* chose the path not to success but to disaster.

About thirty miles off the north-west coast of King William Island Franklin became frozen in for his second winter, the winter of 1846–7. By now his crew must have been suffering from scurvy, and although we shall never know the exact figures it seems probable that winter that a number of them died. With the coming of spring Lt. Gore of the *Erebus* led a party to King William Island, where he built a cairn containing a note that all was well: the inference being that in mid-summer the *Erebus* and *Terror* expected to break free of the ice and continue their passage. But the ice never relaxed its grip. The ships remained frozen in for a third winter, and the situation became suddenly serious. Franklin died; and in the spring of 1848 the *Erebus* and *Terror* were abandoned and the surviving 105 officers and men set out by sledge for the mouth of the Great Fish River. They didn't know much about sledging; no depots were advanced; the sledges were overloaded, and progress was pitifully slow. It wasn't long before men started to die. Soon they were dropping food and tents because they hadn't the strength to carry them farther. They died as they walked. By the time they reached the mainland there can have been no more than thirty or forty of them left. And soon there were none.

They died exactly where King was telling everyone to search for them, and, ironically, in the last few undiscovered miles of the passage for which they were searching.

The Franklin tragedy marked the end of an era. Every year for forty years – from 1818 when the Government acted on Scoresby's letter, to 1858 when the bodies of Franklin's men were at last discovered – there had been at least one major expedition, and sometimes as many as a dozen, either searching for a North West Passage or searching for those who had gone in search of it. And still no-one had sailed through the one tortuous channel which linked the oceans. The Government, the Admiralty and the Society came to the conclusion that the game wasn't worth the candle. They directed their efforts elsewhere.

*Interview with Esquimaux
by Captain Back, R.N.*

The *Journal* reflects this change of attitude very clearly. The first twenty-seven volumes (from 1831 to 1858) all contain either a paper on the search for a passage or a major reference to such a search. After 1858 there is no more than the occasional footnote. The volume for 1859 is a watershed. All 455 pages of it are devoted to a single subject: "The Lake Regions of Central Equatorial Africa, with Notices of the Lunar Mountains and the Sources of the Nile: being the results of an expedition undertaken under the patronage of Her Majesty's Government and the Royal Geographical Society of London in the years 1857–59 by Richard F. Burton."

One chapter in the Society's history had ended. Another was about to begin.

The North West Passage remained inviolate for another fifty years. Then in 1905 a Norwegian, Roald Amundsen, in his diminutive vessel the *Gjoa*, followed in Franklin's wake – or very nearly in his wake: the difference being that instead of heading for the north-west coast of King William Island and being frozen in, Amundsen headed for the north-east coast, and, hugging the shore, edged into Rae Strait. Here he wintered, at the mouth of the Great Fish River, very likely sledging over the graves of some of Franklin's ships' companies in his quest for food; then, in the few days towards the end of August when Rae Strait is free of ice, he sailed westward into Coronation Gulf and thence via Bering Strait into the Pacific. It had taken more than four hundred years for the dream of the fifteenth century merchant adventurers to be realized.

Was the goal worth the price paid for it? Certainly not, if measured in terms of economic or scientific gain; for the passage made no-one his fortune, has never been used commercially, and has added little to our knowledge of the world. Yet man is not motivated by tangible considerations alone. In the last analysis, what drove the explorers north by west, year after year, was neither greed nor patriotism nor the wish for personal aggrandizement, but man's innate curiosity – that "lust of knowing what should not be known" which has led countless pilgrims down countless Golden Roads to Samarkand. A problem had been set, and had to be solved. A challenge had been made, and had to be met. As Everest soaring has to be climbed, and the stars in their courses have to be reached for, so the leads in the ice snaking ever north by west had to be followed. And who can say that by following them man added nothing to his stature?

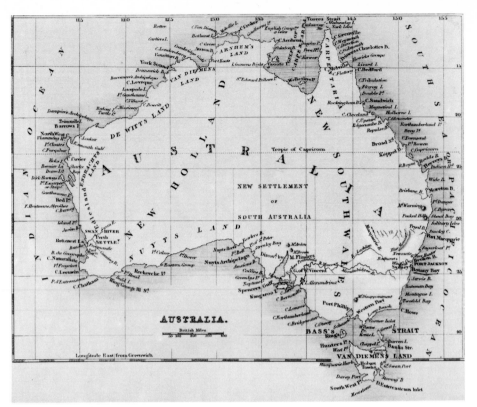

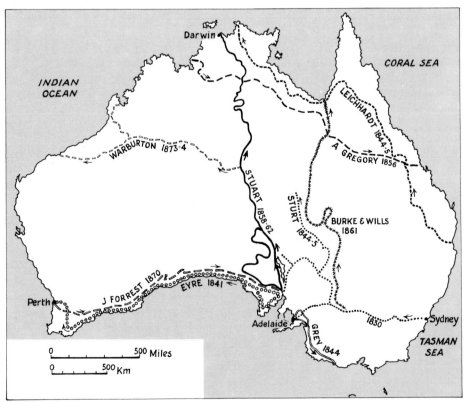

3. The Crossing of the Australian Deserts

THE AUSTRALIAN CONTINENT WAS UNTOUCHED, UNKNOWN AND A LAW UNTO ITSELF; nothing in it seemed to conform to the pattern of the world outside. To paraphrase Alan Moorehead's classic description: on the trees the leaves hung upside down, not so much evergreen as ever-grey; in the outback there were giant birds which never flew, and weird animals which hopped instead of walked; and the alien white man as he moved through the drifts of spinifex often had the feeling that someone or something was watching him expectantly.

It was a land awaiting the kiss of life.

By the early nineteenth century settlers had gained a foothold around the perimeter of this unknown continent; but its interior remained an enigma. Nobody knew what lay at the heart of it – mountain ranges, deserts, or a great inland sea? – because those who ventured into the outback either swiftly retraced their steps or disappeared, unable to survive the heat, the lack of water, and the sheer primordial vastness. By the middle of the century, however, the settlers desperately needed new pastureland for their cattle and sheep. The outback was always on the horizon, always on the periphery of their lives: a challenge. . . .

Within a generation a remarkable series of journeys had unveiled the secrets of the central deserts and filled in the blanks on the map.

Gregory's camp at Depot Creek, a tributary of the Victoria River, painted by Thomas Baines

Watercolour by Conrad Martens, painted between 1835 and 1843: Sydney Harbour seen from Flagstaff Hill, Fort Denison and Government House in the distance. Martens painted many watercolours and oils of Port Jackson, subsequently renamed Sydney

A hundred and fifty years ago, at the time the Royal Geographical Society was founded, Australia was virtually *terra incognita*. Although Flinders had delineated its coastline, and settlements existed around its south-eastern seaboard and at Perth, less than five per cent of the continent had been explored. The other 95 per cent has been aptly described as "a blank", a vast and silent wilderness, immeasurably old, bereft to all appearances of either water or life.

Here, one might have thought, was an ideal canvas on which the young Society could make its mark: one of the last empty spaces on the maps of the world, simply waiting to be filled in.

The omens were propitious. One of the founder members of the Society had a special interest in and affection for Australia. Robert Brown had been Flinders's botanist, and no-one appreciated better than he the unique wonder of the continent's *flora* and *fauna*. If we look at Volume One of the Society's *Journal*, we find that the first three papers are all devoted to Australia – one of them, *On the Botany of the Vicinity of Swan River*, by Brown himself. This early promise, however, was not fulfilled, and the Society never became as active in promoting exploration in Australia as might have been expected. There would seem to be two reasons for this: finance and distance.

The boom period of exploration in Australia was between roughly 1842 and 1862. In these twenty years the number of sheep and cattle in the continent more than doubled,

Collins Street, Melbourne: as seen from the Bank of Australia in 1840

and the finding of new pastureland became an economic necessity for the settlers. It so happened that these years coincided with the nadir of the Society's financial fortunes. During its first few years the RGS had been reasonably affluent; but internal dissensions, a succession of absentee presidents and a series of over-ambitious projects soon brought the young Society to the edge of bankruptcy. It was hard-pressed throughout the forties and fifties to finance expeditions to the Arctic and to Africa, and was reluctant to venture too ambitiously into unknown and yet more distant territory. And how distant Australia must have seemed in those days to a committee sitting in London – "The land is scarcely to be reached," wrote one of the Society's presidents, "except by convict ship or man-of-war." The Society liked to maintain control over the expeditions it sponsored – it had unhappy memories of Alexander in South Africa and Ainsworth in Kurdistan – and it felt, with some justification, that if control had proved difficult in Africa and the Near East, it might prove impossible on the opposite side of the world.

These difficulties dissuaded the Society from ever mounting a major and sustained effort in Australia on the scale that it did in, say, the Canadian Arctic or in Africa. Nevertheless it did help to promote several important expeditions; it publicized the work of all the major Australian explorers, awarding its Gold Medal to no fewer than eleven of them – Eyre, Strzelecki, Sturt, Leichhardt, Burke, Stuart, A. C. and F. Gregory, Warburton, Forrest and Giles; and it sent out the occasional small expedition of its own.

The first of the RGS-sponsored expeditions was that of George Grey.

"We would," the President told the Society in his annual address for 1837, "invite your special notice to an expedition about to proceed to Australia. Two officers of His Majesty's Army, Lieut. Grey and Lieut. Lushington, offered their services to prosecute geographical discoveries in whatever part of Australia the Society would recommend. This opportunity for pressing an important expedition was not lost. A deputation composed of the President, Captain Beaufort and Mr. Murchison waited upon Lord Glenelg (Secretary of State for the Colonies), pointing out the advantages likely to accrue from exploration and recommending in addition to a land expedition a nautical survey. The deputation was most favourably received, and having met with the sanction of the government, a grant of £1,000 was obtained towards the expenses of a land expedition . . . while HMS *Beagle*, just returned from a ten years' survey of the shores of South America, was ordered at the same time to carry out a survey of the northwest coast. . . . This expedition the Society must look to to solve an important geographical problem, namely the existence or the contrary of a great inland sea. This it will do by searching for the entrance to a river which may enable us to obtain access to the interior, and so spread the blessings of civilization throughout this hitherto unexplored country."

George Grey, the leader of the land expedition, was an able and attractive character, who subsequently became the governor first of South Australia, then of New Zealand and finally of Cape Colony. He was hardy, brave and had an empathy with the Aborigines far ahead of his times. He was, however, singularly unsuccessful as an explorer – the archetypal innocent abroad. As his vessel approached Hanover Bay (roughly midway between Darwin and Broome) he was in raptures. "At the first streak of dawn," he wrote, "I leant over the side to gaze upon those shores I had so longed to see." He was in such a hurry to set foot on Australian soil that he put ashore with a small party about five miles to the east of Hanover Bay, intending to walk across a small headland to where his ship would later that afternoon drop anchor. Within a couple of hours he was in trouble. The sun was hot, the light was blinding; his men were unfit and had not been supplied with sufficient water; he lost all three of his dogs, and in mid-afternoon found his way blocked by an unexpected arm of the sea. With more valour than discretion Grey tried to swim across. He was swept by the tide-rip out to sea, and only escaped drowning by becoming stranded on a reef. By the time he had struggled ashore it was dark. He could find neither his ship nor his men. But the Aborigines could, and did, find him; he could hear them calling to one another in the dark. He spent the night huddled miserably in a hollow among the rocks – hardly an auspicious start to his career as an explorer.

His subsequent exploits were equally star-crossed. He had hoped to explore the coast between Hanover Bay and Perth, and to find some great and as yet undiscovered river which he could follow to the great inland sea which he was convinced existed in the centre of the continent; but the monsoon rains and the difficult terrain so slowed him down that he took thirteen days to cover the first ten miles. And when he tried to head inland his difficulties multiplied. His horses died. He was attacked by Aborigines, hit by three spears and seriously wounded. He came to a river (the Glenelg) which he claimed would "be found one of the most important in the continent, second only to the Murray", but which subsequent explorers proved to be a mere stream less than seventy miles in length. And when, at the end of three months, exhaustion and lack of supplies forced him back to his ship, he had covered less than one-tenth of the distance to Perth.

The following year he tried to survey some of the islands off Shark Bay; but again success eluded him. His boats were wrecked, his stores were lost, and he was forced to head back for Perth on foot. His trek soon degenerated into a nightmare, with his men short of food and trying not very successfully to live off the land. It says much for Grey's character that even in this critical situation he retained both his love of nature and his humanity. On 2nd April, on the banks of a river he named the Murchison, he wrote: "The estuary appeared even more lovely than yesterday, and as the heavy morning mists arose, unfolding its beauties to our view, all those feelings came thrilling through my mind which explorers alone can know." A few days later he came across a cache of zamia nuts, hidden in the bed of a stream. His starving companions would have eaten the lot; but Grey insisted they took only a quarter; for he realized that the Aborigines who had made the cache might be relying on it for their survival. On 21st April, exactly a month after losing his stores, he staggered into a settler's house on the outskirts of Perth. He was well-known to the family who lived there; but his hardships had made him so blackened, emaciated and distraught that he wasn't recognized, and was mistaken for a mad Malay, notorious for scavenging food out of the settlers' dustbins.

Grey had some of the qualities of Robert Falcon Scott; it is easier to admire him as a man than as an explorer. The Society, whose Fellows were well able to assess merit in their particular field, awarded him no medal, and published only a very abbreviated account of his exploits in the *Journal*.

An explorer of very different stature was Edward John Eyre. Eyre was an overlander, a tough knowledgeable man, whose experience in driving vast herds of cattle over vaster distances gave him that knowledge of the country which Grey had lacked. For every ten

John Edward Eyre (1815–1901): sheep farmer, explorer and administrator. The picture shows him and his Aborigine guide Wylie arriving at King George's Sound, 7th July, 1841

Four-foot lizard shot by Gregory near the source of the Victoria River

Phasma, male and female, natural size, found on the white-barked eucalypts

miles Grey travelled along the west coast, Eyre was to travel a hundred along the wilder and far more difficult coastline of the south. His explorations were financed not by the Society, but by groups of local settlers, such as the Northern Exploring Committee, who were anxious to find new grazing land. Nevertheless the Society took a keen interest in his work, published a detailed account not only of his travels but also of his geographical theories, gave him its highest award, and towards the end of his life played a major role in salvaging his reputation.

It was in 1841 that he was first mentioned in the Society's *Journal*: "Mr. Eyre," wrote the president, "who left Adelaide in the hope of being able to plant the British standard on the Tropic of Capricorn – that is to say in the very heart of the continent – has met with an unexpected obstacle: a great crescent-shaped lake which he has named Lake Torrens. The length of this piece of water exceeds 400 miles, and its shore, composed of soft mud and sand, can not even be approached." Next year the president reported to the Society again: "Our curiosity respecting the interior of Australia remains unsatisfied, but our knowledge of its seaboard is constantly increasing. . . . After the enterprising Mr. Eyre found his progress blocked by the extraordinary Lake Torrens, he directed his steps west. He left Fowlers Bay on 25th February and working his way along the coast reached King George's Sound on 7th July, having traversed an unknown shore for upwards of 1,040 miles, a journey attended by appalling hardships and the most distressing circumstances."

For this magnificent feat of exploration Eyre was awarded the Founder's medal – the first bestowed for discoveries in Australasia – and the following year, when the medal was presented, the Society was given some idea of what the "appalling hardships and distressing circumstances" had been.

"Seeing that he could not advance to the north," the president told a packed meeting of the Society in its headquarters in Waterloo Place, "Mr. Eyre made preparations for an advance to the west, along the shore, in the direction of King George's Sound. . . . The hardships and sufferings that he experienced in carrying out this project were beyond description; the whole distance being above a thousand miles, full one half of it entirely destitute of water and consequently of herbage or fruit, the only scanty supply of the former in this dreary waste being obtained by digging in the drifts of pure white sand found along the coast at places where the great fossil bank recedes a little from the margin of the sea. Mr. Eyre describes the table-land of the interior to be of the most desolate and barren character imaginable, almost entirely without grass, and destitute of timber. On two occasions the party were entirely without water for seven days, and almost the same time without food. In the latter half of his journey Mr. Eyre was accompanied by only one person, a native of King George's Sound: three other natives having deserted him in despair after they had murdered an overseer. . . . Mr. Eyre confesses that his labours have not been productive of any discovery likely to prove beneficial to the colony; but we as geographers should not be the less inclined to give him our applause, both for the obstacles he overcame and for having sent home so large an addition to our knowledge of this portion of the globe."

A couple of years later, in June 1845, another of Eyre's reports was read to the Society. This was not an account of further exploration, but a theoretical treatise, *Considerations against the supposed Existence of a great Sea in the Interior of Australia*. It was almost unheard of in those days for the *Journal* to publish such an article – as the editor goes to some length to point out: "It is not often that matters of mere conjecture are admitted into the Geographical Journal . . . but the nature of the interior of Australia is a problem of such interest as to warrant the insertion in our publication of the conjectures of one who himself has explored in the country and given the subject his serious consideration."

It is difficult for us today to appreciate how revolutionary Eyre's theories must have seemed to his contemporaries; for most people in those days believed that the centre of Australia must consist of a vast inland lake – a belief engendered by the scarcity of major outward-flowing rivers. To quote Eyre himself: "It is usually thought that the continent is little more than a narrow crust or barrier between an outer and an inner sea, and that the great mass of the interior consists of waters. It is not without the greatest diffidence that I venture to hazard an opinion which I know to be at variance with that generally held. . . . That there is something very singular in the nature and formation of Australia, we have many and strong reasons for believing. It is quite unlike any other part of the world in its geographical character and features. I have never, however, met any circumstances calculated to impress me with the belief that there exists in the interior an extensive navigable sea. On the contrary, I have become acquainted with many facts which have led me to deduce the opposite. . . . First, the hot winds which, in South Australia, always blow out or away from the centre of the continent. To those who have experienced the scorching influence of these winds, which can only be compared to the fiery blasts from a furnace, there can be little probability that such winds can have been wafted over a large expanse of water. . . . Secondly, I have at various points come into friendly communication with the Aborigines who inhabit the outskirts of the interior, and from them I have invariably learnt that they knew of no large body of water inland, fresh or salt; that on the contrary all is arid waste. . . . Thirdly, I infer the non-existence of an inland sea from the likeness observable in the physical appearance, customs, character and pursuits of the Aborigines at opposite points of the continent." He goes on to say that, in his opinion, "the interior will be found generally to be of a very low level and to consist of arid sands alternating with the basins of dried up lakes, or such as are covered only by shallow salt or mud . . . but that there may be detached or higher ranges interspersed among these arid wastes, and that the latter may consist of more fertile land." Seldom has the truth been arrived at so logically, so exactly and with such disarming diffidence, and been so disregarded.

Eyre's subsequent career was distinguished but controversial. He became resident magistrate and protector of Aborigines on the Murray River, where he gained the reputation of being unusually sympathetic in trying to educate and resettle the tribes whose traditional way of life was being threatened by the settlers' hunger for land. In 1846 he left Australia, and became Lieutenant-Governor first of New Zealand and then of Saint Vincent and finally in 1864 governor of Jamaica. A year later there was rioting in the island: rioting which in Eyre's opinion was about to escalate into rebellion. He ordered out the troops. The troops, however, got out of hand, and were responsible for some 600 deaths and the burning of more than a thousand homes. A Royal Commission was appointed and their finding was that Eyre's orders had been justified but had been carried out with excessive force; he was ordered home and relieved of his governorship. It was at this crisis in his career that Eyre was defended by the Royal Geographical Society, and in particular by its president Sir Roderick Murchison. Murchison pointed out to successive courts of enquiry that "our gallant Medallist had for years been the humane friend of the Aborigines of Australia, himself paying for more than one of them to be brought home and educated in England, and that he was not the man to err on the side of unnecessary severity." Eyre's reputation was eventually vindicated, and he ended his days without stigma and with the full pension of a retired governor.

The journeys of Grey and Eyre delineated with some accuracy the western and southern peripheries of Australia, but the "ghastly blank" at the centre remained. Even as late as 1840, except in the south-east corner of the continent, no-one had penetrated for more than a couple of hundred miles into the outback. It was a challenge. "Let any man," wrote Charles Sturt, "lay the map of Australia before him, and regard the blank

Bud and flower of the Gouby or stem tree

Hawk, shot near the camp: length from beak to tip of tail 1'9", spread of wings 4'1"

Charles Sturt (1795–1869): "the father of Australian exploration." The picture is a contemporary sketch of his expedition leaving Adelaide

upon its surface, and then let me ask him if it would not be an honourable achievement to be the first to place foot in its centre." Sturt petitioned the Government to finance an expedition to survey the interior; and their response was positive.

Charles Sturt is an explorer whose stature it is difficult to assess. During his life he was never given the recognition he deserved, and for some years afterwards was regarded as a "mere traveller"; latterly, however, the pendulum has swung to the opposite extreme, and recent writers have described him as "the father of Australian exploration". The truth seems to be that he was a modest likeable man, whose career was blighted by ill health, and whose explorations – through no fault of his own – always fell marginally short of achieving that spectacular success which would have brought him fame. In the late twenties and early thirties he led a number of expeditions which helped to open up the Murray-Darling basin, but the hardships he suffered affected his health, and in particular his eyesight. In 1831 he became totally blind, and a visit to an English surgeon only partially restored his sight. On returning to Australia he held a number of important positions (Assistant Commissioner of Crown Lands and Surveyor-General) but exploration had always been his true love; and he describes his appointment as leader of the 1844 expedition to the interior as the "most gratifying moment of my life". The expedition was a comparatively large one: 15 men, 6 dogs, 11 horses, 30 bullocks, 200 sheep, a boat, a waggon and three drays. It was financed mainly by the Colonial Office, though a number of other organizations also helped—including the Royal Geographical Society, who provided the two new sextants which enabled the expedition's surveyor, James Poole, to plot and record their track with particular accuracy.

Sturt set out from Adelaide in August 1844, determined "to dispel once and for all the mists of doubt which hung over Central Australia". In the event he failed by one degree, a mere 150 miles, to reach the centre of the continent; but his failure was more meritorious than many an easily-won success; for his expedition trekked through and meticulously mapped more than a hundred thousand square miles of some of the most desolate territory on earth – and, with one exception, came back alive.

His *Journal*, read to the Society soon after he returned to Adelaide, paints a vivid picture of the vastness and desolation of the outback.

"October 9th: We have now arrived at the borders of the desert which has so far foiled the most enterprising and undaunted explorers. The natives are not encouraging. They say 'if you go into the desert your bullocks will hang out their tongues, your drays will tip over, and you will die. For there is neither water nor grass in the desert, nor a stick to light a fire with'. . . . November 14th: The ground over which we advanced is covered with pebbles of quartz, ironstone, whinstone and granite – as if McAdam had thrown down here every cart-load of stones he had ever filled. The thermometer stands at 108° in the shade; the heat intolerable, the flies unbearable. The men complain of disordered bowels and sore eyes. . . . January 24th: The thermometer at 118° in the shade. The ranges have now ceased, and we have all around us this level boundless expanse, without a landmark of any kind to guide us. Not that we are going anywhere. For the present we are locked up as firmly as if girt around by ice at the pole, it being impossible to move in any direction in consequence of the dry state of the country. . . . February 13th: We climbed a small sandhill. From the top the view was sufficient to depress the spirits of anyone. The horizon was level as that of the sea; a deathlike hue pervaded the scene; no living creatures save ants were to be seen – even the fly was absent. . . . These deserts are silent as the grave, and surely the most gloomy that ever man has trod. . . . July 9th: So great is the heat that every screw in our boxes has been drawn, the horn handles of our instruments and our combs are split into fine laminae. The lead drops out of our pencils; our hair has ceased to grow, our nails have become brittle as glass. Our flour has lost more than 8% of its weight. We find it difficult to write or draw, so rapidly does the fluid dry in our pens and brushes. The scurvy shows itself upon us all. We are attacked by violent headaches, pains in the limbs, swollen and ulcerated gums. Mr. Poole became worse and worse: ultimately the skin over his muscles became black, and he lost the use of his lower extremities. On the 14th he suddenly expired. . . . September 6th: The Desert was like an immense sea beach. Large fragments of rock were imbedded in the ground as if by the force of waters, while the stones were more scattered, thus shewing the sandy bed beneath and betwixt them. The day was exceeding hot, and our horses' hoofs so brittle that pieces flew off them like splinters when they struck them against the stones. . . . Nothing could exceed the sterile and inhospitable character of this desert, or the hopelessness of the prospect before us. But the moon being full we continued our journey, at times across the white dry bed of the salt lagoons, at other times along the top of the sandy ridges. . . . September 8th: The sky cloudy, but no rain ever falls. We are struggling against difficulties such as are not to be overcome by human perseverance. The floodgates of heaven appear to be closed for ever, so settled is the drought. There appears to be no ending to this gloomy stone-clad plain."

Sturt had struggled through to the edge of the Simpson, perhaps the most forbidding of the Australian deserts. It was impossible to go farther, and he had the good sense to realize it. On the evening of 8th September he turned back. "I was," he wrote, "scarcely a degree from the tropic [of Capricorn] and I can not hide the disappointment with which I turned my back upon the centre of Australia, after having so nearly gained it; but that was an achievement I was not permitted to accomplish."

This was to be Sturt's last expedition. For his health and in particular his eyesight had been permanently damaged, and although he remained in Australia for some years, incipient blindness forced him in 1851 into premature retirement. He went back to England and settled in Cheltenham. The final episode of his life is typical of his misfortune in missing by the proverbial hairsbreadth the fame he so richly deserved. In 1847 the Royal Geographical Society had awarded him its Founder's Medal – "for outstanding services in the course of geographical discovery, for the energy and courage [he] displayed in confronting difficulties of no ordinary character, for the prudence with which further advance was abandoned, and for [his] conciliatory conduct to the natives." This, however, was almost the only recognition Sturt ever received. For, to quote Sir Clements Markham: "His great services were entirely neglected by the Government for a quarter of a century. And justice, when it did come, arrived too late. In May 1869 he received notice that he was to be created a Knight Commander of St. Michael and St. George, but he died on 16th June before the tardily bestowed honour was gazetted."

Sturt's trek to the interior of Australia has certain affinities with Cook's voyage to the periphery of the Antarctic. Both were great negative feats of exploration. For just as Cook dramatically reduced the possible size of a Great Southern Continent, so Sturt reduced the possible size of a Great Inland Sea. Such negative discoveries may lack the glamour of finding something new, but they are neither less arduous nor less important.

It may seem surprising that Sturt was awarded the Society's highest honour for having given up – "for the prudence with which further advance was abandoned". But events were to prove the Society's perspicacity. For the next two explorers who ventured into the great Australian deserts never came back.

Friedrich Leichhardt was an attractive if eccentric character. Born near Berlin, he studied first at Göttingen then at several universities in England, his expenses at the latter being met by his friends the Nicholsons, who also assisted his passage to Australia. He arrived in Sydney in 1842, and soon made a name for himself as a collector of botanical and geological specimens and a lecturer in natural history. When he heard that an overland expedition was being planned from Sydney to Port Essington (near the present site of Darwin) he applied to join the party as naturalist. But the project suffered so many delays that Leichhardt lost patience and conceived the idea of leading an expedition of his own.

His friends – and he was blessed with many – feared for his safety and did their best to discourage him; but businessmen and farmers, anxious to find new grazing lands, showered him with money, provisions and equipment, and it was a well-found expedition which eventually left the Darling Downs in September 1844. Leichhardt was in his seventh heaven. "If you remember," he wrote, "with what longing I visualized this unknown country, you will understand my joy to find myself in a position to see and explore it. I can hardly master my feelings as I march behind the long line of my companions and horses, and say to myself: 'Your perseverance has been rewarded. . . . And what will people say when I appear suddenly resurrected from the grave with a heap of mountain ranges, rivers and creeks in my pocket!'"

Leichhardt is another explorer it is none too easy to assess. On the credit side his expedition covered 1,800 miles, most of which was through unknown territory; he lost only one man (and this through no fault of his); he brought back much information and a fair number of specimens; and he and his companions obviously enjoyed almost every minute of their journey. On the debit side the country through which he trekked was relatively easy, and there is about his travels an aura of curious insouciance, so that one can never quite be certain he wasn't finding his way as much by accident as by design.

His report, read to the Society in 1846, might be describing a different world from the wilderness which had halted Sturt. Of the Mackenzie he wrote: "This is fine country covered with rich grass and herbs and well watered. Open forests and plains well-stocked with game, honey sweet as that of Hymettus, and the air fragrant with wild thyme and marjoram; no country could be better adapted for pastoral purposes...." Of the Suttor: "The grasses are very various, and [there are] at least twenty different species mixed with herbs, which cattle and horses like to feed on. Water is abundant, the water holes being long and broad and covered with duck...." Of the Burdekin: "The tableland is beautifully grassed, of great extent and well provided with water. This country is peculiarly adapted for sheep stations, the elevation being some 2,000 feet, the ground sound and the forest very open...." Of the east coast of the Gulf of Carpentaria: "In this country cattle and horses would thrive exceedingly well. Large plains, limited by belts of forest, extensive box-flats, fine grassy meadows along frequent chains of lagoons, render the country pleasing to the eye of the traveller and inviting to the squatter." Of the joy of the camp: "As the night advances, the Black fellows' songs die away. The neighing of the tethered horse, the distant tinkling of the bell, or the occasional cry of night birds, alone interrupt the silence of our camp. The fire gets gradually dull, and smoulders slowly under the large pot in which our meat is simmering; and the bright constellations of

Friedrich Leichhardt (1813–1849) whose ingenuous enthusiasm cost him his life. The photograph is of Darwin, scene of Leichhardt's triumphant arrival, at the end of the nineteenth century

Robert O'Hara Burke (1820–1861): the first man to cross the Australian continent from south to north

heaven pass unheeded over the heads of the dreaming wanderers."

Leichhardt arrived at Port Essington in triumph after a journey of sixteen months and eighteen hundred miles. Almost at once he picked up a south-bound vessel, and within a few weeks was back in Sydney. "No king," he wrote, "could have been received with greater joy and affection. I believed the whole town would go mad. I was congratulated from all sides." The Society awarded him its Patron's Medal – an award which, in the President's words, "shows that neither distance nor absence nor foreign birth renders the Council unmindful of the merits of a great discoverer." It must have seemed to Leichhardt that his cup had been filled to overflowing. But within a year he had vanished, never to be heard of again.

The applause for his first expedition had barely subsided when he was setting out on his second, attempting to cross the continent from east to west. This time he was not so successful; his party succumbed one by one to fever, his livestock strayed, the streams on which he was relying for water dried up, and he was lucky to extricate himself and his companions alive. Notwithstanding this near disaster, within six weeks he was off again, this time by himself, optimistically declaring that he intended to "follow the Barcoo to the northward, until I come to the Gulf of Carpentaria, then make for the west coast." He didn't realize – until too late – that the Barcoo flowed north only for its first 150 miles: that it subsequently swung west, into the central deserts, to lose itself among the complex and ephemeral waterholes of Cooper's Creek. Here, at the end of some unknown chain of billabongs, the country which Leichhardt loved so dearly extracted a terrible price for his ingenuous enthusiasm.

An even greater tragedy was to follow.

By the late 1850s the whole periphery of the continent had been explored, but the central deserts remained an enigma; Sturt had pushed into them for some six hundred miles from the south, and Gregory for about half that distance from the north and west, while Leichhardt had opened up the north-eastern segment of the continent and proved it to be not so much desert as pastureland. It seemed hardly likely that the unexplored inner core would also contain good pastures; but to settlers hungry for land the possibility was worth looking into. Another spur to exploration was the element of challenge. Sturt's dream of setting foot in the geographical centre of Australia had by now been metamorphosed to the more grandiose dream of crossing the continent from south to north; and in 1860 two expeditions set out to attempt such a crossing – Stuart's, backed by South Australia, from Adelaide; and Burke's, backed by Victoria, from Melbourne. Human nature being what it is, the crossing took on the trappings of a race:

> *"A race! A race! so great a one*
> *The world ne'er saw before;*
> *A race! A race across this land*
> *From south to northern shore."**

And in this haste lay the seeds of tragedy.

The story of Burke and Wills has probably been retold and reconstructed more often than any other episode in Australian history. The facts are beyond dispute – though how one interprets them is another matter. . . . On 20th August, 1860 an expedition led by Robert O'Hara Burke set out from Melbourne. It was a comparatively large and extremely well-found expedition with 27 camels, 23 horses and 15 men: its object being to find a transcontinental route from south to north through unexplored country. There seem to have been dissensions and quarrels from the start. In October the expedition split up, and an advance party pushed swiftly on to Cooper's Creek, reached in mid-

* The Melbourne *Punch*

November. Here a depot was established close to a permanent water-hole, and the expedition split up again, Burke, Wills and two companions setting off on a dash for the Gulf of Carpentaria, nearly a thousand miles to the north. They got there. And it seems to me regrettable that so much attention has been focused on their subsequent failure and death, and so little on this magnificent feat of exploration. In fact they never actually saw the sea, being halted by floods and tropical thunderstorms on the tidal banks of the Bynoe River, some three or four miles from the Gulf. But it would be churlish to deny them the kudos of having made the first transcontinental crossing. Their journey back was slow and arduous, with all four of them growing progressively weaker from debilitation and scurvy. Everything was much more difficult and took much longer than they expected. It was 21st April before they struggled back, in the last stages of exhaustion, to their depot on Cooper's Creek.

It was deserted. All that was left was a message, buried in a bottle. Burke broke the bottle and read:

"Depot, Cooper's Creek, 21st April, 1861
The depot party of the V.E.E. [Victorian Exploring Expedition] leaves this camp today to return to the Darling. . . . We have six camels and twelve horses in good working condition. . . . William Brahe."

The most agonizing thing was the date. The depot party had pulled out that very morning. After travelling for four months and traversing two-thirds of an unknown continent, Burke had missed his companions by no more than a few hours.

They collapsed in the silent and deserted camp, hardly able to believe that after all they had been through they had been abandoned. Wills's entry that night in his diary is understandably bitter. "Arrived at the depot this evening, to find it deserted. Our disappointment may easily be imagined – returning in an exhausted state, after four months of the severest travelling and privation, our legs almost paralyzed, so that each of us found it a most trying task only to walk a few yards. . . . The exertion required to get up a slight piece of ground induces an indescribable sensation of pain and helplessness, and the general lassitude makes one unfit for anything."

They debated that evening whether to try and catch up with the depot party, which they knew must be only a few hours' trek ahead of them. But they were too weak, and they had the good sense to realize it. So they unearthed the meagre supply of provisions which Brahe had left for them, and decided to stay put until they regained their strength, then head for civilization down Cooper's Creek in the direction of Mount Hopeless. It is hard to find fault with this decision; and when a couple of days later they set off down the Cooper, they probably still thought that all was going to be well; for they had two camels and a reasonable supply of food, and there seemed to be plenty of water. However, to quote Alan Moorehead's classic description, "the Cooper is an unpredictable stream. In a year of exceptional rainfall the head of water comes down with a roar, and for a dozen miles across the flat land there is nothing to be seen but a brown flood with the tops of trees appearing above it. But this only happens every ten years or so. Normally the creek fans out into innumerable channels, which soon dry up into chains of waterholes and billabongs; and the further you go down the creek towards Lake Eyre [and Mount Hopeless] the drier it becomes, until in the end every channel peters out into rocks and sand. It does not matter which you follow; always you end up among sandhills and waterless plains of sharp red rocks with an occasional light covering of thorny bushes. It is not sinister country – it is too bright and open for that – but the spaces are vast, the sun pitiless: time becomes an endless continuum and the hours pass in a torpor. Torpor, inertia – this is what overcomes the traveller, especially if he is on foot."

And soon Burke and his companions *were* on foot; for their camels became bogged down in the quicksand surrounding the waterholes and had to be shot. For a while they

(On the facing page)
Baines's paintings: The longboat of the Messenger *running between the reefs of Cape Stewart and the Crocodiles off the North coast of Australia*

Native paintings found in cliffs near the S.E. branch of the Victoria River, 1856

struggled on, growing progressively weaker. Then, realizing that they hadn't the strength to cover the eighty-odd miles to Mount Hopeless, they gave up, and retraced their steps towards their original depot in Cooper's Creek. Again it is difficult to see how they could have acted otherwise. Back at the Creek, they were befriended by Aborigines, who managed for a while to keep them alive with gifts of fish and nardoo seed – "the blacks," wrote Wills, "are very hospitable and attentive." But the Aborigines' kindness could only delay the end, not prevent it. Wills died on about 1st July, Burke perhaps a couple of days later; Gray had died on the return journey from the Gulf; the only survivor was King, whom a relief party found three months later "in an appalling state, burnt by the sun and half-demented with starvation and loneliness."

No-one disputes that these are the facts. What *is* in dispute is how to interpret them; how to apportion the blame.

Most people point a finger at the unfortunate Burke. It is a bit like the inquest which follows an air crash; the obvious person to blame is the pilot – especially if he is dead. Certainly the Royal Commission appointed by the Victorian government was censorious. "Mr. Burke evinced a far greater amount of zeal than prudence in departing from Cooper's Creek before the depot party had arrived, and without having secured communications with the settled districts; and in undertaking so extended a journey with an insufficient supply of provisions [he] was forced into the necessity of overtaxing the powers of his party, whose continuous and unremitting exertions resulted in the destruction of his animals, and the prostration of himself and his companions from fatigue and privation. . . . It does not appear that Mr. Burke kept any regular journal, or that he gave written instructions to his officers. Had he performed these essential portions of the duty of a leader, many of the calamities of the expedition might have been averted."

This may have a weighty and judicial ring to it; but nevertheless it is sophistry! For in

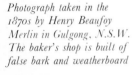

Photograph taken in the 1870s by Henry Beaufoy Merlin in Gulgong, N.S.W. The baker's shop is built of false bark and weatherboard

Another of Merlin's photographs, taken in the spring of 1872, showing the hazards of travel. The waggon has come to grief in Clarke Street, Hill End, N.S.W.

pushing on as fast as possible from Cooper's Creek, Burke was simply following instructions; and how could it have made the slightest difference to the fate of his party if he had kept the most detailed of diaries? The truth surely is that the real culprits were the stay-at-homes, the members of the Victorian Exploring Committee who, firstly, chose Burke as their expedition leader, deliberately overlooking his inexperience and eccentricities, and secondly made it all too plain that they wanted him to be first to cross the continent, for the honour of Victoria. "John Stuart," the Committee chairman wrote to Burke, "has already left Adelaide with an increased number – 12 in all and 36 horses – so it will to a certain extent be a race between you and he." Under this sort of pressure, is it to be wondered that the expedition-leader pushed on as fast as he could? But perhaps the final word in the tragedy of Burke and Wills should be given to the one man whose conduct and ability were at all times beyond reproach: the young and serious-minded William Wills. A few days before he died, Wills wrote in a letter to his father: "Cannot possibly last more than a fortnight. But it is a great consolation, in this position of ours, to know that we have done all we could, and that our deaths will rather be the result of mismanagement of others than any rash act of our own" – a judgment which today is widely if not universally accepted.

The Society awarded its Founder's medal to Burke: "in remembrance of that gallant explorer who with his companions perished after having traversed the continent of Australia from south to north." There was a general feeling that Wills ought to be given a medal too; especially since he was the one geographer in the expedition and it was largely due to his ability that the party had achieved the crossing. The president, Sir Roderick Murchison, however, felt obliged to abide by the Society's rule that only one medal be awarded for any one expedition. So Wills won only the verbal accolade that "nothing less than a medal could have been given to so good a geographer . . . and that his merits will never be forgotten."

John McDouall Stuart (1815–1866) the first man to cross the Australian continent from south to north and return alive

Never is a long time; but it may well be true that for as long as men's hearts are stirred by great feats of endurance, so long will the names of Burke and Wills be bracketed together as among the most tragic if not the greatest of explorers.

A more successful, but almost equally tragic, explorer was John McDouall Stuart. Stuart, it will be remembered, had set out from Adelaide at much the same time as Burke and Wills had set out from Melbourne. He was an experienced campaigner, who had served his apprenticeship with Sturt; and he made three attempts in all to cross the continent from south to north.

On his first journey, in 1860, he passed the Macdonnell Ranges and became the first man to reach the geographical centre of the continent. Here he planted the British flag "on a hill which I named Central Mount Sturt, after the father of Australian exploration, for whom we gave three hearty cheers." He then pushed north into the area round Tennant Creek; but scurvy, lack of water and the hostility of the Aborigines forced him to turn back.

Next year he tried again, with 13 companions and more than 40 horses, in an expedition which coincided with that of Burke and Wills. He got as far as Newcastle Waters, and from there made no fewer than eleven unsuccessful attempts to break through to the Gulf of Carpentaria – a setback which enables us to see Burke and Wills's achievement in proper perspective. Again he was forced to fall back, desperately short of water and provisions, with his health beginning to break down under the strain of continual privation.

In 1862 he was off again, this time with 10 men and as many as 70 horses. "I feel the work more than I did last year," he wrote, "and fear my capability of endurance [is] beginning to give way." He struggled through to Newcastle Waters, and managed this time to discover a chain of waterholes which led him to the Roper River. This he followed to the Gulf of Carpentaria, which he reached some six months after leaving Adelaide. "Stopped the horses," he wrote, "whilst I advanced to the beach, and was gratified and delighted to behold the water of the Indian Ocean. . . . I dipped my feet and washed my face and hands in the sea, as I promised I would do if I reached it." He hoisted the Union Jack in the tallest tree he could find, and left a message: "The exploring party, under the command of John McDouall Stuart, arrived at this spot on 25th July, 1862, having crossed the entire continent of Australia from the Southern to the Indian Ocean, passing through the centre. To commemorate this happy event, they have raised this flag. All well. God save the Queen!"

The journey back was both hazardous and harrowing. The horses were weak, provisions were low, water was scarce and Stuart was afflicted by encroaching blindness and scurvy. On 3rd August he suffered a stroke and was so weakened and crippled that his men feared for his life. After a few days he made a partial recovery, but for the rest of the journey was in constant pain. "What a miserable life mine is now," he wrote on October 7th, "I get no rest night nor day from this terrible gnawing pain; the nights are too long and the days are too long, and I am so weak that I am hardly able to move about the camp." He was carried for a while between two horses on a specially-designed stretcher; then on 27th October he suffered another stroke "of terrible violence". . . . "I have asked King and Nash," he wrote, "to sit with me in case of my dying during the night, for it would be lonely for one man to be there by himself." Again, against all expectations, he recovered, and managed to struggle back to Adelaide. But his health, like that of his friend and mentor Sturt, had been damaged beyond repair. He made his will and returned to England, half-blind, half-crippled and wholly unable to work.

Stuart was one of the greatest – arguably *the* greatest of Australian explorers. He was the first man to reach the centre of the continent, and the first man to cross it and survive; he spent more than ten years in the outback, exploring and opening-up the central deserts; in the expeditions of which he was leader he never lost a man; he was well-liked and generous to a fault – even naming the central point in the continent not after himself but after a friend. The telegraph line from Adelaide to Darwin follows the route that he pioneered, so does the railway to Alice Springs and the Stuart Highway. One would have liked to record that his achievements were recognized and rewarded. On the contrary. Both the British Government and the South Australian Government refused him a pension. Crippled and unable to find employment because of his injuries, in the last few years of his life he was reduced to poverty, and if the Society hadn't come to his aid he would have died destitute. The Society reminded the Colonial Office, in no uncertain terms, of their medallist's achievements. "In no time or country," wrote the president, "has any pioneer more directly advanced the interests of a colony than Mr. Stuart has done for South Australia; whilst as geographers we specially recognize the value of the astronomical observations he made under the severest privation, by which the true features of the interior and the north coast have been for the first time determined." The Society, after some pretty acrimonious correspondence, managed to extract for Stuart a "compensatory award", enabling him to die in a degree of comfort.

Few men have given so much and been given so little so grudgingly in return.

Augustus Charles Gregory (1819–1905) leader of the Society's North Australian Exploring Expedition. Surveyor-General of Queensland

The expeditions of Burke and Stuart finally dispelled the myth of an inland sea and proved that the centre of the continent consisted mainly of desert; the south likewise was known to be little more than a wilderness; the south-east had been settled, and the north-east was about to be settled; so the only places where new pastures might still be found were in the west and north. It was therefore to those areas that exploration was now directed by men such as Gregory, Warburton and Forrest.

Augustus Charles Gregory was the eldest of four brothers, all of whom played an important role in pushing back the Australian frontier. "In 1846," to quote Feeken and Spate's classic work *The Discovery and Exploration of Australia*, "the known grazing land in the west was fully stocked and expansion was checked by the unexplored districts beyond, and so expeditions into the new regions became essential. Augustus Gregory and his brother Frank, both of whom were attached to the survey office, prepared for an expedition to the north of Perth [and] . . . the government provided them with horses and provisions." The brothers covered 953 miles in 47 days, but to their disappointment found the country "extremely dry, with whirlwinds of red dust, immense salt marshes and sandstone cliffs"; they did, however, discover coal, and early in September "had the satisfaction of seeing the first fire of Western Australian coal burning cheerfully in front of [their] camp."

A couple of years later Augustus Gregory was off again, this time with a younger brother and farther to the north. He covered 1,500 miles in 71 days, and discovered the occasional pocket of grazing land – about a hundred thousand acres in the valley of the Bowes River, and twenty thousand acres along the shore of Champion Bay. Once again, however, his most significant discovery was of minerals. "The existence of garnets, iron pyrites and plumbago," he wrote, "which were found in the gneiss, seems to indicate a metalliferous formation, and I have little doubt that a further search would reveal many hidden sources of wealth."

Tree photographed in 1890 showing the camp site of Gregory's expedition to the bank of the Victoria River

Disappointed in the west, Gregory next planned an expedition to the north; and he now found unexpected allies in the Royal Geographical Society and the Secretary of State for the Colonies.

The Society had for years been pressing the Government to survey the Gulf of Carpentaria, and its president now put forward the proposal "that Mr. Gregory be conveyed to the mouth of the Victoria River, and that his expedition should act in concert with a government vessel employed in surveying operations in the Gulf." The idea was well received; and with financial backing from both London and Perth, the expedition was planned on a lavish scale with two ships (the schooner *Tom Tough* and the

Native studies by Thomas Baines, drawn during the North Australian Exploring Expedition of 1855/56. Baines was something of an ethnologist, and his sketches record the Aborigines and their way of life with meticulous accuracy

barque *Monarch*), 50 horses, 200 sheep, provisions for eighteen months, and eighteen men, including a surgeon, a geologist, a botanist and the talented and much travelled artist Thomas Baines, many of whose paintings today grace the walls of the Society's headquarters in London.

Gregory's expedition got off to an unfortunate start. For as soon as she arrived at the mouth of the Victoria, the *Monarch* promptly ran aground and couldn't be refloated for several weeks. Soon the animals on board were dying of thirst. An attempt had to be made to get them ashore; but, to quote Baines's biographer J. P. R. Wallis, "between the barque and the shore flowed a strongish tide across which the animals had to be towed behind boats. Five horses were swept away, one was lost in a mangrove swamp, another escaped and could not be caught and three died aboard ship. Fifty sheep were also taken ashore in the hope that they might be able to reach the rich grass and water at the foot of the hills; but some succumbed to drinking salt water, some perished of sheer weakness and the others were unable to reach the pasture." A few days later and a few miles upriver the *Tom Tough* also got into difficulties. Again to quote Wallis: "She grounded on the south bank, and succeeding flood tides merely carried her from one shoal to another. At length she stuck on a ledge of rock, and in attempts to haul her off she lost an anchor and cable and strained herself so badly that it was feared she would break up. The water rose four feet in her hold, damaging much of the bread and other stores. . . . Sheep died daily, and when at last, after much pumping, running ashore and being warped off, she managed to drop anchor off the camp, only 29 miserable skeletons remained."

To add to their difficulties the members of the expedition quarrelled among themselves, James Wilson the geologist resigning; they suffered from vomiting and ophthalmia, and were several times attacked by the Aborigines. Eventually, Gregory split his unwieldy and contentious expedition into two; one party remaining close to their camp and subsequently sailing in the *Tom Tough* and her longboat along much of the north coast of Australia, the second party exploring first the Victoria River and subsequently cutting across Arnhem Land, the Barkly Tableland and the Gregory Ranges until they came to that part of Queensland which had been opened up by Leichhardt. The distances involved were enormous, Gregory himself covering at least 5,000 miles, often on foot; and although neither party made any dramatic or unexpected discoveries, they did between them map more than five million acres of little-known land and chart more than a thousand square miles of little-known coastal waters. This was a fine piece of exploration; and if one asks why Gregory isn't better known, the answer would seem to lie partly in his character and partly in the character of the country he traversed.

Augustus Gregory doesn't so much emerge from the past as have to be prised from it. He was a man of few words, restrained opinions, sensible judgments, conventional views and pedestrian prose. This isn't to imply that he was not a sound leader and a most meritorious explorer; but his very virtues make his *Journal of the North Australian Exploring Expedition* unexciting reading. And the lack of excitement in his narrative is accentuated by the lack of variety in the terrain through which he travelled. It wasn't unattractive country; it was simply all so very much the same: hundreds of thousands of square miles of desiccated palaeozoic tableland, seldom less than 300 feet in height, seldom more than 900, covered with poor gravelly soil, well grassed but poorly timbered. Take almost any extract from Gregory's *Journal*, and whether it is summer or winter, and whether he is at the mouth of the Victoria, the source of the Sturt, crossing the Barkly Tableland or emerging into Leichhardt's Plains of Promise, his entries could almost be interchanged:

"October 1st, 1855 [near the mouth of the Victoria]. Left camp to search for a practicable route by which the party could cross the MacAdam Range. Pursuing a S.E. course, crossed a stony ridge, and at 8 a.m. came to a creek 20 yards wide, with good pools of water and grassy banks, but the country generally barren and stony. After several unsuccessful attempts, we ascended the hills to the S.E. of the creek, and traversed a very broken country, of sandstone formation till 11, when we reached the head of a creek trending southwards. This was followed down till 1, when we halted for an hour before again proceeding till 4.30, the country being very poor and rising into rocky hills on both banks of the creek. We then entered a wide grassy flat, destitute of trees, bounded on all sides by rocky hills of sandstone of barren aspect. . . . Water is abundant in the creeks, but grass scanty, and the rough surface of the sandstone and the frequent rocky ravines render the country difficult to traverse. Timber is scarce, consisting chiefly of small eucalypt."

"February 7th, 1856 [on their way to the headwaters of the Sturt]. At 6.30 resumed our route to the S.S.W. and reached the head of the creek by 8. Ascending the tableland by an abrupt slope our course was S. for 1 mile, when we came to a large shallow valley extending across our course. Beyond, was a vast slightly undulating plain extending to the horizon, with scarcely a rising ground to relieve the extreme monotony of surface; the county being covered with triodia, small acacia and gum-trees or rather bushes. . . . Though the horses are well shod, they are becoming lame and footsore from continually travelling over rough stony country; more than half of the last 100 miles traversed have been so completely covered with fragments of rock that the soil has been wholly concealed from sight."

"July 27th 1856 [approaching the Barkly Tableland]. Resumed our route at 7, crossing a very rugged ridge of hills, in descending one of which a horse wedged his foot into a cleft of the rock, and falling down was only extricated by beating away the rock with an axe. With some difficulty we extricated ourselves from these rocky ridges, and, crossing a large creek, entered a level plain covered with melaleuca scrub. Crossed two sandy creeks 15 and 20 yards wide, with shallow pools of water. At noon passed a barren ridge of sandstone hills, and entered a grassy plain. . . . The country traversed is of a worthless character; there is little grass and the soil is poor and stony. Eucalypti and triodia are abundant."

"September 4th 1856 [crossing Leichhardt's optimistically-named Plains of Promise]. Continued on a S.E. course through large open plains, thinly grassed. Passed a dry waterhole with a small pool in one of the side channels, but the quantity insufficient for our horses. At noon camped at a shallow waterhole in a grassy flat. Mr. Elsay walked $\frac{1}{2}$ mile to the E, and came to a river 80 yards wide, but, observing some blacks, returned to the camp. . . . The character of the country is inferior, as the grass which covers the plains is principally aristida and andropogon. To the south lay low ridges and stony plains covered with scrub and triodia."

No-one could deny the meticulous accuracy of Gregory's *Journal*. There were however, two ways of interpreting it. The settlers looked at his frequent references to stony soil, bare rock, stunted trees and triodia and decided that the northern reaches of the continent would provide poor grazing for their cattle and sheep. Officials in London, on the other hand, looked at his frequent references to grassy plains, warm climate and many rivers, and decided it was high time the territory was settled. The Society inclined very much to the latter point of view: witness Sir Roderick Murchison's presidential address in the summer of 1858:

"We cannot often expect to grasp so much fresh geographical knowledge respecting this vast country as was laid before us by Mr. Gregory and his associates. . . . Mr. Wilson, the expedition's geologist, estimates that they discovered tracts of not less than 5,000,000 acres in extent which, being covered by grasses and well watered, are especially fitted for pasture and permanent settlement. He points out that no

The North Australian
Exploring Expedition was
more successful on land than
by sea. Its vessels the
Monarch and Tom
Tough were frequently in
trouble. Baines's sketches
show them aground near the
mouth of the Victoria River.
The longboat was also often
at hazard – it is shown
being attacked by Aborigines
who had approached on the
pretext of selling turtle

The Tom Tough, aground in the Victoria River
5.30 PM Sunday Sept 16 1855

Indian Head

other part of Australia possesses so many navigable rivers as this northern seaboard; that the climate, though hot, is by no means injurious to European life; that the grasses are luxuriant, rice is indigenous, fish are plentiful. . . . North Australia ought unquestionably to be occupied without further delay."

For his protracted and far-ranging exploration Gregory was awarded the Society's Founder's medal. History, however, has endorsed the view of the settlers. Fifty years after Gregory's journey, the Northern Territory – an area larger than France, Germany, Italy and the United Kingdom put together – still had a population of less than 3,000; and even today there are fewer people in the whole of this forbidding wilderness than in an average English town.

While Gregory was pushing back the frontier in the north, Peter Egerton Warburton was doing the same in the south. In 1857 Warburton surveyed the sterile approaches to Lake Gardner, and a couple of years later made significant discoveries in the area between Lakes Eyre and Torrens. His greatest expedition, however – that of 1873 – was carried out, not in the south of the continent, but in the centre. It was a remarkable expedition on two counts: when he set out from Alice Springs Warburton was within a few weeks of his sixtieth birthday, and for transport he relied entirely on camels. His objective was "to search for pastoral areas to the west of the overland telegraph line, and if possible to penetrate to the northwestern coast." A glance at the map reveals that his route lay through forbidding territory: first the Macdonnell Ranges, then the Gibson and finally the Great Sandy Desert.

Within forty-eight hours of leaving the Alice, Warburton was "obliged to settle down for the night without water": an entry in his diary which was to be repeated many times during the next eight months. Indeed it would be no exaggeration to say that his journey consisted of long waterless treks, interspersed with short thankful rests at the waterholes which seemed always to materialize just as his party was nearing the end of its tether. He found no new pastures: only a succession of barren ranges, stony deserts and plains knee-deep in triodia – the latter being nicely described by H. W. Bates, the secretary of the Society who edited Warburton's diaries, as "one of the most cheerless objects an explorer can meet. For the country it loves to dwell in is utterly useless for pastoral purposes." Several times the expedition came close to disaster. More than half their camels died. On at least three occasions they were only saved from dying of thirst by following Aborigines to their wells. Warburton himself became so weak that he had to be strapped to his camel's back. "What is to become of us," he wrote, "I do not know. . . ." At the end of six months he had struggled two-thirds of the way to the coast. He had now passed the point of no return; but his provisions were low, and his camels were having to plod across the line of an endless succession of sand-dunes. Progress was unbelievably slow. In a month he made only forty miles to the westward. "Our condition is so critical," he wrote, "that I am determined, should it please God to give us once more water, to risk everything and make a final push for the river Oakover. Some of us might reach it, if not all. . . ." His trek to the headwaters of the Oakover has been well described as a triumph of tenacity, endurance and fortitude. He arrived with his water bottles literally empty, and both his men and his camels in the last stages of exhaustion. "We were all very thankful," he wrote laconically, "to have escaped with our lives out of this most horrid desert." For having traversed nearly a thousand miles of forbidding unexplored and almost waterless terrain, Warburton was awarded the Society's Patron's medal.

The same award was given, a couple of years later, to John Forrest, who has been described as "one of the most successful of all Australian explorers".

Forrest was given command of his first expedition – part of the search for Leichhardt – at the age of twenty-one. From Perth he headed north-east, investigating reports that Aborigines on the periphery of the Gibson Desert had found skeletons and guns. The skeletons, however, turned out to be those of horses, whereas Leichhardt on his last journey was known to have been on foot. "So far as the mystery of Leich[h]ardt is concerned," wrote Forrest, "my expedition was barren of results; but the additional knowledge gained of the country between the settled districts and the 123rd meridian, well repaid me, and those of the party, for the exertions we had undergone."

The following year he took charge of another expedition: keeping close to Eyre's route, though somewhat further inland, along the Great Australian Bight. It was a grim journey parallel to one of the bleakest shorelines in the world. "The cliffs," he wrote, "were terrible to gaze from, and after peering very cautiously over the precipice, we all ran back quite terror-stricken by the dreadful view." This expedition, thanks largely to Forrest's leadership, was successful in that it completed and surveyed its intended route, although it added little to geographical knowledge.

John Forrest (1847–1918): surveyor, explorer, Premier of Western Australia and the first Australian statesman to be raised to the peerage

His third journey was more substantial: a trek of immense distance and difficulty, cutting diagonally across the continent from Shark Bay in the north-west to Adelaide in the south-east. His first stage via the Murchison River was comparatively simple, so was his last stage following the telegraph line to Adelaide; but the long central section across the Gibson and Great Victorian Deserts and the Baker, Cavanagh and Musgrave Ranges lies through some of the most daunting terrain in the continent. Time and again, just when it seemed that he would have to give up, Forrest, like Warburton, managed to locate a waterhole containing perhaps three or four gallons of brackish water: enough to enable him to edge precariously forward, until a couple of days later the same crisis caught up with him again. The President of the Society, when presenting the awards for 1874, paid tribute both to Forrest and to his fellow-explorers.

"The Patron's Medal this year has been awarded to a most meritorious traveller, Mr. J. Forrest, in recognition of his numerous successful expeditions and especially for his survey of the interior from the Murchison River to the line of the Overland Telegraph. Already on eight occasions the Council has awarded its prize of the year to an Australian explorer. For the enormous tracts of uninhabited unknown and often waterless territory, and the difficulty of transit, give a special grandeur and importance to Australian discovery. Never, however, since Macdouall Stuart traversed the continent from south to north has a journey been undertaken of the same magnitude and difficulty as that accomplished by Mr. Forrest and his party; and never certainly has a more conscientious and exhaustive survey been executed along so arduous a route."

This well-deserved tribute marks the end of an era.

There were great Australian journeys after Forrest's – those of the romantic Giles being of particular interest and merit – but with the continent now crossed both from south to north and from west to east, the blank spaces on the map were reduced to little more than small and isolated pockets. The outback had not been conquered nor even tamed – quite possibly it never will be – but by 1880 it was no longer *terra incognita*; there was no longer the possibility of it holding any major surprises, no inland sea nor range of lofty mountains nor belt of luxuriant pasture. And this great feat of exploration had all happened within thirty or at the most forty years.

This point is emphasized by Clements Markham, the Society's long-serving president and historian: "In Australia and New Zealand," he wrote in 1880, "the whole interior of these countries has been discovered and explored since the Society was founded. The maps of 1830 show little more than inaccurate coastlines. Now the arid wastes of Australia have been traversed in various directions, and the whole continent has been crossed from sea to sea, with an amount of brave endurance and indomitable courage which have excited the admiration of geographers, and gained for the explorers concerned the highest honours that the Society can bestow."

In Australia most of the successful exploration had been carried out by the settlers themselves, and the Society had little more than a watching brief. It was a very different story in the other continents: especially in Africa.

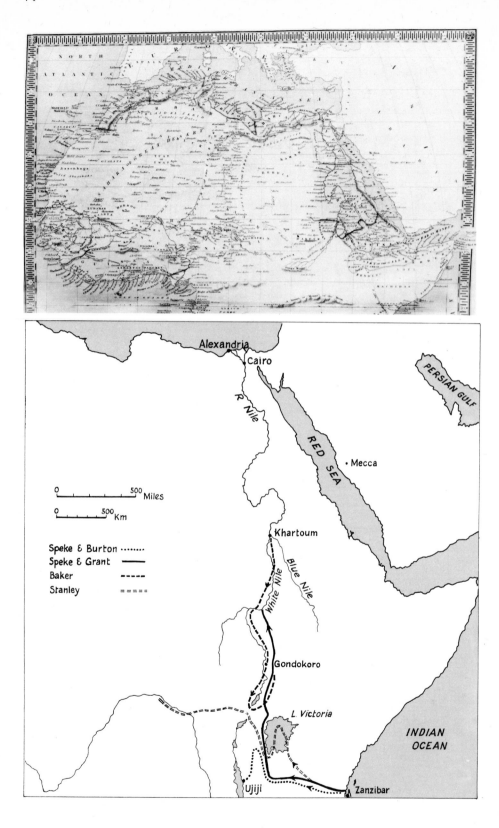

4. The Quest for the Sources of the Nile

ROM TIME IMMEMORIAL THE RIVER HAD BEEN WORSHIPPED AS A GOD; SO PERHAPS
it was not surprising that its conception was veiled in mystery. "Of the sources of the
Nile," wrote Herodotus, "no-one can give any account. It enters Egypt from parts
beyond."

The god had never been known to fail. Year after year, millennium after millennium,
the great brown flood came pouring out of the desert, being swelled by virtually no
tributaries, added to by hardly a drop of rain. Yet each September – the hottest and
driest month of the year – it overflowed its banks, transforming its flood-plain into one of
the richest crop-growing areas in the world. For millions of people, for tens of thousands
of years, the Nile was the be-all and end-all of life.

Yet no-one knew where it came from.

Countless expeditions and a fair number of individuals had attempted to follow the
river to its source. All had failed: defeated by cataracts, swamps, forests of papyrus-reed,
fever, heat and sheer distance. By the middle of the nineteenth century it was generally
agreed that "the source of the Nile is the most important of all geographical questions";
yet less was known about this source than in the days of Ptolemy and Herodotus.

It was a challenge which the Royal Geographical Society was eager to take up.

*Arab slavers taking their
captives to Tete: from
Livingstone's Expedition
to the Zambesi, 1865*

75

The Society played a major role in the explorations of Africa. It sponsored, assisted or honoured nearly all of the great African discoverers – Burton, Speke, Lander, Barth, Baker, Livingstone and Stanley – and hardly a corner of the continent escaped the probing of its expeditions.

The Society's special interest in Africa may have sprung originally from the fact that many of its founder members were members also of Sir Joseph Banks's African Association, an association which was incorporated into the RGS in 1831 and which had a long tradition of training and sending explorers to what was still virtually an unknown continent. In addition to this, the Society's interest in Africa was subsequently fostered by successive governments as part of a deliberate policy. For the government knew that, where exploration led, trade would follow; to the governments of Europe, nineteenth-century Africa was territory ripe for exploitation, and it was therefore always easier for the Society to get financial backing to explore in Africa than in, say, the Arctic or Antarctica.

Three other factors gave impetus to the Society's African activities. The continent was a paradise to the hunter, a challenge to the missionary and an affront to the opponents of slavery.

It may seem odd nowadays to equate exploration with hunting. Yet many of the great explorers of Africa – Galton, Baker and Speke, to mention only three – were also great sportsmen and assiduous collectors of trophies. When Galton went to South West Africa he packed his full hunting kit, and there is a marvellous story of his jumping his ox over a four-foot ditch surrounding a kraal and remarking that "oxen, if you give them time, are not at all bad leapers!" More than one of Livingstone's epic journeys was made in the company of big-game hunters.

Another spur to exploration was missionary zeal. Livingstone is the obvious example. But of almost equal stature as explorers are the German missionaries from Mombasa, men like Krapf, Rebmann and Erhardt, who not only blazed a trail to the snows of Kilimanjaro but restored faith in Herodotus's map, on which the sources of the Nile were shown as three fountains (or lakes) rising astride the Equator in the Mountains of the Moon. Nor should the work of the Jesuits in Abyssinia be forgotten; without their influence the source of the Blue Nile might well have remained almost as well guarded a secret as the source of the White Nile.

As for the opponents of the slave trade, they were numerous, vocal and influential in Victorian England. They repeatedly petitioned the Government to "put an end to this appalling traffic in souls", and backed their demands with considerable sums of money raised at meetings throughout the country. Their concern was an inspiration to many of the greatest explorers – Livingstone and Baker in particular.

Towards the middle of the nineteenth century these powerful but disparate forces were given cohesion and direction by one man: a man whose personality mirrors in a quite remarkable way the factors influencing exploration in Africa. Sir Roderick Murchison was a dedicated sportsman, a dedicated Christian and an outspoken opponent of the slave trade. He was also the *éminence grise* of the Royal Geographical Society, a man who was not only one of the most distinguished geologists in Europe but was utterly devoted to the cause of advancing geographical knowledge. Over a span of twenty years he was the Society's president for no fewer than fourteen, and during his long regime he directed operations in Africa much as Barrow a couple of decades earlier had directed them in the Arctic. Barrow's grail had been the North West Passage. Murchison's was the sources of the Nile.

In his presidential address of 1852 he nailed his colours to the mast.

"In the absence of adequate data we are not entitled to speculate too confidently on the true sources of the White Nile. But judging from the observations of the

(On the facing page)
*The Ripon Falls:
watercolour by Sir Harry
Johnston, 1884*

missionaries Krapf and Rebmann, and the position of the snow-capped mountains called Kilimanjaro and Kenia (only distant from the eastern sea about 300 miles) it may be said that there is no exploration in Africa to which greater value would be attached than an ascent of these mountains from the east coast, possibly from near Mombasa. The adventurous travellers who shall first lay down the true position of these equatorial snowy mountains and who shall satisfy us that they throw off the waters of the White Nile . . . will be justly considered among the greatest benefactors of this age of geographical science."

A few months after this address had been given, Richard Burton returned from his famous pilgrimage to Mecca. Here, it seemed to the Society, was the very epitome of an "adventurous traveller", and they suggested to Burton that he should lead an expedition which would head inland from the east coast and determine the source of the Nile. Burton was interested, but sceptical. He had no time for missionaries. "Krapf has just arrived from Zanzibar," he wrote, "with discoveries about sources of White Nile, Kilimanjaro and Mts. of Moon which remind me of *de Lunatico.*" He suggested that instead of searching for the Nile so far to the south, he should take an expedition through Somalia to the forbidden city of Harar, and the Society somewhat reluctantly agreed. The vicissitudes of this expedition and the Crimean War kept Burton occupied until 1856 when Murchison approached him again, this time with success. In his annual address the president stresses how much the forthcoming expedition was a leap in the dark. "I must call your attention to the limited extent of our knowledge of Equatorial Africa. This extensive region, occupying nearly twenty degrees of latitude, and extending from coast to coast, still remains 'terra incognita'. . . . The source of the Nile lies mysteriously hidden somewhere in this vast unexplored area. Who shall unlock its mysteries? We trust that this question will not long remain unanswered. For the gallant Commander of the expedition to Harar, Captain Burton, has volunteered to proceed from Zanzibar inland towards the Sea of Niassa, and, after exploring its locality, to turn northward towards the Bahr el Abiad [the White Nile]."

Burton's expedition was very much the child of the Society. The Society suggested it, secured a £1,000 grant from the government to finance it, arranged leave for the expedition-members, and drew up precise instructions which the leader was expected to follow. Dorothy Middleton, in her lecture *The Search for the Nile Sources*, emphasizes this latter point. "[There was no question] of the explorers operating on the basis of personal impulse and 'hunch'. The RGS exercised a strict control, and gave very detailed directions which they expected to see carried out. This attitude was part of the African Association's tradition; they were meticulous employers, and [in some cases] actually arranged a course of training before the journey was embarked on. Their instructions in this instance were based on information that had been coming in [to the Society] for some time. There was undoubtedly a large lake inland from the east coast, and there were mountains rather imprecisely indicated, all of which was sketched on a tentative map during discussions at the Society's headquarters in London. Porters were to be collected in Zanzibar. . . . And the Society told Burton to explore first the 'Nyasa' [the Swahili word for lake] and then turn northwards to investigate possible mountains which might give rise to the White Nile."

Burton and his companion Speke set out from Zanzibar in June 1857. They were an unlikely pair: Burton a linguist and scholar whose intellectual accomplishments can only be described as formidable – he spoke 29 languages and probably had a deeper knowledge of Islamic culture than any European alive – Speke a meticulous and painstaking conformist to the beliefs of Victorian England. They recruited, not without difficulty, a motley collection of servants, overseers and porters, and headed west along one of the Arab slave routes. The climate was humid, the terrain rugged, the porters

(On the facing page) *Na 'Mweri (Ripon) Falls: watercolour by John Hanning Speke*

Grant's map of his route from Bagamoyo near Lake Victoria to Gondokoro on the White Nile, signed by J. A. Grant 1863, annotated "This miniature map is the result of a foot march with compass in hand checked only by lunar, J. H. Speke, 26th Feb. 1863"

Livingstone's sketch of the Victoria Falls

recalcitrant; within a fortnight both Burton and Speke went down with malaria. It took them five months, averaging less than four-and-a-half miles a day, to struggle through to Tabora, the great inland market for the slave trade. Here they paused to recuperate: Burton thankful to be in the company of his friends the Arabs, Speke anxious to press on, and in particular to investigate reports of a huge lake to the northward, "a lake which no white man had hitherto set eyes on."

After a month of rest they were again heading inland, if not exactly into the unknown – for the slavers had been here before them – at least into an area unmapped and unvisited by Europeans. They suffered from just about every ill that white men in equatorial Africa are heir to: fever, dysentery, hallucinations, elephantiasis. Burton's legs became paralysed, and he had to be carried everywhere on a stretcher. Speke became both deaf and blind. But somehow they struggled through to "the Sea of Ujiji" – Lake Tanganyika – which they hoped and indeed confidently believed would prove to be the source of the Nile.

They were disappointed. The natives they questioned were unanimous in their verdict. There *was* a great river at the northern end of Lake Tanganyika. But it flowed not out of the lake but into it.

To say that Burton and Speke were disheartened would be putting it a great deal too mildly. After eight months of the most appalling hardships and suffering they had reached their goal, only to find that it didn't contain the prize they had anticipated. They spent three and a half months on the shores of Lake Tanganyika, and even if one makes allowance for their ill health it seems surprising that they never pressed on to the northern tip of the lake and actually saw the Ruzizi River flowing into it. One suspects that Burton at least had had his fill of exploring, and saw no point in having his fears confirmed. So by mid-June, almost exactly a year after leaving Zanzibar, they were back at Tabora.

Here, for the time being, they parted company, Burton, who was primarily a traveller, staying in the trading-centre to write up his notes while Speke, who was primarily an explorer, headed north to try and locate the great lake which no white man had set eyes on.

He found it.

"On August 3rd," he wrote in his diary, "the vast expanse of the pale blue waters of the N'yanza burst suddenly upon my gaze. . . . I no longer felt any doubt that the lake at my feet gave birth to that river the source of which has been the subject of so much speculation and the object of so many explorers."

Speke fixed the exact position of the lake and its height above sea level, was told by local tribesmen that it extended for more than 200 miles to the north. He then went back to Burton and claimed that he had discovered the source of the Nile.

One widely accepted theory of what happened next is that Burton reacted coldly, piqued that it was not he but his subordinate who had solved the mystery of the Nile: that there was a great deal of acrimonious wrangling and the two men agreed not to discuss the question of the Nile until they returned to England: and finally that Speke out-manoeuvred Burton by getting back to England first, where he attracted all the kudos to himself and persuaded the Royal Geographical Society to give him command of a follow-up expedition to explore Lake Victoria more thoroughly.

This interpretation, however, is by no means borne out either by the facts or by the correspondence of the explorers themselves. In Tabora, according to both men's diaries, Burton was thankful to see his companion back; there had been tribal war in the country he had been passing through, and Burton had feared for his safety. Their meeting was "warm and friendly", and to quote Dorothy Middleton "Burton was quite prepared to believe in a great lake to the north and to suppose it part of the Nile system". What he *did* say – and quite rightly – was that Speke had little tangible evidence to support his claim

Sir Richard Burton (1821–1890): explorer, scholar and Orientalist whose rapport with the Arab world made him view Africa and the Africans with a jaundiced eye

to have discovered the source of the Nile: that he had surveyed only a small part of the southern shore of the lake, and that he hadn't actually seen the spot where any river (let alone the Nile) flowed out of it. On their way back to Zanzibar it is true that Burton and Speke "lashed out at one another", and that when they arrived at the coast they had heated words about paying off the porters. There is no evidence, however, that their quarrels had much to do with the Nile. Both men, it should be remembered, were ill, they had been living in one another's pockets for eighteen months, they were both – and here perhaps was the crunch – essentially loners whom circumstances had thrown together. No wonder they were heartily sick of the sight of one another, and that the moment the expedition broke up they went their separate ways, the conventional Speke returning post-haste to London to make a report, the unconventional Burton pausing in Egypt and (to quote his own words written earlier) "living in a house which was a precious scene of depravity, showing what Cairo can do at a pinch and beating the Arabian Nights all to chalks". There is no evidence to support the theory that Speke, in the words of one of Burton's biographers, "sneaked off" to England and ingratiated himself with the Society without Burton's knowledge. Indeed a couple of days after Speke sailed for England Burton wrote to the Society expressly to tell them that "Captain Speke will lay before you his map observations . . . and there are reasons for believing it [Speke's Lake Victoria] to be the source or the principal feeder of the White Nile." Nor does there seem to have been the slightest animosity when, in May 1859, Burton came to London to receive the Society's Gold Medal. On the contrary, in his speech of thanks to the president Burton went out of his way to pay tribute to his companion. "You have alluded, sir," he said on receiving the medal, "to the success of the expedition. Justice compels me to relate the circumstances under which it attained that success. To Captain Speke are due those geographical results to which you have alluded in such flattering terms. Whilst I undertook the history and ethnography, the languages and the peculiarities of the people, to Captain Speke fell the arduous task of delineating an exact topography and of laying down our positions by astronomical observations – a labour to which at times even the undaunted Livingstone found himself unequal."

Yet within a few months Burton and Speke were tearing one another to shreds. It would be idle to pretend that their feud had nothing to do with the Nile; but I suggest that irritants of equal importance were money and the partisanship of armchair geographers.

Burton's expedition – like many which followed it – was under-financed. The £1,000 which the Society provided was nothing like enough to pay for porters provisions and equipment, and the explorers had to provide almost as much again out of their own pockets, something Burton could afford more readily than Speke. It is therefore hardly surprising that the two of them frequently didn't see eye to eye over who was to meet their mounting pile of debts. As for the armchair geographers – men like the pedantic Cooley and the scurrilous M'Queen – they seized on a difference of opinion between the explorers and, to advance their own theories, fanned it into a conflict. This difference of opinion was over something basically very simple. Speke said, "I have found the source of the Nile." Burton said, "Maybe. But you can't be sure." Unfortunately some geographers sprang to defend Burton's view and some Speke's; and in the controversy which followed the explorers found themselves obliged to take up more and more extreme positions, Burton becoming increasingly sceptical and Speke increasingly over-confident.

The Society was in a quandary. Clearly they had to send out another expedition. But whom should they ask to lead it? Burton or Speke?

The president cast his vote for Speke.

This almost certainly upset Burton more than all the popular adulation which was

John Hanning Speke (1827–1864): discoverer of the source of the White Nile, a great explorer, who seemed to have the unhappy knack of making enemies more easily than friends

Slave Market-place, Zanzibar - very difficult to take - slaves & arabs kept running leaving only a line of women slaves whose legs and a face or two may be observed - the women's dr is a blue cotton sheet or cloth tied tight under arms and extending as far as the knees - their heads are cropped as scissors can crop them - very often they have for ornament a hole through the upper lip - at the m they come out very clean - Houses are blocks of coralline earth plastered - an indistinct with Arab houses to the right eyeing the

*Zanzibar Harbour
from door of British Consulate*

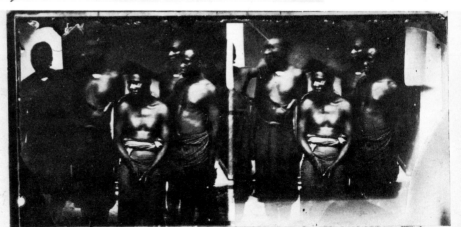

"Wanyamwezis" or natives from the Country of the Moon - heads sha except a moon shaped & very short patch on top of the head - The centre one only w a head dress (a ring of standing out Zebra's Mane) very muscular, tall, fine men - a throatlet of 3 conical or moon shaped ivory is suspended by thread round neck - no coats - a waistcloth to knees

being heaped on his companion. The most distinguished body of geographers in the world passed him over in favour of his subordinate. The Society decided against Burton, partly, I suspect, because they felt that Speke was the better geographer; that when it came to taking observations, making maps and seeing a project through to completion, the tenacious junior officer was more likely to succeed than his erudite senior. And in this they were probably right. But I suggest that two other factors also weighed against Burton. He was, in the eyes of the Society, a bit *too* clever, a bit *too* unconventional, a bit *too* lacking in that *rapport* with the establishment which characterized both the Society itself and the projects it liked to sponsor. The Society preferred a leader who was dull but safe to one who was brilliant but unpredictable. Moreover Burton heartily disliked both Africa and the Africans; he was contemptuous of what he describes as their "cultural and racial inferiority" and was for ever comparing them unfavourably with his friends the Arabs. Burton's Afrophobia is brought out very clearly in the president's 1860 address:

> "The nature of life among the negroes of Eastern Africa as pictured in Captain Burton's pages cannot fail to leave a painful impression on all lovers of the human race. It is not only the reckless cruelty of the people that shocks us, nor their degrading superstitions and incurable indolence, but the picture of one unbroken spread of disunited and drunken savagery over the entire land, connected apparently with fewer redeeming qualities than are possessed by any other race with whom travellers have made us acquainted. In fact it is hard to discover a single trait in East African character, as described by Captain Burton, upon which we are able to dwell with pleasurable recollection. The very features of the land have a repulsive aspect. His description leaves us with the idea of a fever-stricken country, skirted by a low-lying belt of vegetation, dank monotonous gloomy and reeking with fetid miasma."

If this is how Burton saw Africa one wonders if he really wanted to go back? If he wasn't in fact happier sniping at Speke from London than trekking with him through the land which he professed to view with such abhorrence?

Anyhow, it was Speke who got the job. "He has again sailed for Africa," the President told the Society in the spring of 1860, "together with our associate Captain Grant, bound for the discovery of the sources of the Nile. . . . His instructions are to make his way to the point where he before turned back at the southern end of the lake [Victoria] and then to explore to its northern extremity, seeing whether or no it has a northern outlet."

Speke's second expedition had to face somewhat different problems from his first. In some ways it was easier, for he knew the country, he had become at least partially immune to its diseases, and he found Grant an altogether more congenial travelling-companion than Burton. On the other hand, as he neared Lake Victoria he came, for the first time, into contact with tribes who had attained a degree of civilization. He was therefore obliged to be not only explorer but diplomat; and this he didn't find easy.

He arrived at Zanzibar in August 1860, and set about organizing his expedition as he himself put it, "with care expedience and diligence; for I had seen matters go wrong before" (a thinly veiled dig at Burton). Africa, however, is not a continent where things can be done in a hurry. It was nearing the end of the year before he was on his way, and the end of the following year (1861) before he entered the unknown territory of Karagwe at the southern approaches to Lake Victoria.

Alan Moorehead has nicely described Karagwe and its adjoining kingdoms Buganda and Bunyoro as "a tiny capsule of semi-civilization, an oasis of native culture where the most barbarous customs survived in the midst of exceptional sophistication." Speke and Grant were the first white men in history to penetrate this demi-Eden, and it was lucky for them that the king took a fancy to them. King Rumanika was an impressive figure: 6ft 2in, and, according to Speke, "of the best Abyssinian blood and able to trace his lineage from

King David". As evidence of his friendship he offered the explorers the freedom of his harem – though Speke and Grant may have thought it rather took the gilt off the gingerbread that the unfortunate harem girls had all been artificially fed on milk until (like *pâté de foie gras* geese) they were so fat they couldn't stand, but crawled about on the floor of their hut like seals. Speke so far forgot Victorian decorum as to measure one and discover she had a 52in bust. Grant, however, was past taking much interest. For a sore on his leg had become infected; his leg swelled up, and for months he was in such agony that he couldn't leave his bed. So when a message arrived to say that the king of Buganda (at the northern end of the lake) was willing to receive the white men, Speke was obliged to make the journey alone. Grant, the most self-effacing of explorers, made no complaint. "At first sight," he wrote years later, "this appeared to some persons as an unkind proceeding, leaving a helpless brother in the heart of Africa. But my companion was offered an escort to the north, and all tender feelings had to yield to the necessities of the case."

It took Speke and his escort six weeks to reach the court of the King of Buganda; and nothing illustrates the unfortunate explorer's predicament more clearly than the fact that the route he followed was not via the shore of the lake which he had come so far to survey, but through mountain-tracks which were far out of sight of it. He was not so much explorer as prisoner.

Mutesa, King of Buganda, was a bloodthirsty tyrant, who, we are told, strutted about stiff-legged in imitation of a lion. To quote Alan Moorehead: "Hardly a day went by without some victim being executed at his command, and this was done wilfully, casually, almost as a kind of game. A girl would commit some breach of etiquette by talking too loudly, a page would neglect to close or open a door, and at a sign from Mutesa they would be taken away, screaming, to have their heads lopped off. . . . Torture by burning alive, the mutilation of victims by cutting off their hands, ears and

Speke's watercolour of Mgongo Thembo. Without wishing to denigrate Speke, one can see what Burton meant when he spoke of his companion's "Childlike simplicity"

feet, the burial of living wives with their dead husbands – all were taken as a matter of course . . . Mutesa crushed out life in the same way as a child will step on an insect." Speke, very clearly, had to be careful. This doesn't, however, excuse his behaviour during the next six months. Because for almost exactly half a year he remained in Mutesa's court; during this time he witnessed hundreds if not thousands of arbitrary killings; yet only on one occasion did he make any sort of protest, and never once did he say in effect to Mutesa, "killing people is wrong". On the contrary, he made him a present of his rifle. The king, of course, was delighted with his new toy, and when the explorers asked how he had enjoyed a hunting party they were told, "Since his highness couldn't find any animals to shoot, he killed a great number of people." One can hardly imagine Livingstone or Baker – or indeed almost any other explorer – being party to such a way of life for so long, so passively. One reason for Speke's behaviour is, I think, that the source of the Nile had by now become an *idée fixe*, a goal which nothing, no matter how much he had to stretch his conscience, was going to stop him from attaining. Another reason seems to be that for all his sterling qualities as an explorer, Speke as a man had an unattractive side to his character. He was lacking in the milk of human kindness, which perhaps explains why he seemed always to make enemies so much more readily than friends. Be that as it may, at the end of five and a half months Mutesa agreed to consult the oracles to see if they would permit the white men to leave. This involved steaming a fowl and a child, both initially alive, over a cauldron of boiling water. Grant, who had rejoined Speke several months earlier, was visibly shaken; but if Speke felt any emotion he failed to record it. At any rate, the omens (as far as the explorers were concerned) were propitious; and on 7th July, 1862 they were permitted to continue their journey.

Thankful to have seen the last of Mutesa, they headed north, accompanied by an unwieldy retinue of diplomats, warriors, servants and hangers-on. Progress was slow; in ten days they covered less than fifty miles; and by 19th July Speke had lost patience. He decided to make a dash for the Nile. Alone.

It seems, to say the least, a little hard on Grant, who for eighteen months had laboured, suffered and risked his life to reach the river, only to be left behind when his goal was almost literally within sight. However, a good deal of what went on between Speke and Grant defies normal explanation, and we shall probably never know what lay behind Grant's almost feminine acquiescence to his leader's every wish.

So Grant pushed on to the nearby kingdom of Bunyoro, and within forty-eight hours of their parting Speke was standing – as he obviously wanted to stand – alone, on the banks of the Nile.

It was a dream come true.

"21st July," he wrote. "Here at last I stood on the brink of the Nile; most beautiful was the scene, nothing could surpass it! A magnificent stream, from 600 to 700 yards wide, dotted with islets and rocks – flowing between fine high grassy banks, with rich trees in the background where herds of nsunnu and hartebeest could be seen grazing, while the hippopotami were snorting in the water and guinea-fowl rising at our feet. . . . 25th July – I marched up the left bank of the Nile to the Isamba Rapids – extremely beautiful, but very confined. The water ran deep between its banks, which were covered with fine grass, soft cloudy acacias and festoons of lilac convolvuli. The whole was more fairy-like, wild and romantic than anything I ever saw outside of a theatre. . . . 28th July – At last we arrived at the extreme end of the journey, the farthest point ever visited by the expedition. The 'stones' as the Wagenda call them [where the Nile debouched from Lake Victoria] was by far the most interesting sight I had seen in Africa. Everybody ran to see them at once, though the march had been long and fatiguing, and even my sketch-book was called into play. Though beautiful, the scene was not exactly what I expected; for the broad surface of the lake was shut out from view by a spur of hill, and the falls, about 12 feet deep and 400 to 500 feet broad, were broken by rocks. Still, it was a sight that attracted one to it for hours – the roar of the waters, the thousands of passenger-fish, leaping at the falls with all their might, the Wasoga and Wagenda fishermen coming out in boats and taking post on all the rocks with rod and hook, hippopotami and crocodiles lying sleepily on the water. . . . The expedition had now performed its functions. I saw that old father Nile without doubt rises in the Victoria N'yanza, and, as I had foretold, that lake is the great source of the holy river. . . . I christened the 'stones' Ripon Falls, after the nobleman who presided over the Royal Geographical Society when my expedition was got up."

Speke, his ambition slaked, spent an idyllic week at the Ripon Falls, then headed north to rejoin Grant on the borders of Bunyoro.

The explorers' only wish now was to get back to England with the news of their discovery as fast as they could. This, however, proved easier said than done. For a couple of months they were delayed in Bunyoro, more or less in solitary confinement, while the king extracted everything possible from them in the way of promises and "gifts". It was a miserable and frustrating time. "Our situation," wrote Grant, "is little better than that of prisoners in a cell." Eventually, however, when the expedition's cupboard was virtually bare, and Speke had lost even his gold watch and chain to the king's acquisitive fingers, they were told they could leave. They were a bare 200 miles now from the missionary post of Gondokoro on the upper reaches of the Nile, and they didn't expect this last stage of their journey to be difficult, especially as they were expecting help from John Petherick, the British Vice-Consul at Khartoum.

Petherick had been given £1,000 by the Royal Geographical Society, together with somewhat vague instructions to help Speke and Grant with porters and provisions as soon as they appeared on the upper Nile. It was an impossible brief. Petherick had a thousand and one other duties to attend to, and neither he nor anyone else had the slightest idea when the explorers were likely to appear. So throughout the last months of 1862 and the first of 1863 Speke and Grant struggled north, their progress delayed by the hostility of the tribes, the desertion of their porters, and the preoccupation of every settlement they came to with the slave trade. It must have been galling for Speke. Here he was, with news of the greatest geographical discovery of the century – some would say of the millennium – and he couldn't get back to civilization to make it known. Understandably he felt that Petherick was letting them down. It was mid-February before the explorers and their exhausted retinue stumbled into Gondokoro. And even then it was not the Vice-Consul who came forward to welcome them. It was another explorer: Samuel Baker.

With their arrival at the missionary station, Speke and Grant's expedition was to all intents and purposes over. It had been a successful expedition. But its aftermath was anti-climax. And tragedy.

There were, you might say, two tragedies. The first was that of Petherick. He turned up at Gondokoro only a few days after Speke and Grant, and the explorers didn't bother to disguise the fact that they were furious with him. In fact the unfortunate Vice-Consul had had the greatest difficulty struggling through to the mission, he had been so ill he had nearly died (in fact his death had actually been reported both to the Foreign Office and the Society) and seeing that no-one had told him that Speke and Grant were anywhere near the Nile, he could hardly be blamed for not having come to meet them earlier. He at once told Speke that his trade-goods and boat were at the explorers' disposal. His offer, however, was brushed aside. "My good friend Baker," Speke told him coldly, "has supplied me with all I need." One can forgive Speke his initial irritation; for more than two years he had been under enormous physical and mental strain. What is not so easy to forgive is his subsequent vindictiveness; for on his return to England he conducted a personal vendetta against the unfortunate Vice-Consul with such venom that Petherick was eventually removed from his post and was reduced to bankruptcy.

The second tragedy was that of Speke himself.

Before they left the mission Speke and Grant told Baker they believed that another great lake, "where the Waganda go to get their fish", might lie to the west of the Victoria; and they suggested that if Baker could locate this lake he would be performing a valuable service to geography. They gave him all the maps and information they could, then set off for Cairo, pausing only to cable the Society: "Inform Sir Roderick Murchison all is well and that the Nile is settled." They arrived in London in July 1863 to the heroes' welcome they so richly deserved.

The Nile, however, was very far from being settled. For the sceptics took the not unreasonable view that, even after Speke's second expedition, a number of his "discoveries" were still largely guesswork. They pointed out that he had neither surveyed nor circumnavigated Lake Victoria: that he had merely caught a fleeting glimpse of one large sheet of water in 1858, and a fleeting glimpse of another large sheet of water, 200 miles to the north, in 1862, and had assumed that they combined to form the one great lake. They pointed out that he hadn't followed the course of the river which he claimed to be the Nile for more than a few miles from its source: that he had merely found one big river flowing out of Lake Victoria, and another big river 200 miles farther north flowing into Gondokoro and had assumed they were one and the same. And finally they pointed out that there were almost certainly other lakes to the south and west of the Victoria which might be additional and possibly more important feeders of the Nile. These were not unreasonable doubts.

For some time Speke, riding high on a wave of popular adulation, was able to ignore his critics. When he spoke to the Society a few weeks after his return, so great was the applause that several windows in Whitehall Place were shattered. It wasn't long, however, before his unfortunate knack of making enemies began to tell against him. Burton, as might have been expected, remained sceptical, condemning Speke's reports on the Nile as "containing an extreme looseness of geography". The armchair traveller James M'Queen (who had never been out of England in his life) stirred up trouble by publishing a series of bigoted and scurrilous attacks on Speke's character. And the crowning blow for the luckless explorer must have been when the formidable Dr. Livingstone entered the lists against him. "Poor Speke," the doctor wrote, "has turned

Drift in the Great Fish River, below Cradock. Painted by Thomas Baines, 1868

his back upon the real sources of the Nile . . . his river at Ripon Falls was not large enough for the Nile.''

I think that Livingstone became involved in the controversy largely because of his special *rapport* with the Society. Ever since 1850 when they had published an account of his trek through the Kalahari Desert, the Society had regarded Livingstone as their *beau idéal* of an explorer; like Scott half a century later, he epitomized all those virtues which they esteemed most highly – patriotism, a firm committal to Christian values, and a burning desire to advance geographical knowledge. He was also a close personal friend of Sir Roderick Murchison. Murchison, by the spring of 1864, was becoming disenchanted with Speke, and by voicing his own disapproval Livingstone was also voicing that of the Society.

Speke's relationship with the Society makes sad reading. They had backed him to the hilt: had sponsored him, financed him, given him command of their expedition, arranged for him to have the companion of his choice, and on his return to England had accepted his findings without cavil. He was *their* explorer. Speke, however, didn't do a great deal for the Society in return. First he involved them in his vendetta with Petherick. Then he antagonized them by publishing the story of his expedition not in the Society's *Journal*, but in the rival magazine *Blackwood's*. This was rank ingratitude. The Society, displeased with the controversy between their chosen explorer and his detractors, invited Burton and Speke to thrash out their differences in the polite but erudite atmosphere of a meeting of the British Association, to be held at Bath in September 1864. It would have been a confrontation to remember. But the evening before it was due to take place, Speke died in a shooting accident on his cousin's estate.

His death, like his life, was fraught with controversy. Inevitably – although this was officially denied at the time – there were whispers of suicide.

Grant wrote one obituary: "Captain Speke was pure-minded, honourable, regardless

"Overhauling the giraffes", from Baker's The Albert Nyanza, *Vol. 1. Like many of the early explorers of Africa, Baker was an enthusiastic hunter*

"The last charge" from Baker's The Albert Nyanza, *Vol. 1, published 1866*

of self and self-denying, with a mind always aiming at great things and above every littleness. He was gentle and pleasing in manner with almost childlike simplicity, but at the same time extremely tenacious of purpose." Burton wrote another: "Lieutenant Speke was uncommonly hard to manage. To a peculiarly quiet and modest aspect and an almost childlike simplicity of manner he united an immense and abnormal fund of self-esteem. He ever held, not only that he had done his best on all occasions but that no living man could do better."

The truth about Speke must surely lie somewhere between the eulogy and the diatribe. Certainly it cannot be denied that for all his failings and unlovability he was a great explorer. His claims may in part have been based on conjecture, but they turned out in every instance to be right. He discovered the major source of the Nile; and this, in the words of the Society's valedictory was "a great and daring achievement of which Englishmen may ever be proud".

Speke's death served to underline the fact that the Nile was still known only in part. One source had been discovered; but no-one could say with any certainty if this was the only or indeed the principal source. More exploration was needed; and the hopes of the Society now rested on Baker (who was already on the spot) and Livingstone (who was planning an expedition to the area west of Lake Tanganyika).

Samuel Baker was described by his fellow-explorer Stanley as "that magnificent and sensible man", and the adjectives are well-chosen. For Baker comes leaping at us out of the past like the larger-than-life hero of a *Boy's Own Paper* adventure yarn, and always at his side – and this really *was* extraordinary in the 1860s – stood a young and beautiful girl, later to become his second wife, the Hungarian Florence Ninian von Sass. Florence shared every danger with her husband-to-be, suffered every hardship, several times saved his life, and emerges in more ways than one as quite the most attractive of the explorers who went searching for the sources of the Nile.

Baker was born in London in 1821 – the same year as Burton – the son of a wealthy ship-owner. He had led an incredibly full and eventful life before suddenly turning up at the age of 40 with a beautiful young girl in perhaps the least-known and most dangerous corner of the earth: the upper reaches of the Nile. "In March 1861," he subsequently told the Society, "I commenced an expedition to discover the sources of the Nile. . . . From my youth I had been inured to hardships in tropical climates, and I had a hope, mingled with humility, that even as the insignificant worm bores through the hardest oak, I might by perseverance reach the heart of Africa." The sheer audacity of the enterprise demonstrates the "magnificent" side of Baker's character. The thoroughness of his preparations demonstrates the "sensible" side. For Florence and Samuel spent the next eighteen months exploring not the White Nile but the Blue, gradually acclimatizing themselves to local conditions, doing valuable research on the Nile sediments, testing equipment, and learning not only Arabic but as many central African languages as they could find people to teach them. It was during these preliminaries that they met and became friendly with Petherick; and when the Vice-Consul was taken ill and reported dead, the Bakers were asked if they would press on up the Nile in the hope of making contact with Speke and Grant. This fitted in with their plans very well; although when they did eventually make contact, Samuel must have listened with mixed feelings to the explorers' account of their discoveries. "Does not one leaf of the laurel remain," he is said to have asked them, "for me to pluck?" The answer was of course that a very large leaf indeed remained: he could prove the existence or otherwise of the Luta N'zye, the great lake bordered by salt licks which had been reported to the west of the Victoria, and which, it was suspected, might well be another and possibly even the principal feeder of the Nile.

With the object of finding this lake Samuel and Florence left Gondokoro on 26th March, 1863.

Their adventures during the next two years make wonderfully exciting reading. Indeed Baker's report to the Society and his book *The Albert N'yanza* contain the classic ingredients of just about every African adventure story that has been written from that day to this. "Here," as Alan Moorehead puts it, "is Allan Quartermain in his broad-brimmed hat setting forth into the jungles with a young and lovely girl at his side, and they face every hazard with marvellous determination. When wild beasts charge, Baker with deadly aim stops them in their tracks. At the outset of the journey he quells a mutiny by striking down the ringleader with his fist. As they advance, all their baggage animals die and they are forced to ride oxen, their food supplies fail and they are reduced to eating grass, fever lays them prostrate for weeks on end, deceitful guides mislead them, hippopotamuses overturn their boats, the slave-traders cheat them, the tribes attack with poisoned arrows, and they are never for long out of hearing of the war-drums."

Through it all the incredible Mrs. Baker never flinches. "She was not a screamer," her husband* tells us. When she hears stealthy footsteps approaching their hut at night she quietly touches him on the sleeve and he reaches for his revolver. In a tight spot, the explorers I'd like best to have at my side would be the Bakers. Extracts from *The Albert N'yanza* give us some idea both of their difficulties and of the way they faced them.

March 1863: of an incipient mutiny:

"I was determined to insist upon the punishment of the ringleader. I went towards

Sir Samuel White Baker (1821–1893) explorer, discoverer of the secondary source of the Nile, hunter, suppressor of the slave trade and Governor-General of the equatorial regions of the Nile

* *Samuel and Florence were not in fact married at the time of their journey up the Nile. In spite of exhaustive research Florence's origins remain shrouded in mystery, though the most widely accepted story is that Samuel bought her at a slave market in the Balkans. They were married at St. James's, Piccadilly, in 1865 on their return to London. Queen Victoria, who was clearly not amused, refused to allow Florence to be presented at court.*

him with the intention of seizing him; but he, being backed by upwards of forty men, had the impertinence to attack me. To stop his blow, and to knock him into the middle of the crowd was not difficult, and seizing him by the throat I called for a rope to bind him; but in an instant I had a crowd of men upon me to rescue their leader. How the affair would have ended I cannot say; but as the scene lay within ten yards of my boat, my wife, who was ill with fever in the cabin, witnessed the whole affray, and seeing me surrounded, she rushed out, and in a few moments was in the middle of the crowd. Her sudden appearance had a curious effect, and calling upon several of the least mutinous to assist, she very pluckily made her way up to me. Seizing on the indecision that was for the moment evinced by the crowd, I shouted to the drummer-boy to beat the drum, and at the top of my voice ordered the men to 'fall in'. It is curious how mechanically an order is obeyed if given at the right moment. About two-thirds of the men fell in, the remainder retreated with the ringleader. The affair ended in my insisting all formed in line and the ringleader being brought forward. In this critical moment Mrs. Baker, with great tact, implored me to forgive the ringleader if he kissed my hand and begged for pardon. This compromise completely won the men over."

Lady Baker, who accompanied Samuel – though to Queen Victoria's outrage not yet married to him – on his search for the source of the Nile. Her courage, tact and charm on more than one occasion saved their expedition from disaster

January 1864: in King Kamrasi's court at Mrooli, between Lakes Victoria and Albert:

"I again requested Kamrasi to allow us to leave. In the coolest manner he replied, 'I will allow you to go to the lake as I promised, but you must leave your wife with me!' At this moment we were surrounded by a great number of natives, and my suspicions of treachery appeared confirmed by this insolent demand. If this were to be the end of the expedition I resolved that it should also be the end of Kamrasi, and, drawing my revolver I held it within two feet of his chest, and told him that if I touched the trigger not all his men could save him. . . . I explained that in my country such insolence would entail bloodshed, and that I looked upon him as an ignorant ox who knew no better, and that this excuse alone could save him. My wife, naturally indignant, had risen from her seat, and made him a little speech in Arabic (not a word of which he understood) with a countenance about as amiable as Medusa. . . . Whether this little *coup de théâtre* so impressed Kamrasi with British female independence that he wished to be off his bargain, I cannot say; but with an air of astonishment he said: 'Don't be angry. It is my custom to give my visitors pretty wives, and I thought you might exchange. But if you don't like the idea, there's an end to it.' This very practical apology I received sternly, merely insisting upon starting our journey."

February 1864: on the last stage of their trek to the Albert N'yanza:

"Marching along the south bank of the Kafoor River, we came to an area of marsh, so covered with thickly matted water-grass that a natural floating bridge about two feet thick was established over it, and upon this waving and unsteady surface the men ran quickly across, sinking nearly up to their ankles although beneath the vegetation there was deep water. I begged Mrs. Baker to follow me across, as quickly as possible and precisely in my track. I had completed barely a fourth of the distance when, looking back, I was horrified to see her standing in one spot, sinking, gradually through the reeds, her face distorted and purple. Even as I perceived her, she fell, as though shot dead. In an instant I was by her side; and with the assistance of eight or ten of my men, I dragged her like a corpse through the yielding vegetation, just keeping her head above water, until we scrambled across to the other side. I laid her under a tree, and bathed her face with water, as for the moment I thought she had fainted; but she lay perfectly insensible as though dead, with teeth and hands firmly clenched, and her eyes open but fixed.

"I sent off a man in haste to recall an angarep upon which to carry her. . . . At length it came, and after changing her clothes, we carried her mournfully forward as a corpse. Constantly we had to halt and support her head, as a painful rattling in her throat betokened suffocation. At length we reached a village, and halted for the night. I laid her carefully in a hut, and watched beside her. I opened her clenched teeth with a small wooden wedge, and inserted a wet rag upon which I dropped water to moisten her tongue, which was dry as fur. . . . It was impossible to remain in this spot, or the men would have starved. So [next day] she was laid gently upon her litter and we started forward on our funeral course. I was broken-hearted as I followed by her side,

Livingstone's steam-launch the Ma Robert *(nicknamed "The Asthmatic") built for exploring the Zambezi River by John Laird of Birkenhead. Drawn by S. Walters, 1858*

The Satanic Escort: watercolour by Samuel Baker: "Ugandans with spears and shields surrounding SB, riding ox, and his escort on their way to the Albert Nyanza, 1864"

through streams, thick forest, and valleys of tall papyrus grass, which, as we brushed through them, waved over the litter like the black plumes of a hearse. . . . We halted at a village, and again the night was passed in watching. I was wet, coated with mud from the marsh, and shivering with ague; but the cold within was greater than all. She never moved. I had plenty of fat, so I made four balls of about half-a-pound, each of which would burn for three hours. A piece of a broken water-jar served as a lamp, pieces of rag as wicks. So in solitude the night passed away as I sat by her side and watched. Was she to die? Was so terrible a sacrifice to be the result of my selfish journey?"

For three days Florence never moved. Then, on the fourth night, came the crisis.

"The morning was not far distant; it was past four o'clock. I had passed the night replacing wet clothes on her head and moistening her lips, as she lay apparently lifeless on her litter. I could do nothing more. In abject misery in that dark hour I beseeched an aid above all human, trusting alone to Him. . . . Morning broke; my lamp had burned out, and cramped with the night's watching, I rose from my seat and went to the door of the hut. I was watching the first red streaks that heralded the rising sun, when I was startled by the faintly uttered words, 'Thank God!' She had woken from her torpor, and with a heart overflowing I went to her bedside. But her eyes were full of madness. She spoke, but her brain was gone!

"I will not inflict a description of her seven terrible days of brain fever, with its attendant horrors. The rain poured in torrents, and day after day we were forced to travel on, through want of provisions. Every now and then we shot a few guinea-fowl, or procured a little wild honey from the forest; but the deserted villages contained no food, for we were on the frontier of Uganda, and M'tese's men had plundered the district. For seven nights I had not slept, and although weak as a reed had marched beside her litter by day. Nature could resist no longer. When that night we reached a village, she had been in violent convulsions successively. It was all but over. I laid her down within a hut, and fell by her side, insensible with sorrow and fatigue.

"The sun had risen when I woke. I had slept, and horrified as the idea came to me that she must be dead and I had not been with her, I started up. She lay pale as marble, and with that calm serenity which the features assume when the cares of life no longer act upon the mind. But, as I gazed upon her, her chest heaved gently, not with the convulsive throb of fever, but naturally. She was asleep. And when, at a sudden noise, she opened her eyes, they were calm and clear. She was saved! When not a ray of hope remained, God alone knows what helped us. The gratitude of that moment I will not attempt to describe."

March 1864: the sighting of the Albert Nyanza:

"For several days our guides had told me that we were very near to the lake. I had noticed a lofty range of mountains some distance west, and had imagined that the lake lay on the other side of these; but I was now informed that the mountains formed the western frontier of the N'zye, and that the lake was within a day's march. . . . That night I hardly slept. . . . 14th March – The sun had not risen when I was spurring my ox after the guide, who, having been promised a double handful of beads on arrival at the lake, had caught the enthusiasm of the moment. The day was beautifully clear, and having crossed a deep valley, we toiled up the opposite slope. I hurried to the summit. And the glory of our prize burst suddenly upon me! There like a sea of quicksilver, far beneath us, lay the grand expanse of water – a boundless sea-horizon on the south and southwest, glittering in the noonday sun. . . . It is impossible to describe the triumph of that moment. . . . The path to descend to the lake was so steep and dangerous that we were forced to leave our oxen, and descend on foot. I led the way, grasping a stout bamboo. My wife, in extreme weakness, tottered down, supporting herself on my shoulder and stopping to rest every twenty paces. After a descent of about two hours, weak with fever but for the moment strengthened by success, we gained the level plain below the cliff. A walk of about a mile through flat sandy meadows of fine turf, interspersed with trees and bushes, brought us to the water's edge. The waves were rolling upon a white pebbly beach. I rushed into the lake, and thirsty with heat and fatigue but with a heart full of gratitude, drank deeply from the sources of the Nile."

The Bakers spent several weeks exploring the northern end of the lake, which they named the Albert Nyanza, discovering both the entrance of the Victoria Nile and, a few miles to the north-west, the exit of the Albert Nile. On the latter they found what is perhaps the most spectacular feature in all the 4,000 miles of the river's course.

"Our guide informed me that we should terminate our voyage that day at the great waterfall.

As we proceeded, the river gradually narrowed to about 180 yards; we could hear the roar of water . . . and upon rounding a bend, the most magnificent sight burst suddenly upon us. On either side the river were beautifully wooded cliffs rising abruptly to a height of about 300 feet; rocks were jutting out from the intensely green foliage; and rushing through a gap that cleft the rock, the river, contracted from a grand stream, was pent up in a narrow gorge; roaring furiously through the rock-bound pass, it plunged in one leap of about 120 feet perpendicular into the dark abyss below. The fall of water was snow-white, which had a superb effect as it contrasted with the dark cliffs that walled the river, while the graceful palms and wild plaintains perfected the beauty of the view. This

(On the facing page)
Some of the Zanzibar and other natives of Mr. H. M. Stanley's party, sketched at Government House, Cape Town, 1st November, 1877, by Catherine Frances Frere

Rhinoceros attacking horse: a watercolour by Samuel Baker: April 1862

(Overleaf) Bushmen hunting a herd of heterogeneous game. Painting by Thomas Baines, 1858

Some of the Zanzibar & other Natives
of H.H. Mr Stanley's Party Nov. 1.
sketched at ... Government House Cape Town 1877.

3 Saladie · 4 Majuara · 5 Smaustry · 6 Hassina · 7 Badazulee · 8 Bestemessie · 9 Mamawuzer · 10 Binkilamazenee · 11 Mamiamoti · 12 Yanja · 13 Mamifana ·

was the greatest waterfall of the Nile, and, in honour of the distinguished President of the Royal Geographical Society, I named it the Murchison Falls, as the most important object throughout the course of the river.

"The boatmen, having been promised a present of beads to induce them to approach the fall, succeeded in bringing the canoe to within about 300 yards of the base, but the power of the current and the whirlpools rendered it impossible to proceed farther. There was a sandbank on our left which was literally covered with crocodiles, lying parallel to each other like the trunks of trees prepared for shipment." (Baker shot one of the crocodiles; and the report of his rifle so terrified the rowers that they dropped their paddles, and the canoe drifted out of control against a bank of reeds.) "Hardly had we touched, when a tremendous commotion took place in the rushes, and in an instant a great bull hippopotamus charged the canoe, and with a severe shock, striking the bottom, lifted us half out of the water. The natives yelled with terror . . . and the hippopotamus, proud of having disturbed us but doubtless thinking us rather hard of texture raised his head to take a last look at his enemy, then sank too rapidly to permit me a shot."

The discovery of the Albert Nyanza was the culmination of the Bakers' achievements in exploration. It was, however, the better part of a year before they managed to struggle back to Gondokoro. And when they got there, there was no welcoming committee to greet them, no supplies and no mail. For they had been away so long that everyone had given them up for dead.

Shortly before they landed in England Baker was told that he had been awarded the Gold Medal of the Society – one can't help wishing it could have been given to him and Florence jointly. A knighthood followed. So did enormous popular acclaim for his books. No-one, however, could say that success went to Baker's head. He never lost his simplicity. His report, for example, which was read to the Society in November 1865, is almost unique among those of expedition leaders in that he doesn't overplay but actually underplays the importance of his discoveries. "For myself," he told the packed assembly in Whitehall Place, "I claim no honour as the discoverer of a source, for I believe the mighty Nile may have a thousand sources. The birthplace of the river lies among the great chain of lakes bosomed among the mountain ranges of Equatorial Africa. Fifteen hundred feet below the general level of the country, in this precipitous depression lies the great reservoir of the Nile. I will not enter upon vain theories of a connection between [these great lakes] . . . nor indulge in wild hypothesis. I wish only to lay before the world this simple and straightforward narrative of my expedition for the benefit of geographical science, trusting that nearly five years in Central Africa may have been of service in determining the great basin of the Nile."

We can see now that Baker's discovery did in fact reveal the basic truth about the origin of the Nile – that the river emerged from Lake Victoria at the Ripon Falls and flowed north-west into Lake Albert, passing over the Murchison Falls en route; that it subsequently emerged from Lake Albert, and then, fed by the waters of both lakes, flowed over a succession of rapids on the way to Gondokoro. In the 1860s, however, there were still a number of imponderables. Nobody knew how large Lake Albert was, whether it was part of a chain of lakes, whether it was connected to Lake Tanganyika, and whether these lakes were the source not only of the Nile but also the Congo (or Lualaba); there was also the possibility – and this was Livingstone's pipedream – that another major source of the Nile would be found among the north-flowing rivers to the west of Lake Tanganyika.

It was to solve these remaining problems that the Society decided to sponsor yet another expedition. Murchison, in his presidential address of May 1865, explains very clearly the background and objectives of this latest undertaking. "Considering the doubts and uncertainties which still prevail respecting the true watershed of Central Africa, I proposed to our Council that we endeavour to remove these obscurities by

(On the facing page)
Victoria Falls with stampeding buffaloes, painted by Thomas Baines, July 1862. "There," wrote Baines, "within 70 yards of us are a hundred buffaloes. . . . They turn and rush towards the fall, crashing through palm brake and rotten wood till at full speed they gain the rocky headland, and we hold our breath in fear lest they should rush over. Now they halt on the very edge, their dark forms stand out in bold relief against the misty clouds. . . . I lose no time in committing to paper my impression of the herd halting short in their headlong career on the very face of the cataract"

The Murchison Falls: the most spectacular feature in the 4,000-mile course of the Nile, "named in honour of the distinguished president of the Royal Geographical Society". Murchison also had a town in New Zealand named after him, a mountain range and a river in Australia, and a sound in Greenland

promoting an expedition up the White Nile. Political circumstances, however, render it but too certain that the ardent desire of Geographers must for the present be postponed. Until some stop is put to the misconduct of traders in pillaging and making slaves of the natives, no hope can be entertained of realizing our anticipations. . . . In the meantime, it has been deemed desirable to carry out an examination of the region lying between the Lake Nyassa of Livingstone and the Tanganyika of Burton and Speke, by sending a well-considered expedition to that part of Africa. The Council therefore agreed to a proposal of my own that the tried and successful traveller Livingstone should be the leader of such a survey."

To understand why Livingstone was the obvious choice for this new expedition we need to go back a little in time.

David Livingstone was born at Blantyre, near Glasgow, in 1813, and reared in what Dorothy Middleton describes as "virtuous poverty"; at the age of ten he was working as a piecer in the local cotton mill, and it tells us a good deal about his character that he spent his first week's wages in buying a Latin grammar. By the time he was 25 he was both a qualified doctor and an ordained missionary, and was about to sail for Africa to join Robert Moffat at his famous mission at Kuruman, not far from the Orange River. There is no evidence to support the suggestion that he arrived in Africa "filled with a burning desire to explore its mysteries"; indeed his original ambition had been to go to China. However, the mission station at Kuruman soon proved too restricted a field for him – partly perhaps because before long he found himself married to Moffat's daughter, Mary! – and during his first decade in Africa Livingstone worked his way steadily north. Establishing Christian settlements as he went. In the late 1840s, accompanied by the big-game hunters Oswell and Murray, he crossed the Kalahari Desert and reached the hitherto unexplored Lake Ngami. It was this, his first true piece of exploration, which brought him to the attention of the Society who secured for him an award of £20. Again the way Livingstone spent his money tells us something about his character; not on his wife or children but on buying himself a chronometer to enable him more accurately to fix his latitude. In 1852 he sent his family home to Britain and embarked on the great trans-African journey which first brought him to the attention of the world.

This journey was remarkable on several counts: it was a truly epic feat of physical endurance, it gave the world its first account of the great watershed of central Africa, and the observant doctor recorded in his diary much valuable scientific and geographical information. But perhaps most remarkable of all was the rapport he established with the people.

He loved both Africa and the Africans.

"I have often thought," he wrote, "in travelling through [this] land, that it presents pictures of beauty which angels might enjoy. . . . Green, grassy meadows, the cattle feeding, the goats browsing, the kids skipping, the groups of herdboys with miniature bows, arrows and spears; the women wending their way to the river with watering pots poised jauntily on their heads; men sewing under the shady banians; and old grey-headed fathers sitting on the ground, listening to the morning gossip, while others carry trees or branches to repair their hedges; and all this flooded with the bright African sunshine, and the birds singing among the branches before the heat of the day has become intense, form pictures which can never be forgotten." A very different appraisal from Burton's!

It was because Livingstone loved the Africans so dearly that he hated the slave trade so deeply.

This trade, carried on by the Arabs and connived at by the Portuguese, was the bane of both eastern and western Africa – "this open sore of the world" Livingstone called it, and with good reason, for the cruelty and suffering that it engendered were beyond belief. Indeed it would not, I think, be any exaggeration to say that the slave trade was the principal *raison d'être* for Livingstone's travels. For initially he had pushed north from

David Livingstone – born Livingston – (1813–1873): missionary and explorer. Many of his European colleagues found him "difficult to meddle with"; but he loved and understood the African way of life, exemplified in the sketch below of the homestead of the Bari tribe

Mupundu tree, under which Livingstone's heart is buried. Photograph by P. Weatherley, 1898. After Livingstone's death his heart and viscera were removed and buried in a tin box under the tree which was inscribed
LIVINGSTONE
MAY 4, 1873
Souza Mniasere
Chuma Uchopere
His African friends – it would be quite wrong to describe them as porters – then dried and wrapped the rest of his body in calico and carried it over 1,000 miles to Zanzibar; from there it was taken for burial in Westminster Abbey. The carved bark of the tree is now in the Society's home in Kensington Gore

the Orange River to escape the trade; his trans-continental journey was undertaken with the idea of opening up Angola to legitimate commerce in the hope that this would combat the trade, and his subsequent exploits were based on the idea that a combination of commerce and Christianity would eventually extirpate it.

The story of his journey across the continent is soon told. He set out from Linyanti; (close to the junction of present-day Botswana, Namibia and Zambia) with a handpicked group of Makololo companions – not, it ought to be stressed, hired porters. It took them six months to cross the unexplored plains where the Congo to the north-west and the Zambezi to the south-east have their origins. On reaching Luanda on the coast he was offered a passage back to England in a naval frigate; but this he refused, for he had promised his Makololo companions that he would take them back to their homeland. The return journey was begun in September, 1854, and as they retraced their steps, often hampered by torrential rains, news of their journey percolated through to England. Back in Linyanti, Livingstone decided to complete his crossing of the continent by following the Zambezi eastward to the Indian Ocean. It was his hope that the rivers of Africa in general and the Zambezi in particular would serve as arteries for commerce, and it must have seemed to him as he followed the course of the great river partly by canoe and partly on foot, that he had found a route which traders could follow; for apart from the Victoria Falls – which he was almost certainly the first white man to visit – the Zambezi appeared to be navigable for most of its length. What he didn't realize was that in one of the few places where he was obliged to leave the river – between Zumbo and Tete – the Kebrabasa rapids form a complete barrier to navigation. He arrived at Quelimane on the coast of Mozambique in the spring of 1856, having, in three years, travelled virtually one and a half times across the continent, and in May he set sail for England. Seldom before or since has so large a blank space on the map been so comprehensively filled.

Back home, Livingstone found himself a popular hero and regarded as an authority on all things African. The Society awarded him its Gold Medal, and eagerly sifted through and published the mass of new geographical material in his notebooks and diaries; and it was not long before a very real and lasting friendship sprang up between Livingstone and Murchison. Both men were Scots, both were dedicated Christians, dedicated patriots and dedicated geographers; and for the rest of his career Livingstone – like Scott a couple of generations later – became the chosen child of the Society. In 1858 he returned to Africa as the leader of an official government expedition to open up the Zambezi as a highway into the interior.

The Zambezi expedition is an unhappy chapter in the Livingstone story. For like many of the greatest explorers, Livingstone was essentially a loner, and he lacked the ability to weld together and lead a party of disparate interests and personalities. The venture was bedevilled from the start by misunderstandings, incompatibilities and fever. Their specially-built launch, the *Ma Robert*, had so much trouble with her boilers that she was dubbed "The Asthmatic"; the Kebrabasa rapids proved insurmountable; Livingstone and the artist Thomas Baines fell out in no uncertain manner; and the crowning disaster was the death of Mary Livingstone from fever. To quote Dorothy Middleton: "The Zambezi expedition did break new ground and laid foundations for better things to come, but it disappointed the high hopes pinned on it, and was wound up in 1863."

Livingstone returned to England, and almost immediately became involved in the Burton/Speke controversy over the sources of the Nile.

This was an issue on which Livingstone had a reasonably open mind, and together he and Murchison worked out a scheme whereby he should lead an expedition hoping to strike inland up the Rovuma River, visit Lakes Nyasa, Tanganyika and Victoria, and "clear up once and for all the tangled question of the Nile sources and the inter-relation of the central lakes and rivers". This was a tall order, especially for a man in his fifties who was suffering from chronic fever and diarrhoea and incipient pneumonia of the right lung. The expedition was financed jointly by the Government, the Society and the philanthropist James "Paraffin" Young. It was modestly equipped, because it was not expected that such an experienced traveller, covering terrain that was basically familiar, would need to be away for long – which goes to show how mistaken planners can be.

Livingstone arrived at the mouth of the Rovuma in April 1866, and headed upriver in the direction of Lake Nyasa, which he reached at the end of four months' journey. This lake and the River Shire, which drains out of it into the Zambezi, was a favourite hunting ground for the Arab traders. "Found a slave party here," Livingstone wrote in his diary, "and went to look at the slaves . . . eighty-five were in a pen formed of dura stalks (*holcus sorghum*). The majority were boys of about eight or ten; others were grown men and women. Nearly all were in the taming-stocks; a few of the younger ones were in thongs, the thong passing round the neck of each." For the next five years, as one of his biographers writes, "Livingstone was to see almost daily evidence of the slavers' work in the deserted and burnt villages, and in the brutalized bodies of slaves lying abandoned on the forest-paths." This was the facet of African life which he abhorred most vehemently. But ironically, he could make no protest. For with his health deteriorating and his food soon exhausted, his expedition became almost totally dependent on the Arabs for their supplies and indeed for their survival. What gave him strength during these last five nightmare years was his almost mystical obsession with the source of the Nile. He became convinced that it lay not in the great lakes at all, but somewhere among the northward-flowing rivers to the west of them; for he had read in Herodotus that "the fountains of the Nile rise midway between two hills with conical tops, and half the water runs north into Egypt and half to the south." So for five years, becoming progressively weaker and sicker, Livingstone wandered through the thickly-forested country to the west of Lakes Tanganyika and Nyasa, ever asking the natives if they knew of two such hills. The answer was always no. But Livingstone never gave up. Stanley tracked him down on the shore of Lake Tanganyika, and begged him to come home; but the doctor accepted Stanley's supplies more readily than his advice, and, replenished, set out on the final stage of his impossible journey. He died about 3rd May, 1873. And it is perhaps typical of his determination and courage that he died not *in* his bed, but kneeling across it, in prayer.

Livingstone has been described as "the Society's most-favoured explorer". From the moment in 1850 when they recommended Queen Victoria to present him with £20 for his first great journey to Lake Ngami, to the moment in April 1874 when his body lay in the Society's map-room before being carried to Westminster Abbey, they supported him, sponsored him, and encouraged him both as geographer and missionary. As regards the Nile, his contribution was negative – he merely proved it unlikely that the river rose anywhere except in Lakes Victoria and Albert. His early discoveries, however, were of the greatest significance. And of even greater significance was the manner in which his voice reverberated out from the forests of Equatorial Africa in protest against the slave trade. He shouldered the burden and made himself the conscience of the world. Some of his biographers have put forward the view that on his last expedition the Society awarded him an inadequate grant, packed him off on an impossible mission, and then abandoned him. The facts, however, do not substantiate this interpretation. His grant of £500 was, by the standards of the day, not ungenerous; he didn't have to be talked into going back to Africa, this was what he wanted; and far from abandoning him, the Society financed three expeditions to search for him – E. D. Young's in 1867, Dawson's in 1872 and Cameron's in 1873, while James Young and the RGS between them sent yet another expedition up the Congo. The British consul at Zanzibar also made repeated efforts to get through to him with supplies. The theory that no-one cared about

Livingstone's coffin lying in the map room of the Society before being taken to Westminster Abbey, April 1874

Harry Morton Stanley – born John Rowlands (1841–1904). His magnificent feats of exploration were marred by the carnage he all too frequently left in his wake. His treatment of those who stood in his path is typified by "The Fight with the Avisibba Cannibals" from his book In Darkest Africa, *Vol. I*

Livingstone except the altruistic Gordon Bennett of the *New York Herald* and his reporter Stanley is very wide of the mark.

It was, nevertheless, Stanley who succeeded in finding him. And it was Stanley who managed to clear up the last remaining doubts about the sources of the Nile.

When he first arrived in England, after his famous meeting with the doctor at Ujiji, Stanley received a hero's welcome from the public but a frosty reception from geographers. Men of science in general and members of the Society in particular disliked his brashness, mistrusted his eloquence, and found it hard to forgive him for finding Livingstone when their own expeditions had failed. The atmosphere thawed a little when the Society in 1873 presented him with its Gold Medal; but it was not until Stanley had completed his epic journey across the continent in 1877 that the pundits were prepared to recognize him as a serious explorer as distinct from a journalist in search of a scoop.

In November 1874 he struck inland from Zanzibar determined to fit together the final pieces in the jig-saw of the Nile. He had been financed – and right royally – by the *New York Herald* and the *Daily Telegraph*, and his expedition (356 men, eight tons of supplies, and the sections of a 40-foot steel boat) was by far the largest and best-equipped ever to land in Africa. He reached Lake Victoria, assembled his boat and carried out a careful circumnavigation, proving that the lake had only one major intake, the Kagera, and only one major outlet, the Nile. "So Speke," he wrote, "can claim the full glory of having discovered the largest inland sea on the continent of Africa, also its principal affluent and outlet. I must also give him credit for having understood the geography of the countries we travelled through better than any of those who so persistently opposed his hypothesis." This was vindication for Speke beyond all possibility of dispute.

Stanley next turned his attention to Lake Tanganyika. Again he assembled his vessel the *Lady Alice*, circumnavigated the lake and found that it had no outlet which could possibly be connected with the Nile. This was an important if negative discovery; for it proved that the Victoria and the Albert were the only major lakes which could claim to nurture the Nile.

Only one issue now remained to be clarified. A great tributary of the Nile (or even the mainstream itself) might still be found among the northward-flowing rivers which lay inland of Lake Tanganyika. There were many great rivers in this area. In particular there was the Lualaba. Livingstone had stood more than once on the bank of this mighty torrent, had watched it flowing broad and strong to the north, and had hoped it was the Nile but feared it might be the Congo. "Am filled with doubt and perplexity," he had written in his journal. "Am oppressed with apprehension that after all it may turn out I have been following the Congo." These doubts Stanley was now determined to resolve; and Alan Moorehead's account of how he resolved them can not be bettered. "The story of Stanley's voyage in the *Lady Alice* down the Lualaba and the Congo to the Atlantic is one of the great epics of African adventure. For many months he had no notion of where the river was eventually to take him – it might have been northwards into Egypt or anywhere into the vast unexplored regions to the south – but having once started he had to go on. His account of the voyage in *Through the Dark Continent* reads like some chronicle of the early Spanish conquistadors, for he was overtaken by every possible disaster: shipwreck and starvation, the attacks of the riverside tribes and the loss of all his supplies, and finally the drowning of his last surviving white companion, Frank Pocock. Nine hundred and ninety-nine days after leaving Zanzibar the survivors emerged like ghouls from the jungles at the mouth of the Congo, and here the little community of European traders brought them back to life. But by the time they had struggled through to the Atlantic of the original 356 members of the expedition only 114 remained."

Without doubt Stanley must rank as one of the most successful-ever explorers; although some people, disliking his ruthless treatment of the natives, felt that his success was achieved at too high a price.

At much the same time as the American was fighting his way down the Congo, a very different sort of exploration was taking place on the headwaters of the Nile, where in the area between Lakes Victoria and Albert a cosmopolitan group of surveyors – the Italian Gessi, the German Emin and the American Mason – were putting the final touches to Gordon's meticulous mapping of the river. Once this work had been completed, there remained only two small pieces of the jig-saw to fit into place. No-one as yet had explored the southern reaches of Lake Albert, nor had located Ptolemy's Mountains of the Moon.

It was the ubiquitous Stanley who filled in these last two blanks on the map. In 1887 he led yet another expedition, across the continent, this time from west to east, his declared objective being to rescue Emin Pasha who, like Gordon before him, had been cut off by the Mahdist uprising; although in fact his main preoccupation was to open up the Congo for a variety of sponsors, including the Imperial British East Africa Company, the Egyptian government and King Leopold of the Belgians, who between them, secretly or otherwise, provided the expedition with most of its funds. The Society still regarded Stanley with mixed feelings. No-one now doubted his ability as an explorer; but the severity with which he treated the Africans – tribes who opposed him were taught the error of their ways by gunfire – earned him many enemies, and there was some doubt as to whether the Society wished to be associated with his venture. In the end, after a succession of heart-searching debates and a number of resignations, the Council voted Stanley £1,000 on the understanding that he supplied them with the geographical findings of his expedition straight from the field. This arrangement he scrupulously adhered to; and his despatches from the Congo are among the most exciting and graphic ever to be published in the *Journal*. His expedition, lavishly equipped and forcefully led, managed to work its way through the forests and swamps of the Congo basin until it

Charles George Gordon (1833–1885). Soldier, mystic, suppressor of the slave trade and surveyor of the upper reaches of the Nile

The Ruwenzori: the Mountains of the Moon, which Ptolemy suspected more than 2,000 years ago fathered the River Nile. Discovered by Captain G. N. Humphreys – though the credit is often erroneously given to Stanley

came to Lake Albert, that "boundless sea-horizon", which had hardly been visited by Europeans since Baker first set eyes on it. The explorers surveyed the southern reaches of the lake and found the River Semliki which connects it to the smaller Lake Edward. Then, in May 1888, the last piece in the jig-saw was slotted into place as they sighted a great range of snow-capped peaks, very nearly astride the equator – the Ruwenzori, Ptolemy's Mountains of the Moon. All these discoveries Stanley recorded with great accuracy on maps, which he forwarded with his despatches direct to the Society. Then in the spring of 1890 he returned to London, to a triumphant reception at the Albert Hall: a reception at which the press, the Society and the Prince of Wales vied with one another in showering him with the honours he undoubtedly deserved.

"Thus," to quote the Society's historian H. R. Mill, "with impressive ceremony and an abundance of good will, the Royal Geographical Society celebrated the completion of the task it had so long laboured upon in settling the great features of African orography."

The delineation of the Nile was without doubt the Society's crowning achievement in Africa. The Nile, however, represented only one facet of the Society's many-splendoured work. For virtually all the major mountain ranges, rivers and lakes in

Africa were made known to Europeans and laid down on the map as a result of
expeditions made under the auspices of the RGS. In 1840, shortly after the Society was
founded, a committee member had referred to the centre of Africa as "virtually a blank
on the map, a mysterious region exciting the curiosity of geographers and explorers".
Within fifty years the continent had been crossed and recrossed from all points of the
compass, all its major lakes had been accurately surveyed and all its major rivers had
been followed from mouth to source. It is interesting to note how many of these
discoveries the Society was directly involved in. As regards the Lakes: Beke and Lake
Tana, Barth and Lake Chad, Burton and Lake Tanganyika, Livingstone and Lake
Nyasa, Speke and Lake Victoria, Baker and Lake Albert and Stanley and Lake Edward.
The list of rivers is equally impressive: apart from the Nile there was Lander and the
Niger, Alexander and the Orange, Livingstone and the Zambezi, Du Chaillu and the
Ogowé, Rohlfs and the Benue, Stanley and the Congo, Erskine and the Limpopo and
Johnston and the Rufiji. One can only echo the words of Sir Clements Markham, that
"this long array of gallant and brilliant achievements with which our Society has been
connected has wrought a marvellous change on the map of Africa".

*Approaches to the
North Pole*

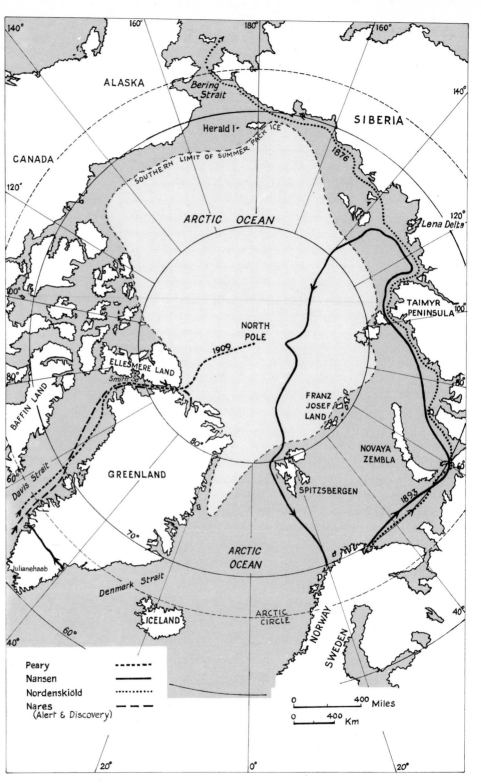

Peary
Nansen
Nordenskiöld
Nares
(Alert & Discovery)

5. The Conquest of the North Pole

T HE POLES ARE THE FARTHEST AND MOST DESOLATE EXTREMITIES OF THE earth, and to be the first creature to set foot on them presented a particular kind of challenge to a particular kind of man.

In their quest for other geographical goals explorers usually had to deal with more problems than the difficulty of the terrain – the hostility of an existing population for example, disease, or nationalistic rivalry – but the attainment of the Poles was like a straight fight between two unencumbered protagonists.

This sort of fight had a special appeal to those men whose single-mindedness of purpose enabled them to set all other considerations aside and concentrate every effort on the attainment of one specific goal. It was not by chance but by character that Peary became the first man to set foot on the North Pole and Amundsen on the South.

The Pandora *nipped in the ice-pack in Melville Bay, 24th July, 1876. Painting by W. W. May*

109

The year 1880 marked the RGS's fiftieth anniversary. Since its conception at a fashionable club dinner and the financial crises of its adolescence, the Society had grown enormously in size, importance and prestige. Its president-to-be, Sir Clements Markham, indicates how much it had achieved already and how much it hoped to achieve in the future:

"The progress that has been made in the science of geography since the Society was founded is only partially shown by a comparison of an atlas of 1830 with the maps of the present day. For this progress is not alone comprised in the discovery and delineation of unknown countries. Its range is far wider. There have also been great improvements in the methods of investigation, in the systematic arrangements of facts, in cartography, and in the construction and use of instruments. . . . [All the same] the most striking advances have been made in the field of discovery, and in completing our general knowledge of the earth's surface, preliminary to more detailed surveys."

Markham goes on to deal with the Arctic in particular:

"Glancing first at the regions around the North Pole, only unconnected strips of coast line had been traced in 1830 along the shore of Arctic America, and nothing was known of the regions between Barrow Strait and the continent. Our knowledge of the eastern sides of Greenland and Spitzbergen, of Novaya Zamlya and of the surrounding seas was vague and inaccurate, and the enormous area of Northern Asia was virtually unknown. Now, the whole coast of Arctic America has been delineated, and the remarkable archipelago to the north explored . . . considerable portions of the East coast of Greenland and the south shore of Franz Joseph Land have been discovered; the Union Jack has been advanced to 83°20'N, and Nordenskiöld has achieved the north-east passage.

"However, much remains to be done. The interior of Greenland presents a problem of the deepest interest, while the discovery of its northern shore has been an object of ambition for three centuries. The extent of the Polar Ice is unknown. The exploration of Franz Joseph Land and of the lands north of Siberia will be an important addition to knowledge, and the whole physical economy of the Polar Region must gradually be brought to light. . . . In the Arctic there is still important and difficult work to be done, and it is the duty of our Society to promote and further it by every means in our power."

It is surprising that the attainment of the North Pole was not included in Markham's list of tasks to be accomplished; especially since his friend and cousin Albert Markham, when second-in-command to Nares, had man-hauled his sledges to latitude 83°20' – farther north than man had ever been before. The fact, however, is that the North Pole never seems to have had quite the same attraction for British explorers as the South; perhaps because their repeated failures in the search for a North West Passage had made them view work in the Arctic with a jaundiced eye. The greatest journeys in the far north were therefore made not by the British (the exploits of Parry, McClintock and Nares notwithstanding) but by the Scandinavians: men like Nordenskiöld, Sverdrup, Amundsen, Nansen, Rasmussen and Stefansson, whose exploits drove home the point, first made by Rae, that man *could* come to terms with and live in the Arctic, provided he had the wit and the knowledge to understand it.

This comparative lack of interest in the North Pole is reflected in the pages of the *Journal*, which devotes twice as much space to the Antarctic as to the Arctic, and more than six times as much to exploration in Africa and Asia. Indeed in the years 1830 to

1880 no more than a couple of dozen papers were read on North Polar exploration, and the majority of these were either theoretical or devoted to the work of the Russians. In 1838 and 1844, for example, the Society listened to an account of Pachtussoff's survey of the north coast of Novaya Zemlya, and an account of Middendorf's explorations, *On the shore of the Great Frozen Sea*. In the 1850s, in contrast, papers were read on such theoretical topics as *The Origin of Icebergs* or *The Supposed Discovery of a Polar Sea*; and it was one of these basically academic papers which sparked off renewed interest in reaching the Pole.

In 1865 the Society listened to a lecture by Captain Sherard Osborn *On the Exploration of the North Polar Region*. Osborn divided his talk into three parts: "First: the direction from which a Polar exploration should be undertaken. Second: the mode in which such an exploration should be executed. And third: the scientific results likely to accrue from such an exploration." On each count he hit the nail unerringly on the head. He discounted the conventional idea of striking at the Pole as Parry had done from Spitsbergen, and advocated an expedition which would sail up the Davis Strait, would enter Smith Sound and would then work its way along the weather shore of Ellesmere Island until its advance was halted by ice. He calculated that a ship following this route should be able to penetrate to within 450 miles of its objective before becoming frozen-in. The final dash for the Pole should, he suggested, be made by dog-drawn sledge. This last idea was, to British eyes, something of an innovation; for although the technique of travelling by sledges pulled by huskies had been pioneered by Company factors and perfected by McClintock during the search for a North West Passage, both the Admiralty and the Society were too conventionally minded to give it their support – Markham for example throughout his life championed the use of man-drawn sledges. Osborn produced statistics to prove that in the Arctic long distances had frequently been traversed safely and swiftly by dog-drawn sledge – "Hamilton, for example," he told his audience, "covered 1,150 miles in only 70 days with a dog sledge and only one man"; he also quoted McClintock as telling him, "I regard the Pole as being within the reach of this generation; for knowledge, as you know, is power in sledge-travelling" – a dictum so far ahead of its time that it seems never to have attracted the attention it deserves.

It was partly as a result of Osborn's paper that the Society began to press the Government to play a more active role in polar exploration. And the Government responded. As soon as Nares returned from his round-the-world voyage in the *Challenger* he was given command of the *Alert* and *Discovery*, and ordered to explore the approaches to the Pole via Smith Sound, and to restore to Britain the "farthest north" record which Hall, at the cost of his life, had recently achieved for America.

Nares's expedition was the last major British naval assault on the North Pole to be launched in the nineteenth century. It epitomized both the best features of British exploration and the worst. On the credit side, it was meticulously planned and carefully equipped – the Society, for instance, provided Nares with a full resume of all its papers on Arctic geography and ethnology, while McClintock himself personally designed the sledges; its personnel demonstrated, yet again, the uniformly high standard of British seamanship; while its younger officers (Albert Markham in particular) showed endurance, courage and initiative far beyond the call of duty. On the debit side, it displayed an inflexible adherence to traditional methods. As Jeanette Mirsky rather unkindly puts it: "The expedition achieved success in spite of the antiquated techniques of travel employed, which were hardly different from those of Parry. It would seem as though the British naval mind was incapable of learning the lessons that the Arctic had been for generations expounding." An example of this failure to move with the times was the expedition's diet. It had been demonstrated on many occasions that the best way to remain healthy in the Arctic was to live, like the Eskimos, off the land, and that failing this antiscorbutics (*i.e.* vegetables containing vitamin C) were essential. Yet Nares and

Foreign Postage.

NEWS OF THE ARCTIC EXPEDITION.

SUPPLEMENT
TO
THE ILLUSTRATED LONDON NEWS, NOVEMBER 4, 1876.

THE NORTH POLE EXPEDITION: SKATING RINK AT THE WINTER QUARTERS OF H.M.S. DISCOVERY.

The illustrations on these pages are from the special editions of The Illustrated London News *published in November 1876 to commemorate the voyage to Ellesmere Island of the* Alert *and the* Discovery, *and the attainment of Markham's "Farthest North"*

his men spent little time hunting, and their daily rations are quoted as being: "16 ozs. pemmican, 14 ozs. biscuits, 4 ozs. bacon, 2 ozs. potatoes, $\frac{1}{2}$ gill of rum, 1 oz. chocolate, 2 ozs. sugar, $\frac{1}{2}$ oz. tea, $\frac{1}{8}$ oz. salt, $\frac{1}{2}$ oz. pepper, $\frac{1}{4}$ oz. onion and curry powder." No wonder they soon succumbed to scurvy.

The story of the expedition is a compound of heroism and near disaster. The *Alert* and *Discovery* sailed from Portsmouth in May 1875. They called at Proven in Greenland and took aboard 55 dogs, then stood north into Smith Sound. Ice conditions were bad, and Nares needed all his very considerable skill to get his ships into winter quarters off Ellesmere Island before the sea froze solid. He had hoped during the winter to advance on the Pole by dog-drawn sledges over relatively smooth ice. But it was not to be. His dogs, we are told, "all either died or ran away, victims of *piblokto* – a peculiar sort of madness." As for the ice: far from being smooth, it proved to be "tortured pack-ice, with ridges thirty feet high". Clearly the Pole was beyond their reach. Nares, however, was determined to advance as far as possible. He sent his sledges north, drawn not by dogs but by men; and in spite of the most terrible conditions, his ship's companies managed to chart both the north-west coast of Greenland and the north-east of Ellesmere Island. David Mountfield, in his *History of Polar Exploration*, describes both their achievements and the price they paid for them: "The sledging parties suffered frightful privations. They often had to travel six miles to gain one, chiefly because the whole party was needed to move a single sledge. They went down with scurvy, an affliction Hall had avoided by living on an Eskimo diet, and suffered from snow-blindness. Markham's party reached a new 'farthest' north of 83°20′, but he had to abandon one of his boats and regained the ship with half his party unable to walk. A second party, exploring the Ellesmere coast, was in an even worse state. A group from the *Discovery* explored the Greenland cost, and were reduced by scurvy, cold and exhaustion to crawling on all fours." It was only thanks to their commander's fine seamanship that the expedition managed next spring to extricate itself without loss of life.

One important result of Nares's expedition was that it pioneered the approach-route to the Pole which was used thirty years later by Peary. Another result, less obvious but certainly no less important, was that it determined, tragically, the path which British polar exploration was to follow for the next generation. For as Markham listened to his cousin's account of how he and his companions had man-hauled their sledges over the ice, it seemed to him that the *camaraderie* among the men striving by their own physical efforts towards a common goal epitomized all that was noblest in exploration, and when in later years he became the power behind the Society – a figure even more influential than Barrow had been in the 1830s or Murchison in the 1850s – this was the style of exploration that he championed, this was the mantle that he sloughed off onto his protégé Robert Falcon Scott.

And he left Scott another legacy from the Nares expedition – a mistrust of dogs. It is by no means clear what happened to Nares's dogs; that is to say, it isn't clear to what extent their *piblokto* was pathological and to what extent it was due to the explorers' inability to handle them. Anyhow, they were a failure – a failure which prejudiced those in power against them. And this prejudice led to a fundamental weakness in all British polar expeditions of the late nineteenth and early twentieth century. They neglected the best – indeed what was at that time the only feasible – method of travelling, by dog-drawn sledge.

This weakness, however, was not immediately apparent; for in the 1870s and 1880s most assaults on the Pole were still launched by sea. In 1869, for example, the Society listened to a report by the Finnish explorer Nordenskiöld on his efforts to force a passage through the ice to the north of Spitsbergen: a report which he ended with the words: "The only way to approach the Pole is that proposed by the most celebrated Arctic authorities in England, viz., that of – after having passed the winter at Smith Sound –

(On the facing page)
Two paintings of Lieutenant Albert Markham, R.N., reaching what was then the world's "farthest north" – 83°20′26″, on 12th May, 1876. Above, by Markham himself: below, The Most Northerly Encampment by Captain R. B. Beechey, R.N.

continuing the journey towards the North on sledges in the spring." Nordenskiöld, however, didn't follow his own advice; for it was not in the north-west but in the north-east that he achieved the success for which he is today best remembered – the *Vega*'s discovery in 1878 of a North East Passage. Nordenskiöld had already won the Society's highest award for his previous work in the Arctic, so to commemorate his latest feat the Founder's Medal was given to the *Vega*'s navigating officer, Lt. Palander of the Swedish Navy. And seldom can an award have been better deserved; for the *Vega*'s voyage lasted two nerve-racking years, during which she was continually hugging an uncharted shore, on nine days out of ten enveloped in either snow or fog; indeed so hazardous was navigation that a ship's boat had most of the time to be rowed ahead of the *Vega* to take soundings.

The immediate result of Nordenskiöld's voyage was that it channelled exploration into an area which up to now had received little attention: the Kara, Laptev and Siberian Seas, to the north of Asia. Into this desolate wilderness Gordon Bennett of the *New York Herald*, the man who had sponsored Stanley, now directed another expedition, this time under George Washington De Long.

De Long, a lieutenant in the US Navy, had all the attributes bar one of a successful explorer; he was tough, sensible, tenacious, brave and a first-class leader of men; he also had a sense of humour – a virtue not enjoyed by all that number of polar explorers. The only thing he lacked was luck. The Society played no part in the preparations for his expedition, and when it was over, like nearly everyone else at the time, they gave him less credit than perhaps was his due. Markham alone seems to have had the perspicacity to realize the expedition's importance, for in an address to the Society he describes it as "one of the most important of all polar voyages" and De Long's *Diary* as "perhaps the most interesting of all polar documents".

In August 1879, in his vessel the *Jeanette*, De Long pushed through the Bering Strait and hopefully "set course for Wrangel Land and the Pole". Within forty-eight hours he was beset by pack ice. Within a week he was trapped fast as a fly in amber. His diary gives us a good idea of his predicament.

Winter quarters of the Discovery

"September 6th – This is a glorious country to learn patience in. I am hoping to get the ship to Herald Island to make winter quarters. But as far as the eye can range is ice, and not only does it look as though it had never been broken up, it looks as though it never will. Yesterday I hoped that today would make an opening for us; today I hope that tomorrow will do it. . . . At 1 p.m. the fog lifted, and we saw a chance of making about a mile towards the island. Spread fires again and commenced forcing a way through, ramming whenever we were opposed, and with good effect. Ramming a ship through ice from ten to fifteen feet thick is of course impossible, but whenever a crack or narrow opening showed between two floes we could by judicious ramming and backing and ramming again shove them apart enough to squeeze through. . . . At 4.20 however, we had reached solid flows again, and with the fog closing in we came-to with our ice anchor."

What followed had the inevitability of a Greek tragedy whose end is writ plain in its beginning, For twenty-one months the *Jeanette* was held fast in the grip of the ice. She was battered, squeezed, listed, tugged this way and that and subjected to a thousand unbearable pressures. At last, in the summer of 1881, she began to break up. She was abandoned in good order, and almost everything of value was transferred to sledges or boats. All the same, De Long and his men were in trouble; for the *Jeanette* had gone down more than 500 miles from the coast of Siberia, and in ice which was drifting slowly but inexorably northwestward, away from the shore. In appalling weather the three ship's boats and five sledges headed south, their path over treacherous and uneven ice covered

(On the facing page) Wally Herbert's photographs evoke both the loneliness and the beauty of the Arctic (above) *"The sun returns through haze, teams heading north."* (below) *Sledging over hummocked ice*

George Strong Nares (1831–1915): naval officer, explorer and hydrographer, and his ship the Alert *nipped in the ice off Cape Beechey*

by two foot of water and slush and criss-crossed by sea lanes over which the sledges had to be floated and by solid floes over which the boats had to be hauled. They were shrouded in fog and lashed by sleet. The ice tore the men's boots to ribbons – within ten days they were walking barefoot. They were making for the mouth of the Lena, where De Long's maps indicated a number of villages. What he never knew – until too late – was that his maps were inaccurate; the villages were wrongly placed and, what is more, were inhabited only during the summer, so that even as the desperate men were struggling towards them, the Russians were pulling back for the winter to the comparative shelter of the hinterland. Eventually, after ten weeks of appalling privations, the boats were scattered by a violent gale. One foundered, and her crew were never heard of again. One was cast up on the east side of the Lena delta, providentially close to the one village which was still inhabited. But De Long wasn't so lucky. His boat was driven onto the north-west tip of the delta; there were no villages here, no food, no shelter; and between the first day of October and the last De Long and his men perished one by one of starvation, cold and physical exhaustion.

Their story, however, was not over, for almost exactly three years after the *Jeanette* had foundered off the coast of Siberia, her wreckage was washed ashore on the opposite side of the world, on the south-west coast of Greenland.

To the question "How did the wreckage get there?" Carl Lytzen, a Danish official in Julianehaab, supplied a precise if unexpected answer. First he satisfied himself that the wreck was, beyond all possible doubt, that of the *Jeanette*. Then he pointed out that because of what was already known about the currents of the Arctic, the remains of the vessel could have reached Greenland by only one route, "borne for a great circle distance of over 3,000 miles – nearly as far as from North Cape to the Cape of Good Hope – by a powerful west-flowing current almost directly over the Pole." Lytzen ended his report with the prophetic words: "It will be seen therefore that although Polar explorers are bound to become embedded in the ice, yet this same ice will drift them across the Pole and will eventually bear them out to safety. It would therefore not be impossible for an Expedition to drift from Siberia, with the ice, right through to southern Greenland, provided such an expedition was prepared to spend several years under way."

Lytzen's theories were soon put to the test by the Norwegian Nansen, in what has been described as "by far the most adventurous programme [of exploration] ever brought to the notice of the Society".

Fridtjof Nansen was born at Froen, near Oslo, in October 1861. He was one of those fortunate men on whom the gods seem to have lavished every possible blessing. Six feet tall, fair-haired, blue-eyed and of magnificent physique, he combined kindness and gentleness of character with a keen scientific brain and considerable organizing ability. He was on several counts a great man – as explorer, scientist, artist, writer, politician, Nobel prizewinner and humanitarian – but probably the happiest years of his life were the decade 1887–97, when, in his physical prime, he led the two great expeditions which established his fame as an explorer: the first crossing of the Greenland ice-cap, and the first crossing of the Arctic Ocean.

In the early 1880s it was generally believed that the centre of Greenland consisted of alternate mountain ranges and valleys. Nansen put forward a different theory: that it consisted of a relatively flat ice-cap, which it should be possible to cross on skis. The experts laughed at him. But it was Nansen who had the last laugh, for in the summer of 1888, together with five companions, he skied across the 500 miles of the Greenland plateau in less than three weeks.

Soon after his return, he decided to put another theory to the test: Lytzen's theory that a ship could be drifted icebound across the Pole. Having been proved right once, it might have been thought that when Nansen put forward this second proposal he would be listened to respectfully. However, the Norwegian Government alone had the courage

Fridtjof Nansen (1861–1930): explorer, scientist, writer, artist, statesman and humanitarian; and his ship the Fram *frozen into the ice during their epic three-year drift across the Arctic Ocean*

*Baron Nils Adolf
Nordenskiold (1832–1901)
geologist and Arctic
explorer: first to sail through
the North East passage in
command of the* Vega – *the
latter photographed in her
winter quarters, by
Lieutenant Palander 1879*

and vision to give him their backing; in the rest of the world his idea was received at best
with scepticism, at worst with hostility.

The Society listened to him with respect but misgivings. On 14th November, 1892 he
read his historic paper *How can the North Polar Regions be Crossed?* to a meeting which was
attended by just about every living British Polar explorer of note. However, in the
discussion which followed only the veteran McClintock voiced his approval. "I think,"
McClintock said, "this is the most adventurous programme ever brought to the notice of
the Society. Dr. Nansen is a true Viking, and one cannot but admire his splendid
enthusiasm. . . . He has fully described his ship, and I think she should accomplish all that
any vessel can do. . . . I wish Dr. Nansen complete success." Other speakers were less
enthusiastic – "All very well in theory, but extremely difficult in practice" (George
Nares); "Highly dangerous . . . the ice will go through the ship no matter how she is
constructed" (Alan Young); "I must speak discouragingly of the project. The *Jeanette*
relics may well have drifted to Greenland via another route entirely: i.e. via Smith
Sound" (Admiral Richards). And the Society's feelings were summed up by Sir Joseph
Hooker: "The project involves the greatest danger. May I express the hope that Dr.
Nansen will dispose of his admirable courage, skill and resource in the prosecution of
some less perilous attempt." This scepticism was to some extent mitigated by the obvious
good-will of Nansen's British critics, and by the Society's donation of £300 towards his
expenses. There was no such good-will from American critics who, spearheaded by
General Greely, attacked Nansen with a bitterness which today seems incom-
prehensible. "It strikes me," wrote the cantankerous old general, "as incredible that the
plan advanced by Dr. Nansen should receive encouragement or support. For it seems to
be based on fallacious ideas and to foreshadow barren results. Dr. Nansen has had no
Arctic experience . . . and it is doubtful if any hydrographer would treat seriously his

theory of polar currents, or if any Arctic traveller would endorse his scheme." It is possible to attribute Greely's initial reaction to ignorance, and to forgive it. It is not so easy to forgive the malicious and completely unjustified attacks which the General launched on Nansen after his return, when he accused the Norwegian of "deliberately quitting his comrades in [an] ice-bound ship, thus deviating from the most sacred duty of a commander". The Americans, then, offered Nansen neither encouragement before his expedition nor praise after it. They disassociated themselves from his venture. And for this history has taken an ironic revenge. For although the voyage of the *Jeanette* and the drift of the *Fram* were in fact complementary, they are not nowadays associated with one another in people's minds; so that while the Norwegian Nansen and his ship the *Fram* are household names, his American precursors who died pioneering the route he was to follow are forgotten.

Nansen prepared for his expedition with unprecedented thoroughness. His ship, designed by the Scotsman Colin Archer, has been rightly described as "a masterpiece of craftsmanship, ingenuity and attention to detail". His supplies were sufficient for five years; and to quote Nansen himself, "every single item has been chemically analysed and was properly packed – even bread and dried vegetables being soldered down in tins as a protection against damp." His scientific instruments – many lent by research institutes and some by the Society – were of the latest and best. His crew had been hand-picked from more than two thousand volunteers. And when, in June 1893, he took the *Fram* out of Oslo, Nansen was leading one of the best-planned, equipped and victualled expeditions that ever put to sea.

Events were to prove both Lytzen's theory and Nansen's patience. For in a voyage which has been described as "the greatest human exploit of the nineteenth century" the *Fram's* twelve-man all-Norwegian crew took their vessel from the Bering Strait to the Barents Sea via the centre of the Arctic Ocean: a three-thousand-mile three-year drift across the roof of the world. This was a magnificent achievement on several counts. The *Fram* reached 82°30'N, closer to the Pole than a ship had ever stood before. Nansen and his companion Johansen left their vessel and sledged to 86°13'N, and this again was the closest to the Pole that a man had ever set foot. Nansen's paintings and descriptions of the Arctic have seldom been bettered. And, most important of all, the voyage of the *Fram* proved beyond all possible doubt that the Arctic consisted not as had been previously supposed of land, but of deep uncluttered ocean; while the data which was collected daily enabled the scientists of many disciplines to begin a detailed study of the whole Polar region.

It is pleasant to record that the British Polar explorers who had viewed Nansen's project with such misgivings were the first to congratulate him on his triumph. The Society paid him the unprecedented complement of sending both its President and Secretary to Norway to welcome him home; and a few months later, before a vast audience in the Albert Hall, he was given an enthusiastic welcome and a specially designed gold medal – only the second such presentation to be made in the Society's history.

While Nordenskiöld, De Long and Nansen were opening up the eastern reaches of the Arctic, the Americans were active in the west.

In the 1850s Kane had made important discoveries in the area of Ellesmere Island and north-west Greenland; though he somewhat tarnished his image by reporting a vast and non-existent open sea to the north of Smith Sound, a report which was to give false hope to explorers for more than a generation. In the 1860s and 70s the eccentric but persevering Hall embarked on a series of expeditions which culminated in his briefly holding the record for "farthest north", in the loss of his ship the *Polaris*, and his death – or was it his murder? – through arsenic poisoning, off the coast of Greenland.

Hall's death was perhaps one of the factors which led Karl Weyprecht, in 1875, to deliver his famous address to the German Scientific Association in which he made an

Charles Francis Hall (1821–1871) American Arctic explorer, who died mysteriously of arsenic poisoning having passed Markham's "farthest north"

Adolphus Washington Greely (1844–1935): American army officer and Arctic explorer, attained another "farthest north" and with a handful of men survived perhaps the most horrifying of all explorers' ordeals, frozen-in off Cape Sabine for the Arctic winter without food – except, it has been claimed, their companions

impassioned plea for international co-operation in Polar research. There was, Weyprecht argued, far too much emphasis on spectacular feats of exploration, such as reaching the farthest north or being first at the Pole; what was needed was teamwork, objectivity and disinterested research. Weyprecht was clearly right; and his suggestions did lead in 1882 to the first International Polar Year, an event which foreshadowed the more ambitious and more successful attempts at co-operation of the present century.

Ironically, it was as part of the programme for Weyprecht's International Polar Year that the United States sent an expedition to Ellesmere Island: a venture which can only be described as the epitome of chauvinism. This expedition consisted of twenty-six officers and men of the US Army commanded by Lieutenant Greely, and had the dual objective of collecting scientific data and breaking Markham's record of "farthest north".

To start with all went well, and in the summer of 1882 Markham's 83°20′N was duly passed by about four miles. That winter, however, the expedition ran into difficulties, not because of its own shortcomings, but because of the incompetence and indifference of the authorities at home who failed to send the relief ship and supplies on which Greely was relying. To quote Paul Victor's *Man and the Conquest of the Pole*:

> "As the ship which had been promised did not come to pick them up, Greely attempted to head south. After a terrible journey he reached Cape Sabine where he built a cabin. With hope and provisions running out he and his men could only wait. Scurvy broke out. One man was shot for stealing another's food. And the others died one by one in an infernal atmosphere of hatred and cannibalism.
>
> "When the men of the sealing ship *Thetis* put ashore at Cape Sabine in June 1884, they found a terrible scene. Greely's tent had collapsed. None of those underneath could move; but incredibly six men were still alive. One had his jaw hanging free and was blind; another was without hands or feet and had a spoon attached to the stump of his arm; Greely, on hands and knees, his hair in pigtails, resembled a skeleton, his joints bulbous and swollen. All the food that remained was two repulsive-looking jars of 'jelly'."

Coming in the wake of the Franklin disaster and so soon after the death of Hall and De Long, this latest catastrophe confirmed the malign reputation of the Arctic throughout the English-speaking world. It was only by slow degrees that the exploits of the Scandinavian explorers caused people to re-assess this reputation and arrive at a more balanced view of the regions surrounding the Pole.

Few journeys did more to dispel the myth of the Arctic's invincibility than Amundsen's conquest of the North West Passage in his diminutive vessel the *Gjoa*. The word conquest is used deliberately. For Amundsen was one of a new breed of explorer – tough, patient, dedicated, immensely capable, frequently ruthless – who began to emerge in the last decades of the century: men who made a career out of exploration. He was not, like Nordenskiöld or Nansen, primarily a scientist engaged in research; he was not, like Greely or Scott, primarily a serving officer put in charge of an expedition in the course of his duty; he was certainly not an amateur. He was, to quote David Mountfield, "a clever thorough man, who set out methodically to make himself an expert in all the techniques of travel and survival in the polar regions". In 1903, after the most meticulous preparations, he set out to force his way through the North West Passage.

In the *Journal* he describes both his ship and his plan.

> "We shall be eight men all told. Our vessel, the *Gjoa*, has already given proof of its solidity, and has been further strengthened by heavy bulkheads of timber and a two-inch sheathing of planks. She is fitted with a petroleum motor, and can make about 4 knots. She is 47 tons register, 70 feet long and 20 broad. It may seem that the vessel is

small, and indeed it is one of the smallest which has ever set out for a long polar expedition; but the choice was made after full consideration. Many will object that such a vessel cannot force its way through the ice, and that the space is too cramped for both members of the expedition and for provisions. To this I reply that it has never been my intention to charge the ice with the *Gjoa*. My idea is to trust to patience, and steal through when there is opportunity. The sounds and straits we must try to pass through are small and narrow and full of drift ice. The many attempts made to force a way through have all failed. Experience proves that one must watch one's opportunity, and that a small vessel, requiring less room and being easier to manoeuvre, has the advantage. What, then, has not been accomplished with large vessels and force, I will attempt with a small vessel and patience.

"We sail in May for Disko Island, off the coast of Greenland, where, by permission of the Danish Government, we shall buy Eskimo dogs. From here a course will be set past Melville Bay to Lancaster Sound. We then turn south through Prince Regent's inlet to Belliot Strait, between Boothia Felix and North Somerset. Magnetic observations will be taken as frequently as possible . . . and if these indicate that we are in the neighbourhood of the magnetic pole, two men will be put ashore with provisions for two years, and the materials necessary for building a magnetic observatory and house. The plan is to use packing cases for the house, and these have therefore been specially made, all grooved and tongued and of the same size. By filling them with earth and placing them one above another, walls may be speedily raised."

There follows a sentence which illustrates that meticulous attention to detail which enabled Amundsen to succeed where those before him had failed: "To avoid disturbances in the magnetic observations, the cases are put together with copper nails."

Roald Amundsen (1872–1928): arguably the world's most professional and successful explorer. First to set foot on the South Pole and first to navigate the North West Passage in the diminutive Gjoa – the latter from a painting by Honsheen

He goes on to describe in detail the scientific observations he hoped to make, the route he expected to follow and the schedule he intended to keep to.

Almost exactly four years later he was reading another paper to the Society: this time an account of his voyage *To the North Magnetic Pole and Through the North-West Passage*. Bearing in mind his predecessors' repeated failures in the Canadian Arctic, one might have expected the account of his expedition to be one of difficulties, frustrations and delays. Yet, amazingly, not only did Amundsen complete his scientific work *in toto* and succeed in navigating the North West Passage for the first time in its entirety, he did it all exactly according to plan. His address to the Society, in February 1907, was a singularly happy occasion. He paid tribute to the work of his predecessors – "the British seamen who here, as in most other parts of the world, have taken the lead and showed us the way" – and the Society responded by giving him an enthusiastic reception; its President spoke of the "intense admiration we feel for Captain Amundsen and his exploit", suggested naming a gulf in his honour, and presented him with the Society's Gold Medal – all of which is worth bearing in mind, in view of the unfortunate *faux pas* committed a few years later after the Norwegian's achievements in Antarctica.

While Amundsen was setting up his observatory at the magnetic pole, another equally determined man was locked in a twenty-three-year struggle with the geographic pole.

Robert Edwin Peary was born in Pennsylvania in 1856, and, like Amundsen, he became interested in the Arctic at an early age. Indeed he was still at school when he wrote an article on the subject of polar exploration: an article which contained the precocious but undoubtedly correct judgment that the old Royal Naval style of expedition "had had its day . . . and that the use of a small party, depending largely on native assistance, will put us far ahead in the race". Peary's choice of the word "race" is significant, and gives us the clue to his character: he was intensely competitive. David Mountfield's description of him cannot be bettered. "He was strongly built, with powerful chest and shoulders, and always kept himself fit; indeed his concern with 'manliness' would today seem not far short of obsessive. Photographs show him confronting the camera with steely gaze, eyes slightly narrowed, jaw out-thrust; his weight rests on one leg, the other being set slightly forward at an angle . . . a pose familiar in Roman statues and portraits of Victorian generals. The image, however, was not phony: Peary was as tough as he looked."

In 1886, after only his second visit to the Arctic, he set his sights on the Pole. What followed was not so much a quest as a war; a bitter and protracted battle which could end only with the Pole conquered or Peary dead. A summary of his expeditions illustrates both the difficulty of his self-appointed task and the tenacity of his character.

In 1886 he tried to cross the Greenland ice-cap, but managed to advance no more than a hundred miles before his sledge crashed into a crevasse and he was nearly killed.

In 1891–2, accompanied by his wife and his black man-servant, he spent a year with the Eskimos of Smith Sound. From them he learned how to travel on skis, with his provisions carried on lightweight sledges drawn by dogs: a technique which he referred to as "the Peary method", and which was undoubtedly the best way of travelling in the Arctic. During this expedition he crossed the Greenland ice-cap, and advanced as far as Independence Bay (82°N).

In 1893–5 he tried to head north from Independence Bay; his expedition, however, was overtaken by a succession of disasters; and when the calving of an iceberg swamped his supplies he was stung into the classic cry of defiance: "The fates and all hell are against me, but I'll triumph yet." After a journey of unbelievable hardship and hazard, he struggled back to base with only one dog left out of thirty, and his two companions near-dead from exposure.

In 1896 he was again in north Greenland, and again unable to advance beyond 82°N.

He did, however, discover three enormous meteorites – the largest weighing over 1,000 lbs., which he shipped back to the United States.

In 1897–9, disheartened by repeated failures in Greenland, he tried a new approach: via Smith Sound, the Kane Basin and the north-east coast of Ellesmere Island: the route used by Nares and Greely. He managed to force his way through to Fort Conger, which had not been visited since the *Thetis* evacuated survivors from the Greely disaster. It was bitterly cold, with temperatures down to −70°F; Peary's toes became frostbitten; seven had to be amputated, and he was dragged back to his vessel, the *Windward*, strapped to a sledge.

In 1900 he again wintered at Fort Conger; and though his feet were still tender and he found it difficult to stand upright, he made a long and arduous journey by sledge parallel to the north coast of Greenland. Before this journey it had been thought that Greenland might be connected to the little-known North-East or Franz Land; it was Peary who proved beyond all possible doubt it was an island. He was still unable, however, to make much headway towards the Pole, because the ice was drifting steadily east and consisted of great crumbling pressure ridges, many of them thirty feet high. This confirmed Peary in his belief that Ellesmere Island would be the most promising starting point for future expeditions.

In 1902 he set out from Fort Conger with two dozen sledges and more than a hundred dogs. In accordance with "the Peary method", the supporting dog teams cached supplies along their line of advance and one by one returned to base, eventually leaving Peary with only a couple of companions to make the final assault. They headed across the ice from Cape Hecla (one of the most northerly points of Ellesmere Island); but the going was rough, with huge ice-ridges and deep snow through which the dogs could hardly haul themselves. After three exhausting weeks, during which they covered little

(Above left) *Five flags at the Pole;* (Above right) *Robert Edwin Peary (1856–1920) in his genuine and original North Polar costume, and his ship the* Roosevelt, *against the face of Cape North Glacier: all from the Hubbard edition of Peary's book* The North Pole

more than a hundred miles, they were engulfed by a blizzard of such ferocity that it opened up leads in the ice. Peary struggled on to 84° 16′N; then, realizing that his goal was beyond reach, he returned to Ellesmere Island. "My dream of sixteen years is ended," he wrote despondently. "I close the book."

In 1905, however, he was back again: this time aboard the *Roosevelt*, a tough wooden-hulled vessel of 1,500 tons designed by Peary himself and paid for by the President of the United States and the Peary Arctic Club.

The attainment of the pole was now becoming for America a matter of national prestige. To quote Peary: "The *Roosevelt* was built of American timber in an American shipyard by an American firm with American metal, and constructed on American designs. Even the most trivial items of supply were of American manufacture." All through the summer this sturdy all-American vessel battered her way through the ice-floes of the Kane Basin, encouraged by her captain with cries of "Rip 'em, Teddy! Bite 'em in two!" The *Roosevelt* did indeed rip and bite to such effect that she managed to reach the north-east tip of Ellesmere Island, farther north than a ship under way had ever penetrated before. Here she was frozen in, while Peary prepared for his most ambitious assault yet: twenty-seven drivers and 120 dogs. He set out from Cape Hecla in February 1906, and to start with all went well. The Peary method of travelling, however, had been perfected on land-ice not sea-ice, and on the unstable and ever-shifting surface of the Arctic Ocean the expedition soon ran into difficulties. Their supply dumps drifted away, and instead of the usual methodical advance, the dog-teams found themselves bunching together at the open leads. Peary succeeded in establishing a new "farthest north" of 87°06′; but with the temperature down to − 50F, his men suffering from ophthalmia and his dogs dying of exhaustion, he was forced yet again to give up. And this time he almost left his decision too late. For by the time he turned back the ice was thin, treacherous and drifting rapidly east; his retreat was slow, and he and his companions reached land with only two dogs left out of 120, and virtually no food. They owed their lives to a wandering herd of musk ox, three of which were shot and their "flesh gobbled warm and raw".

In 1908 Peary, now aged 52, was back for what he himself described as "one last try". The *Roosevelt* again forced her way into winter quarters off the north-east tip of Ellesmere Island, and on 28th February, 1909 the assault began. The ice was in better shape than in previous years, the weather favourable, and the twenty men and 140 dogs made steady progress. The Peary method worked better on this occasion, with some teams turning back as soon as they had blazed a trail and cached supplies, the dogs being slaughtered for meat as their work was accomplished, and the main assault party of Peary and four Eskimos being carefully nursed – during the first four weeks of their advance they slept each night in igloos which had already been built by the teams ahead of them. A month after leaving Ellesmere Island Peary passed his previous "farthest north", and a couple of days later the support parties turned back, leaving Peary, his black man-servant Hanson and four Eskimos to make the final dash.

They were now a bare hundred miles from the Pole; and Bob Bartlett, the skipper of the *Roosevelt*, who in the last month had done sterling work pioneering the trail, begged Peary to let him join the assault party. Peary, however, in a gesture reminiscent of Speke's denial of Grant at the headwaters of the Nile, refused. It is possible to justify his refusal – just as it is possible to justify Speke's – on the grounds of expediency; but it has been uncharitably suggested that something else may have been behind it: that Peary might not have wanted to share his triumph with another white man.

A week later he stood at the Pole. "The Pole at last!!!" he wrote in his diary. "The prize of three centuries, my dream and ambition for twenty-three years. *Mine* at last. I cannot bring myself to realize it." He spent twenty-four hours at and around the Pole. He took soundings – no bottom was found at 10,000 feet – and made no fewer than thirteen observations from different points. He built a snow cairn, raised the American flag which he had been carrying with him for fifteen years, and gave three hearty cheers, while the Eskimos did a ritual dance, chanting "*Ting neigh timah ketisher!*" ("We're there at last!"). He left an account of his expedition in a glass bottle, and wrote a postcard to his wife. Then he headed back for the *Roosevelt*, which he reached on 27th April after a surprisingly easy journey.

Hardly anyone nowadays doubts that Peary got to the Pole; or that he was the first man to do so. This, however, was certainly not the case in 1909. For as the *Roosevelt* that summer stood south down the coast of Greenland, her crew sighted three figures man-hauling a sledge. They turned out to be a white man and two Eskimos, in the last stages of exhaustion. They were taken aboard and fed; and when asked who they were and where they had come from, the white man said matter-of-factly: "I am Dr. Frederick Cook. And I have come from the North Pole."

Frederick Cook is an enigma. He was a competent doctor, a likeable man and an explorer of no mean stature who had accompanied Peary on several of his earlier expeditions and was one of the first men to winter in the Antarctic (aboard de Gerlache's vessel the *Belgica*). One would *like* to believe him. It would, however, be idle to deny that there was an element of instability in his character, and that his writings – out of which he made a fortune – contain flights of fancy more suited to a novel than to the factual report of an expedition.

The *Journal* of the Society, in October 1909, gives a very fair summary of his claim:

THE NORTH POLAR EXPEDITIONS OF COMMANDER PEARY AND DR. COOK

Within a few days of one another telegrams appeared in the press from Dr. F. A. Cook and Commander R. E. Peary, each of which announced that he had reached the North Pole. At present we propose only to summarize the narratives of the two explorers, in order of their appearance, reserving any criticism or expression of opinion till farther information is available.

DR. COOK'S NARRATIVE

On September 1st telegraphic messages from Lerwick announced that the steamer *Hans Egede* had arrived there from the Danish settlements in Greenland where it had taken on board the American explorer Dr. F. A. Cook who reported that he had reached the North Pole on April 21st, 1908 [i.e. almost a year before Peary]. Dr. Cook had gone north on board a schooner belonging to Mr. J. R. Bradley in the summer of 1907, prepared to attempt to reach the Pole if a favourable opportunity offered, and had organized his equipment accordingly. When the schooner returned south, Dr. Cook remained at Etah [a settlement at the approaches to the Kane Basin], in company with Mr. Francke, and sent back word that he intended to make a "dash" for the pole by way of Nansen Sound, which separates Ellesmere Land from Axel Heiberg Land to the west. He started from Etah early last year, accompanied only by some Eskimos and their dogs, and on March 17th sent back despatches from Cape Hubbard, the northernmost point of Axel Heiberg Land. In these despatches he stated that he hoped to be back in June ... but in the autumn there was still no news of him. It was feared that Dr. Cook must have lost his life while attempting to reach the Pole, and the news that he was alive and had succeeded in attaining his object, came as a complete surprise.

The following summary of his experiences after leaving Cape Hubbard is compiled from despatches he cabled to the *New York Herald*. The journey over the ice was begun

*Smith Bay, Ellesmere
Island: the starting point of
many attempts, including
several by Peary, to reach
the North Pole*
(Inset) *Dr. Frederick
Cook, about whom there is
still a mystery – did he
actually reach the North
Pole a year before Peary?*

from Cape Hubbard on March 18th, but it was not until three days later that Dr. Cook commenced "the crossing of the circumpolar pack". The last of the supporting parties returned from this point, and Dr. Cook continued in company with only two Eskimos and twenty-six dogs. The low temperature and persistent winds were very trying; nevertheless long marches were made, and the "big lead which separated the land-ice from the central pack was crossed with little delay". The weather did not favour the taking of accurate observations; but on March 30th the sky partially cleared, and "over the western mist was discovered a new land". According to his observations, Dr. Cook was then 84°47′N, 86°36′W.... Being anxious to continue his northern march, Dr. Cook did not turn aside to explore the land he sighted. He states that he now found himself beyond the range of all life. The surface of the pack-ice began to offer less and less trouble, and long distances were covered every day. On April 8th he secured observations which gave his position as 86°36′N, 94°2′W. At this point of his narrative he states: "Much of our hard work was lost in circuitous twists around troublesome pressure lines and high irregular fields of very old ice. The drift, too, was driving eastward with sufficient force to give some anxiety.... Beyond the 86th parallel the icefields became more extensive and heavier, the crevasses fewer and less troublesome, with little or no crushed ice thrown up as barriers. From the 87th to the 88th parallel much surprise was caused by an indication of land ice. For two days we travelled over ice which resembled a glacial surface. The usual sea-ice lines of demarcation were absent, and there were no hummocks or deep crevasses. There was, however, no perceptible elevation and no positive sign of land".... Later on Dr. Cook says: "Signs of land were still seen almost every day, but they were deceptive illusions ... due to the atmospheric magic of the midnight sun". Finally, on April 21st, Dr. Cook states that the first corrected altitude of the sun indicated that he had reached

89°59′46″N. "We advanced the 14″, made supplementary observations and prepared to stop long enough to permit a double round of observations. The temperature was −38°. . . ."

Cape Hubbard, as shown on Commander Peary's map in his book *Farthest North*, is in 81°15′N; so that to have reached the North Pole on April 21st Dr. Cook must have covered 525 geographical miles in 35 days – an average rate of progress of 15 miles a day.

The return march was commenced on April 23rd. With fair weather and good ice, long distances were at first covered; but below the 87th parallel the character of the ice changed greatly, and violent gales were encountered. Observations on May 24th indicated that the party had reached the 84th parallel in the neighbourhood of the 97th meridian west. The ice was much broken and there was an easterly drift. The 83rd parallel was reached, then foggy weather ensued which lasted twenty days. At the end of this time the party found themselves far down in Crown Prince Gustav Sea, to the west of Axel Heiberg Land, and separated therefrom by broken ice interspersed with so much open water that it was impossible to reach the island. Ultimately winter was passed at Cape Sparbo, on the coast of North Devon Island. And early this year the crossing to the west coast of Greenland was effected [where Cook was picked up by the *Roosevelt*].

The controversy which followed was bitter and protracted. Peary denounced Cook as a fraud and a liar. Cook, in contrast, behaved impeccably; "there is honour enough in it," he told the press, "for both of us." Contemporary opinion was overwhelmingly on the side of the doctor; a newspaper poll in Pittsburgh for example indicated that 73,238 people regarded Cook as the conqueror of the Pole, and only 2,814 Peary.

This verdict time has reversed.

The first nail in Cook's coffin was when the Royal Society of Copenhagen pronounced his claim "Not Proved"; a second nail was when the Royal Geographical Society tacitly agreed; a third was when he was convinced of fraud in a not very savoury scandal concerning oil shares.

Today probably not one person in a thousand has heard of the man who in his hour was hailed as the greatest American explorer of all time. Yet a residue of doubt remains; a lingering suspicion that Cook *could* have been telling the truth. And it is interesting to note that his staunchest supporters have always been those who knew the Arctic best. Among his contemporaries, Greely, Sverdrup, Amundsen, Nordenskiöld and Nansen all believed him; and today the man who is probably the world's greatest authority on polar sledging, Wally Herbert, prefers his claim to that of Peary. Certainly two facts – both in Cook's favour – are worth bearing in mind. His critics usually dismiss his story on two counts: his report of land where it is now known that no land exists, and his lack of scientific observations. Yet on the first count it should be remembered that the history of polar exploration, in both the Arctic and Antarctic, is full of erroneous sighting reports – Ross's "discovery" of the mythical Croker Mountains is only one such instance; also that Cook did qualify his report by saying he frequently saw "signs of land" but these "often turned out to be deceptive illusions". On the second count, it does not seem to be generally known that when he was picked up off the coast of Greenland Cook *did* have additional observations with him, but that Peary refused to allow his notes and instruments to be brought back aboard the *Roosevelt*; they had therefore to be cached in Greenland, and were subsequently lost.

All therefore that can be said without fear of contradiction is that Peary almost certainly reached the North Pole in April 1909, and that Cook may possibly have reached it a year before him.

No such doubt surrounds the conquest of the South Pole.

6. The Race for the South Pole

IN ITS EARLY YEARS THE SOCIETY PLAYED ONLY A MINOR ROLE IN OPENING up the Antarctic, being inhibited by the two factors which had also curtailed its activities in Australia: distance and finance. Of these, finance was the greater stumbling block.

The Society understood very well the importance of promoting exploration in the little-known reaches of the Southern Ocean. One of its first secretaries, John Washington, wrote a memorandum on this subject to the Admiralty: a memorandum which helped to bring about the highly successful expedition led by James Clark Ross. But when it came to financing Ross, not only was the Society unable to afford to buy him equipment, it couldn't even afford to buy him dinner, the minute-book recording that "no funds were available for such a purpose"!

So for more than fifty years the Society's contribution to exploration in the Antarctic was restricted to publishing reports – including articles by Biscoe, Enderby and Charles Darwin – and awarding medals – in 1833 to Biscoe, in 1842 to Ross and in 1848 to Wilkes. Then, in the last decade of the century, the years of inactivity were superseded by a sudden burst of research-cum-exploration, with expedition after expedition landing on, pushing into, and finally penetrating to the very heart of what had hitherto been an unknown continent.

In this great leap into the unknown no man played a more important role than the Society's President, Sir Clements Markham.

"All of us gathered round the colours, a beautiful silken flag. . . . And placing it on the spot, gave the vast plateau on which the Pole is situate the name of 'King Haakon VII Plateau'" from Captain Amundsen's Narrative.

Sir Clements Robert Markham (1830–1916): writer, geographer and for many years doyen of the Society. His passion for exploration nurtured British interest in the Antarctic

(On the facing page) *Two views of Erebus. Above:* HM Ships Erebus *and* Terror *off Cape Crozier, painted by J. E. Davis during Sir James Clark Ross's expedition to the Antarctic (1839–1843). Below: "Pressure ridges at the foot of Mount Erebus, photographed from close to Scott Base during the New Zealand Antarctic Research Programme (1976–1977)." Photograph and caption by Jeremy Sutton-Pratt*

The first man to sight the mainland of Antarctica was almost certainly the Russian explorer Thaddeus von Bellingshausen, in January 1820; although it is possible that an unknown American sealer may have caught an earlier glimpse of the continent and failed to make the discovery known – for sealing was a secretive and highly competitive calling. For almost a couple of decades the New England sealers had the approaches to Antarctica to themselves. Then in the late 1830s three major expeditions came south, each hoping to discover and be first to set foot on a virgin continent: d'Urville for France, Wilkes for America, and Ross for Great Britain.

D'Urville sighted Adélie Land in January 1841, landed on an offshore island, unfurled the Tricolour, drank a bottle of Bordeaux (doubtless a good vintage, since he was an explorer of impeccable taste), and took possession of the nearby coast in the name of France.

Wilkes also sighted the continent in January 1841, a little farther to the east. His ships had been in a poor condition when he set out, and were now near-foundering; but Wilkes was a man of great determination, and in one of the most hazardous and physically demanding voyages ever made he followed the coast of Antarctica for more than a thousand miles, before he too landed on an offshore island and claimed the adjacent territory for the United States.

The British expedition, meanwhile, in the last of the epic voyages to be made wholly under sail, broke through the pack-ice of the Ross Sea and for several weeks stood close inshore past the magnificent ten-thousand-foot peaks of the Prince Albert Range. Then Ross also landed, "gave three hearty cheers, and took possession of the newly-discovered lands in the name of our Most Gracious Sovereign, Queen Victoria."

All three explorers had followed tradition by claiming the territory they discovered for their respective countries. They cannot, however, have rated what they found very highly. For the Antarctic coastline is the bleakest in the world and quite unsuitable for colonization; the spirit of scientific investigation was not yet sufficiently powerful to offset the new continent's remoteness and desolation, and so for almost half-a-century Antarctica was ignored. In what has been termed "the Age of Averted Interest" almost the only people to penetrate the tempestuous sea-lanes of the Southern Ocean were sealers and whalers.

It was the whalers who, towards the end of the century, helped to bring about a sudden revival of interest in the Antarctic.

Throughout the early part of the nineteenth century seamen of a dozen nations had combed the oceans of the world in search of the slow-moving right and sperm whales, as many as 600 vessels a year putting out from New England alone. When the right whales had been reduced to near extinction, the predators turned their attention to the rorqual whales (the fin, sei, humpback and blue). The rorquals, however, were a good deal faster than the rights – a blue can swim at a steady 25 knots – and the whalers who hunted these magnificent creatures with the conventional hand-harpoon and rowing-boat didn't have a great deal of success. Then a Norwegian businessman, Svend Foyn, perfected a special sort of harpoon gun. To quote F. D. Ommanney, himself both explorer and whaler, "Svend Foyn's deadly invention was taken up by the Norwegian whalers in 1880, and gave them a worldwide supremacy which lasted until 1950. It took the glamour, but also the danger and hardship out of whaling, and led to the mass slaughter of the rorquals." Before 1880 most of the whaling ships which had penetrated the Southern Ocean had met with little success as we can learn from a report by Alexander Fairweather: "From all points of view the expedition was a disappointment. We saw no Right Whales, but all around us spouted the fast-swimming Rorquals, and our experienced skippers were well aware that our tackle was inadequate for killing them. Eventually in our frustration we were reduced to hunting seals." After 1880, however, the situation changed. Whaling once again became commercially viable.

"Tilted" Bergs off the Barrier. Jan. 25. 1902. E.A.W.

More and more vessels converged on Antarctica, and their voyages stimulated both discovery and research. In 1892 the Scottish whaler *Balaena*, commanded by Bruce, discovered Active Sound. In 1894 the Norwegian whaler *Jason*, commanded by Larsen, made important discoveries off the coast of Graham Land. In 1895 the Norwegian whaler *Antarctic*, commanded by Bull, made a discovery of another kind; one of its seamen, Carsten Borchgrevink, landed on an island in the Ross Sea and found the rocks coated with lichen – the first indication that the continent supported any form of life.

The nations of Europe began to take a sudden if belated interest in Antarctica and the seas that encircled it. In 1895 a meeting of the International Geographical Congress declared that "the most important piece of exploration still to be undertaken is that of the Antarctic", and the Congress – which was attended by several members of the Society – went on to urge that "scientific teams be sent out there in view of the vast addition to knowledge which would result".

So by the turn of the century men had two reasons for heading south: commercial gain, and the accruing of scientific knowledge. To these there was soon added a third reason: rivalry, either national or personal.

Patriotism was still widely regarded as a virtue in the 1890s and was a contributory factor to the launching of many expeditions. Both Nansen and Amundsen, for example, were conscious of their country's need for national heroes at a time when Norway was seeking its independence from Sweden; and it would be idle to pretend that Markham, the driving force behind British exploration, was not motivated by the wish to see the Union Jack advanced towards the South Pole as his cousin years earlier had advanced it toward the North. This national rivalry was about to be heightened and given a cutting edge by the newly emerging type of professional explorer. Men like Amundsen, Borchgrevink and Shackleton wanted to achieve great feats of exploration not only for their country but for themselves. They were – in the best sense of the word – adventurers, men who were willing to go to almost any lengths to achieve their goal. So there were soon two types of expedition heading south, those interested in scientific research and those interested in establishing a personal record. (The tragedy of Scott has its roots in the well-known British penchant for compromise; he tried to do both.) This dichotomy was not, however, immediately apparent; for so little was known of Antarctica, and so physically daunting were its terrain and climate, that the earliest expeditions were hard pressed to do more than survive.

First on the scene was a Belgian naval officer, Adrien de Gerlache, whose ship the *Belgica* has the distinction of being the first exploring vessel to winter in the Antarctic. The *Belgica* had a number of men aboard who were subsequently to become famous: Frederick Cook as doctor, Roald Amundsen as mate, and the Polish meteorologist Henryk Arctowski, whose observations revealed the basic pattern of Antarctica's weather. And it is interesting to note *en passant* these men's opinion of their American doctor. "His behaviour won the respect, indeed the admiration, of us all. . . . He was the most popular man on the expedition. . . . Upright, honourable, capable and conscientious in the extreme – such is our recollection of Frederick Cook." De Gerlache and his men spent a terrible two years frozen into the pack-ice at the approaches to Alexander Island. They suffered from poor circulation, palpitations and melancholia; one died, two went out of their minds. The survivors, however, brought back valuable scientific data, and proved that men could – albeit at a price – live through the Antarctic winter.

The Belgians were followed by the British: not a big officially-sponsored expedition, but a small nine-man party commanded by Borchgrevink and financed by the publisher Sir George Newnes. Borchgrevink was an adventurer in the same mould as Shackleton, and he always had the same difficulty as Shackleton in getting official backing. The Society, for example, looked at him askance, Markham referring to him as a

Carsten Egeberg Borchgrevink (1864–1934): at the time he was given little official backing or recognition, but he is now generally recognized as the precursor of Scott

(On facing page) *Tilted bergs off the barrier: Jan. 25th 1902: a watercolour by E. A. Wilson*

"White out: a blizzard at Cape Evans; Christmas Day, 1976." Photograph and caption by Jeremy Sutton-Pratt

HM Ships Erebus *and* Terror *wearing to clear a pack of ice, painted by J. E. Davis, 1843*

"meddlesome interloper". It is possible to see Sir Clements's point of view; he was trying at the time – without a great deal of success – to persuade the government to finance a big two-ship scientific expedition, and the last thing he wanted was for funds to be siphoned off on a subsidiary enterprise. Nevertheless, there should have been room in Antarctica for both types of expedition, and Markham's high-handed dismissal of anyone who wasn't a serving naval officer is one of the less attractive features of his regime. It is pleasant to record that although frowned on by the establishment, Borchgrevink met with success and was eventually awarded the Society's Gold Medal. His party spent the first-ever winter on the mainland of Antarctica, did a small amount of research, charted the Ross Sea and made a successful sledge journey across the ice-shelf which established a new "farthest south". And it is interesting to note that Borchgrevink seems to have put his finger on the inherent weakness which bedevilled British Polar expeditions; for he included in his party two Lapps who had the specific job of handling dogs. On Borchgrevink's return to England, his decidedly racy accounts of his adventures which appeared in the popular press provoked acid comments from academic circles. Nevertheless future explorers found his charts accurate and his comments perspicacious. Scott followed where he led.

As Borchgrevink was leaving Antarctica three other expeditions were arriving. 1901 had been designated "Antarctic Year" by the International Geographical Congress, and to mark the occasion Germany, Sweden and Great Britain all launched major expeditions.

The Germans, aboard the *Gauss*, were commanded by Erich von Drygalski, a protégé of Neumayer. Drygalski was a professor of geography at the University of Berlin, and his expedition was wholly scientific and not in the least interested in achieving personal records or claiming new territory. They landed in a little-known part of the continent, Kaiser Wilhelm II Land, almost due south of Kerguelen Island in the Indian Ocean, and carried out an extensive and extremely valuable programme of research.

The Swedish expedition, aboard the *Antarctic*, was commanded by Otto Nordenskjöld, nephew of the explorer who first traversed the North East Passage. This also was planned as an exclusively scientific expedition, although their adventures proved in the event both hair-raising and heroic. For the *Antarctic* became trapped by the ice and was unable to evacuate her scientists as planned. They were therefore obliged to spend a second winter at their base off the coast of Graham Land; and, what was worse, three of them were marooned at the approach of winter midway between base and ship, with neither food, fuel nor shelter. "When it became clear," wrote their leader Andersson, "that the ship would not return, we build ourselves a stone hut. Since our food was inadequate, we killed about 100 penguins to supply us with fresh meat. Since we had no fuel, we burned seal blubber. And the winter passed uneventfully and without accident." Simple words that don't so much describe as conceal an epic. Eventually, thanks to a series of extremely fortunate coincidences, the expedition was rescued and returned in triumph to Sweden, their leader continually stressing not their adventures but their wealth of specimens and observations, data which, in his own words, "confirmed Antarctica to be a vast refrigerated storehouse of knowledge".

The British expedition, once it got to Antarctica, proved an outstanding success. Its birth, however, was fraught with difficulty, and if it hadn't been for the Society it would never have been born at all. Markham, in an address to the International Geographical Congress, gives a very fair account of its conception.

"In 1893 the Royal Geographical Society determined to promote the cause of Antarctic exploration in earnest, and to persevere until its objective was attained. It was felt that a thoroughly efficient expedition must consist of two vessels commissioned by the government, officered and manned by the navy, and under naval

Mount Erebus and dome cloud, with icicled glacier in foreground, photographed by Herbert Ponting (1871–1935). Ponting was one of the first photographers to use his camera to produce not merely a representation of what he saw but a work of art. His pictures of the Antarctic, often taken and developed under conditions of appalling difficulty, have seldom been equalled and never bettered; his work did much to arouse and maintain public interest in Antarctica

discipline. After a considerable lapse of time the government came to a decision, and declined to undertake an enterprise of such magnitude. The Society, having secured the co-operation of the Royal Society and the approval of other scientific bodies, then resolved to appeal to its Fellows for funds to enable an Antarctic expedition of less magnitude to be fitted out. An appeal was made, and the result up to the present has been a subscription of £40,000. This enterprise was cordially supported by the press; and, seeing the importance that was attached to it by public opinion, the government has been induced to grant annual sums to double the amount raised by private subscription."

What Markham didn't tell the Congress was that an unfortunate rift soon developed between himself representing the Royal Geographical Society and John Murray, representing the Royal Society. The rift was caused by the fact that Markham was basically an explorer, Murray basically a scientist. What Murray wanted, to quote his own words, was "a steady continuous laborious and systematic survey of the whole southern region". He favoured waiting until funds were sufficient to send two ships; he wanted the expedition manned and led by scientists; and he wanted no heroics, no aiming at a "farthest south" or making a dash for the Pole. Markham, on the other hand, felt that if two ships couldn't be afforded one should be sent right away; he insisted on a naval expedition, and he very definitely wanted its objectives to include exploration. The outcome was a compromise, but a compromise in Markham's favour. He got his single ship the *Discovery*, and he got his naval personnel. "Our vessel will be built of oak," he told the Congress, "with ice-casing of greenheart. She will be 172 feet long and 33 broad, with a displacement of about 1570 tons. She will carry 240 tons of coal, and have an engine of 450 horse power. . . . Her engine will be right aft, so as to allow a magnetic observatory to be built before the mainmast which shall have no iron within 30 feet. Provision will also be made for deep-sea sounding and dredging. There will be two houses on deck for biological work and a laboratory below. There will be accommodation for six executive officers, three civilians and thirty-nine men. . . . The ship will be prepared for wintering, and extensive journeys are contemplated."

Markham's final triumph was that he was empowered to select the expedition leader. In many ways he made a surprising choice. For Commander Robert Falcon Scott had no scientific qualifications and no experience of either the Arctic or the Antarctic. He had first come to Sir Clements's notice in 1886. . . . "When I was on board the *Active* in the West Indies," the president subsequently wrote, "the lieutenants got up a cutter race. The boats were to be at anchor with awnings spread. They were to get under way and make sail, beat up to windward for a mile, round a buoy, down mast and sail, pull to the starting point, anchor and spread awning again. The race tried several qualities. For a long time it was a close thing between two midshipmen, Scott and Parker. However, Scott won . . . and on the 5th he dined with us. He was then eighteen, and I was much struck with his intelligence, information and charm of manner." This description pinpoints Scott with exact if unintentional precision. He was not a scientist in the mould of his contemporaries Drygalski or Nordenskjöld, and he was not an adventurer in the mould of Shackleton or Amundsen; he was an able and conscientious naval officer who found himself unexpectedly in the course of duty put in charge of what Markham not unreasonably describes as "one of the most important geographical enterprises ever conceived". What happened in the years to come has tended to obscure the truly magnificent achievements of those who went south with Scott on his first voyage in the *Discovery*.

The expedition was, thanks almost entirely to Markham, one of the best equipped ever to leave the British Isles. The *Discovery* herself had been specially built in the shipyards of Dundee. Scott had personally supervised the choice of stores, examining the

Lunar Corona, Cape Evans, McMurdo Sound: May 14th, 1911. A watercolour by E. A. Wilson, presented to the Society by Mrs. Wilson in 1917

food containers one by one and rejecting 265 out of 11,000. Clothing and sledging equipment had been bought in Norway, and included such exotic items as bales of Lapland grass and sleeping bags of reindeer hide, while the scientific equipment included the most up-to-date thermometers, pressure gauges, seismographs, spectrometers and sounding apparatus, together with a gas-filled balloon for observation. On 3rd August the Society gave the explorers a farewell dinner; on 4th August the King and Queen made a ceremonial inspection of the *Discovery*, and next day the expedition stood south out of the Thames. Almost exactly five months later they were forcing their way through the Antarctic pack-ice and dropping anchor in McMurdo Sound. Here, in the shadow of the volcanoes Erebus and Terror, they built observation posts on the ice-shelf and allowed themselves to become frozen in for the winter.

It was almost two years before, in June 1903, Markham was able to tell a packed meeting of the Society how his expedition had fared. . . .

"The winter passed cheerfully," he reported, quoting a despatch from Scott. "There were plenty of amusements; also plenty of hard work. Mr. Bernacchi tended his magnetic instruments with zealous care, and took regular observations with the electrometer. The temperature and salinity of the sea water at various depths was ascertained. Mr. Hodgson was indefatigable in all weathers, keeping holes open in the ice for his nets and fish-traps. Dr. Wilson's work on vertebrates is exceedingly valuable, and his biological collections form one of the great features of the expedition. The meteorology is under the charge of Lieut. Boyd, and nothing can exceed his care and diligence. A series of observations for two years, more than 500 miles farther south than any ship has wintered before, will be most valuable.

"As the sun began to return, the magnificent range of mountains to the west began to appear in surpassing grandeur. And in September the early spring travelling commenced, although the cold was even more intense than in the autumn, with the thermometer always $-40°$ and once as low as $-58°$. . . . Many sledging journeys for short distances were conducted by the scientific staff, chiefly with the object of geological investigation; but the greatest results were obtained from the southern and western parties."

Markham goes on to describe the two journeys – the first by Scott, Shackleton and Wilson, the second by Armitage and Skelton – which set the pattern for the tragedy to come.

On 2nd November Scott and his companions set out for the Pole. They took three sledges and nineteen dogs, and hoped for the first part of the journey to use depots which had already been laid along the line of their advance. Progress was slow. On good days they covered up to eighteen miles; but when the snow was deep and the ice rough they advanced no more than four or five miles. The dogs grew progressively weaker: to quote Scott's diary: "15th November dogs began to fail. . . . 12th December dogs unharnessed. 1st January dogs useless." Soon the men were hauling the sledges themselves. Each sledge, however, was so heavy that it needed their combined efforts to shift it; every stage of their journey had therefore to be covered three times. They suffered from snow-blindness, exhaustion and hunger. Shackleton developed a racking cough and was intermittently spitting blood. They struggled on to $82°15'$ – more than 200 miles farther south than man had ever been before. Then they turned back. They very nearly left it too late. For their dogs died one by one, and all three men grew progressively weaker with scurvy. By the time they had struggled through to the most southerly of their depots (which they might easily have missed) they had enough food left for only 48 hours. This, to quote Markham, was "a story of heroic perseverance unmatched in polar annals, opening up a new and hitherto unknown world in the far south".

Of almost equal difficulty was the westward journey, led by Armitage and Skelton.

They were away for 52 days, covered 600 miles, and, again to quote Markham, "had to drag 240 lbs per man, first over sea ice, then up a snow-filled valley to the foot of the mountains. . . . Crampons, blocks-and-tackle, ice-axes and crowbars were needed as they climbed the ice-slopes with loaded sledges, and travelled many miles over the bare blue glaciers, often amidst magnificent scenery, eventually reaching an elevation of 9,000 feet. No dogs were used. The sledges were man-hauled every foot of the way."

To Scott, as he prepared for his second Antarctic winter, the key point about these journeys had been the behaviour of the dogs. On one journey, they had failed and very nearly cost him his life; on the other, success had been achieved without them.

The expedition's first two years in McMurdo Sound had been successful, but they hadn't been easy. Neither their dogs nor their motor sledges had worked as effectively as they had hoped; one man had died, several had shown symptoms of scurvy, and they were short of fresh meat. They could without doubt have survived another winter unaided. But the fact that a relief-vessel got through to them with supplies enabled Scott to stay on for a third year in far greater comfort and safety than would otherwise have been possible.

The ship that came to relieve them was the old Norwegian whaler, the *Morgen*, built by Svend Foyn and purchased by Markham with funds raised almost entirely by the Society. Markham could never forget the fate of Franklin and Greely; and when Balfour's parsimonious government refused to pay for the support vessel which Scott had been promised, the redoubtable old campaigner set about raising funds himself. Members of the Society had already contributed over £50,000 towards the *Discovery*; they now raised as much again to purchase and provision the *Morgen*, renamed the *Morning*. Most of the money was given by Fellows; but contributions also came in from all over the world, including £50 from the Prince of Wales and five shillings from a boy in Australia who had been saving the money to buy himself a bicycle. The *Morning*, most ably commanded by William Colbeck, forced her way through the ice to within six miles of Scott's base in McMurdo Sound, unloaded provisions (including the much-needed fresh meat) and evacuated the sick and injured. Among the latter was Shackleton, who had been ordered home by Scott but who left only with the greatest reluctance. As David Mountfield puts it: "It looked as though he had failed; and he was determined to return, and to obliterate the memory of his humiliation by a glorious march upon the Pole. On the day that the *Morning* carried Shackleton away from Antarctica, the basis was laid for a great polar career."

The *Discovery*'s third year was devoted almost entirely to research. Scott may not have been a scientist himself, but he was keenly aware of the importance of his team's investigations and, like the good commander he was, he took an interest in and actively encouraged his men in their work. Indeed he became so involved in the research programme that when the *Morning* and the *Terra Nova* arrived next summer with orders to lift his expedition off the ice-shelf, he, like Shackleton, left Antarctica only with the greatest reluctance.

He returned home to a hero's welcome. What most excited the public was that he had blazed a trail to the Pole. The real value of his expedition, however, lay in the vast amount of data brought back by his scientists: data which takes up more space on a library shelf than the entire twenty-four volumes of the *Encyclopaedia Britannica*, and which, together with the information brought back by Drygalski and Nordenskjöld, forms the basis for man's understanding of the southernmost continent.

Scott used three types of transport: dogs, ponies and motor sledges. He cared deeply for his animals and gave most of them names — above "Osman", centre "Victor". But, to paraphrase his own words, each type of transport failed him

For one man it was a dream come true. For more than forty years Markham had championed the cause of exploration, first as the Society's secretary then as its vice-president and latterly as its president. In Africa he had helped to promote the work of men like Livingstone, Burton, Speke and Stanley; in Asia of men like Rawlinson, Trotter, Montgomerie and Hooker; and now in the Antarctic it was his protégé Scott

(Above) *Capt. Scott at the ice crack, photograph by Ponting, 8th October, 1911*

(Above right) *The* Discovery *frozen-in for winter quarters. Observation Hill in the background*

who had opened up a new world and ushered in a new era of scientific investigation. Markham was now 74; and he chose the hour of his triumph to hand over the helm of the Society to a younger man. It was, however, one thing to relinquish the trappings of power and another its substance. Markham was a man of forceful character and decided views – about 90 per cent of which were probably right – and even after he had resigned from the presidency he continued to work behind the scenes for the furtherance of the policy that he believed in. This policy was the sponsoring of a select number of major expeditions to Antarctica under the aegis of the Navy. It is hard to find fault with such a policy. It had, however, an unfortunate corollary: that Markham opposed all other expeditions which didn't fall into what he termed "the right category". As in the past he had fulminated against Borchgrevink as "a meddlesome interloper", so he was in the future to fulminate against Shackleton as "an absolute cad": an attitude due partly perhaps to the fact that as a man grows old he becomes increasingly inflexible and clings with increasing tenacity to that which he believes to be right.

So when the Scottish explorer Bruce proposed an investigation of the Weddell Sea, he received little support from either the Government or the Society; his expedition was financed by the industrialist Andrew Coats. In the same way, when Shackleton proposed an assault on the Pole, the Society gave him only lukewarm encouragement and three chronometers; he had to rely on the patronage of William Beardmore and on money raised by a whirlwind series of lectures. Nevertheless, he came within a hairsbreadth of success.

Shackleton emerges from the Antarctic blizzards as possibly the most attractive and certainly the most controversial of polar explorers. He was, to quote his official biography, "a lonely fighter, often at odds with officialdom and always short of funds . . . an outsider, a pathfinder, a man who inspired his companions to efforts beyond the apparent limits of human endurance, a born leader who never (on any of his expeditions) lost a man." Those who sailed with other commanders often regarded Shackleton as little more than an extrovert showman; but those who served under him once never wanted to serve under anyone else.

He left England in the autumn of 1907 aboard the *Nimrod*, a diminutive forty-year-old sealer. His destination was the South Pole; but before he had crossed the equator he ran into the sort of problem which would never have arisen had he enjoyed official backing. Here is David Mountfield's account of what took place. "Shackleton's original plan was to establish his headquarters where the *Discovery* had wintered in McMurdo Sound. . . . In the spring of 1907, however, Scott, writing from Gibraltar where he was in command of a warship, informed Shackleton that he was contemplating a second expedition to the Antarctic, and would therefore be grateful if Shackleton would establish his base elsewhere. . . . Shackleton, quite correctly, gave way to Scott's prior claim, and switched his destination to the Bay of Whales." Mountfield's account may be a simplification, but it contains the pith of the matter. And the more one thinks about it, the more one wonders that Scott should ever have made such a demand, as though Antarctica were forbidden territory in which only the chosen few should be permitted to set foot. Yet having said this, it should be pointed out in fairness to Scott that his attitude merely reflected that of officialdom in general and his mentor Markham in particular – witness a letter written that spring by Sir Clements regarding a proposed Polish expedition: "I certainly should have been much annoyed if that fellow Arctowski had gone poaching down in our preserves; but I believe he has not got any funds. Foreigners, anyhow, never get much beyond the Antarctic Circle" – an opinion which must at the time have caused de Gerlache and Charcot to raise their eyebrows and Amundsen subsequently to smile.

Anyhow, to quote a favourite phrase of Edward Wilson, *l'homme propose, le bon Dieu dispose*. For when Shackleton arrived in the Bay of Whales in January 1908, he found that

(Inset) Sir Ernest Henry Shackleton (1874–1922) inspired explorer and leader. Markham may have mistrusted him, but those who served with him once never wanted to sail with anyone else. His ship the Nimrod *was dilapidated, weighed less than 200 tons, and cost only a fraction of Scott's* Discovery *or* Terra Nova

*Frank Wild (1874–1939)
one of the few seamen to
rise from the lower deck to a
position among the elite of
Antarctic explorers. Lifelong
friend and devotee of
Shackleton*

the ice-barrier had shifted and the inlet where he hoped to drop anchor had
disappeared. For two days the *Nimrod* beat frantically to and fro, in constant danger
from the ice, trying to find alternative quarters for the winter; but without success; and in
the end Shackleton was forced to run for the one and only place of safety, McMurdo
Sound. He broke his undertaking to Scott only after the deepest heart-searching: "I
never, never knew", he wrote to his wife, "what it was to make such a decision as the one
I was forced to make last night." Scott was angry, though he never made his feelings
public. Markham was furious, and never trusted Shackleton again.

The *Nimrod* expedition achieved two notable successes and one even more notable
near-success. On 10th March, 1908 a party of six men stood on the summit of the 13,000
foot active volcano Mount Erebus which had never before been climbed; and on 16th
January, 1909 David, Mawson and Mackay became the first men to set foot on the
South magnetic pole. What really caught the imagination of the public, however, was
Shackleton's assault on the geographic pole, a resumé of which was given by the
President of the Society on the explorers' return. A close packed audience in the Albert
Hall were told:

"On 29th October, 1908, Mr. Shackleton headed south, accompanied by Adams,
Marshall and Wild. They took with them four ponies, four sledges, light equipment
and provisions for ninety-one days. A supporting party travelled with them for the
first few days, and then returned to winter quarters. The four men pushed south with
all possible speed, and, in spite of dangerous crevasses and a soft surface, they made
rapid progress. On 26th November they passed the previous 'farthest south', twenty-
four days after leaving their winter quarters. By this time they were sighting new land,
for they were taking a line further east than the previous expedition. At intervals they
killed a pony and established a depot, leaving provisions and some of the meat to
carry them over the return journey. They continued to discover ranges of new
mountains as they moved south, and as the direction of these mountains was south-
east, it became evident they would have to find a way through. On December 3rd
they climbed a mountain 4,000 feet high, and from its summit saw what they believed
to be a royal road to the Pole – an enormous glacier stretching southwards. There was
only one pony left by this time, and, taking this animal with them, they started the
ascent of the glacier, which proved to be seamed with crevasses. Progress became very
slow, for disaster threatened at every step. On December 7th the remaining pony was
lost down a crevasse, very nearly taking Wild and a sledge with it. . . . Finally the
party gained the inland plateau, at an altitude of over 10,000 feet, and started across
the great white snow plain towards the Pole. They were short of food, having cut
down their rations to an absolute minimum; the temperature at the high altitude was
extremely low, and all their spare clothing had been deposited lower down the glacier
to save weight. On January 6th they reached lat. 88°S, after having taken the risk of
leaving a depot of stores on the plateau. Then a blizzard swept down on them, and for
two days they were unable to leave their tent, suffering from frostbite even in their
sleeping bags. When the blizzard moderated they felt that they had reached their
limit, for their strength was greatly reduced and their food almost done. They
therefore pushed on for five hours, planted Queen Alexandra's flag in lat. 88°23', took
possession of the plateau for the King and turned their faces north again. . . . They
were desperately short of food, nearly worn out, and dysentery added to their
troubles. On the morning of January 26th, while still thirty miles from their depot at
the foot of the glacier, they ran out of food, and marched until two o'clock on the
following afternoon with nothing but a little tea to maintain their strength. . . .
Thereafter they reached each depot with their food entirely finished, until on March
1st they at last struggled back to the *Nimrod*."

(Top) *Shackleton's motor car which "travelled well on sea ice but could not be used on the soft snow of the Barrier; it covered over 400 miles laying depots"*

(Centre) *Shackleton's Manchurian ponies were more successful than is generally realized. If the expedition hadn't lost their last pony down a crevasse in the Beardmore glacier they would almost certainly have reached the Pole*

(Bottom) *"The penguins," wrote Shackleton, "enjoyed this novel experience. It was the first time they had heard 'Waltz me around again, Willie'!"*

This was a magnificent piece of exploration on two counts. Firstly, Shackleton got to within 97 miles of the Pole, a far greater advance beyond the previous "farthest south" than had ever been made before; and secondly, he had the good sense and moral courage to know when to turn back, for had he pushed on even for another twenty-four hours he would undoubtedly have suffered the fate of Scott.

Congratulations poured in from all over the world – letters from Nansen, Nordenskjöld and Amundsen being particularly unstinting in their praise – and the Society now found themselves basking in the reflected glory of an expedition which in fact they had done little to support. They made amends first by confirming Shackleton's observations and then by awarding him one of the few special gold medals ever to be struck. Yet there were still those who appeared to grudge the explorer his success. "I cannot quite accept his latitudes," wrote Markham. "For 88°20′ they must have gone, dragging a sledge and on half rations, at the rate of 14 miles a day in a straight line, up a steep incline 9,000 feet above the sea, for 20 days. I do not believe it." And a few days later the Secretary of the Society wrote to Cuthbert Bayes the medal maker: "We do not propose to make his medal so large as that which was awarded to Capt. Scott, and this I suppose would make a difference in your estimate." The Society of course had to be exceedingly careful about what discoveries it endorsed, and it did eventually endorse Shackleton's, and agree to make his medal the same size as Scott's. But these straws in the wind indicate the residue of disapproval which was never entirely absent from the Society's relations with Shackleton.

They had no such reservations about the next explorer who came to them for help. For in 1908 Scott decided once again to head south.

If asked to make a list of famous explorers, I think that almost everyone would include Robert Falcon Scott. Yet his achievements, although considerable, were not all that outstanding – one can think of many explorers who achieved more – Magellan, Humboldt, Nansen, Cook, James Clark Ross, Amundsen, Livingstone, to mention only a few. Scott's greatness lay not so much in what he did, as in the manner in which he did it, and in particular in the manner in which he met his death. As a biographer expressed it: "His supreme achievement is that he touched the imagination of his country as no other man has done this century. He imposed upon the public his own set of values – yet not as his own, but as the standard by which England should measure the worth of action. To the very end, when we can look into his mind, we find him constantly at watch on himself, for ever keeping himself up to the mark, never content to let himself rest or slacken." He was the devotee of a discipline which nowadays is out of fashion:

> "Stern daughter of the voice of God!
> Oh, Duty, if that name thou love
> Who art a light to guide, a rod
> To check the erring and reprove. . . ."

And although duty today may not be such a powerful god as it was to Scott's generation, there is no denying it is a virtue without which the world would be very much the poorer.

The story of Scott and Amundsen and their very different experiences in quest of the Pole is so well known that little new remains to be written about their actual journeys. It is now common knowledge that the one succeeded because he used and ate his dogs, and the other failed because he didn't use them. The records of the Society, however, do help us to see some aspects of the story in a fresh perspective.

Scott's second expedition to the Antarctic was different from his first in that it was a private not a national undertaking. One might have thought that this would have made things easier for him, would have enabled him to choose his purpose, route, equipment and personnel himself; and for a less conscientious man this would probably have been the case. Scott, however, was all too aware of the fact that different people who gave money to his expedition expected different things of it. He explained to the Society:

"There is a sharp difference of opinion as to the value of Polar exploration, and as to what is expected of Polar expeditions. The general public count success only in degrees of latitude. On the other hand there are better informed and eminent men who have a contempt for all results but that which accrues from the advanced scientific study of the regions visited. Within these limits there is every shade of opinion. . . . I submit that the effort to reach a spot on the globe untrodden by human feet and unseen by human eyes, is in itself laudable: that there is something more than mere sentiment in its attainment; it appeals to our national pride and the maintenance of great traditions, and its quest becomes an outward and visible sign that we are still a nation able and willing to undertake difficult enterprises, still standing in the van of the army of progress. . . . But there are various ways in which such a project can be undertaken. It is possible to conceive the record of a journey to the pole which would contain only an account of the number of paces taken, the food eaten or the clothes worn. The interest of such a record, however, would be entirely marred by disappointment that so rare an opportunity to add to human knowledge had been missed. It becomes, therefore, the plain duty of an explorer to bring back something more than a bare account of his movements; he must bring back every possible observation of the conditions under which his journey has been made. He must take every advantage of his unique opportunity to study natural phenomena, and to add to the edifice of knowledge those stones which can only be quarried in the regions he visits. This cannot be achieved by a single individual or by a number of individuals trained on similar lines. The occasion calls for special knowledge and special training in many branches. I have entered into these preliminary explanations to show the objects I have had in view when organizing the expedition. I have arranged for a scientific staff larger than that carried by any previous expedition, and for a very extensive outfit of scientific instruments and implimenta . . . and I believe the more intelligent section of the community will heartily approve of the endeavour to achieve the greatest possible scientific harvest which circumstances permit."

Edward Adrian Wilson (1872–1912). Physician, artist and explorer. A man who had no enemies and many friends

Everything that Scott says is right, every sentiment that he expresses is eminently reasonable. Yet the sum total of his wisdom was folly. For while Antarctica would certainly have yielded its treasures to Scott the scientist, and would almost certainly have yielded its Pole to Scott the explorer, the continent was far too formidable to yield anything to an adversary who divided his forces in an effort to win both.

And if Scott's basic plan contained within it the seeds of tragedy, the equipment which he took south provided the opportunity for these seeds to germinate. It was a question of transport.

As had been the case with the *Discovery* expedition, one of the last functions the explorers were invited to before they sailed was a luncheon in the King's Hall, Holborn, given by the Society. It was a magnificent occasion, attended by the country's most eminent geographers and travellers, including Sir Clements Markham, now in his eightieth year. It must, for the grand old man of British exploration, have been a wonderfully happy moment: just the sort of expedition he had always favoured, led by his protégé, setting out on just the sort of mission he approved of – to quote his Godspeed to them, "to scatter the paths of science with the spoils of Nature's southern secrets". And yet ironically it was largely because of their adherence to Markham's views on sledge travel that the expedition ended in tragedy. Markham had no time for dogs. And if this today seems at the best surprising and at the worst folly, the fact is that his view was shared by the vast majority of his British contemporaries. In particular, a succession of great naval expeditions – those of Parry, Franklin and Nares – had all found their dogs more trouble than they were worth. It is therefore hardly surprising that Markham should have championed the traditional method of man-hauled sledging as practised by

Mears and Oates at the blubber stove, May 26th, 1911

the great explorers of the past. Scott shared his mentor's mistrust of dogs on practical grounds, and had an additional aversion to using them on humanitarian grounds. As Markham himself put it: "With regard to dogs, there were two ways of treating them: one way was to bring them all back safe and well, and the other way to get the greatest amount of work possible out of them and then use them as food. Scott had an unconquerable aversion to the employment of them in the second way." And as if to confirm this Scott wrote: "No journey made with dogs can approach the sublimity of a party of men who succeed by their own unaided efforts. Surely in this (latter) case the conquest is more nobly and splendidly won."

So when Amundsen headed south in the *Fram*, he took with him nineteen men and ninety-seven dogs. They had one objective: the Pole. And one watchword, "dogs first and last". But when Scott headed south in the *Terra Nova*, he took with him sixty-five men, thirty-three dogs, nineteen Siberian ponies, three motor-sledges and a vast quantity of scientific equipment. He had a variety of objectives which he hoped to achieve by travelling in a variety of ways. The wonder is not that he failed to be first at the Pole, but that he came as close to success as he did.

As the *Terra Nova* stood south that summer, most people in the British Isles were confident that Scott would one day return in triumph having conquered the Pole. The news that Amundsen had changed course and was also heading south did not at the time cause a great deal of anxiety.

Apart from a brief message to say that they had dropped anchor safely in McMurdo Sound, almost the first news the Society had from the expedition was a letter from Edward Wilson. And this letter demonstrates very clearly the difference between Scott's expedition and Amundsen's. It was dated October 31st, 1911.

"This is the last opportunity I shall have for sending any letter home by the *Terra Nova* . . . for she will almost certainly leave before we can return from the long sledge journey south on which we start tomorrow.

"The following is an epitome which Captain Scott asked me to make out. . . . The self-registering meteorological instruments have given a continuous record of pressure, temperature, wind velocity and direction; and these records have been checked every four hours by eye observations. A pressure-tube anemometer has given interesting records which will throw light on the character of Antarctic winds. The upper atmosphere has been investigated by means of small balloons, which have shown the direction of upper currents to a height of 6 miles and the temperature up to $1\frac{3}{4}$ miles. An almost unbroken record of the magnetic elements has been obtained, and absolute magnetic observations have been made every week. All through the winter the aurora was observed every hour. Atmospheric electricity has also been studied. Ice work and physiography have afforded much field work. Land-forms now appearing in fresh state with receding glaciation are being studied in relation to similar time and weather-worn structures of other parts of the world. The discovery of interglacial periods of vulcanicity gives additional interest to the study of this volcanic region. The mainland offers a rich field for petrology, with an abundance of mineral-bearing quartz veins; but no economic minerals yet found. Winter quarters provide an excellent field for work on ice, in miles of the glacier front. The hut stands on a cape formed largely of massive moraine with lava flows from Erebus. Pendulum observations for value of gravity have been carried out. A tide gauge has given a continuous record. Marine biological work has been carried on throughout the winter at a hole kept open in the sea-ice for nets, water samples and sea temperatures. Quantitative and qualitative observations of minute organisms at various seasons give interesting results. The parasitology of seals, penguins, other birds and fish available has already given good results, and new protozoa have been found."

Wilson goes on to outline the extremely arduous work undertaken throughout the winter by various members of the expedition, ending with a reference to his own three-man trek to Cape Crozier, "to get to the emperor penguins at a time when their eggs would provide embryos fit for cutting." This was probably the most hair-raising and physically demanding journey ever made, immortalized by Cherry-Garrard in his classic description of Polar travel, *The Worst Journey in the World*.

It is obvious from Wilson's letter that Scott and his men spent a very different winter to that enjoyed by the Norwegians, now encamped some 400 miles to the east in the Bay of Whales. Amundsen was so determined his men should be 100 per cent fit for their coming assault on the Pole that he forbade the taking of meteorological readings by night so that they could sleep undisturbed.

And it was from Amundsen and not from Scott that the Society next had news: the unexpected news that he had reached the Pole. It was a blow to British pride; but few doubted that where the Norwegian explorer had led, the British explorer would soon follow. At a meeting on 11th March the Vice-President told the Society:

> "Since our last meeting we have heard that the courageous Norwegian explorer Amundsen, who is known to many of us here present and who has done such excellent work in the Arctic, has succeeded in his endeavour to reach the South Pole. On this occasion I do not think I need do more than read the telegram which our President Lord Curzon has today sent him. The telegram runs as follows. 'On behalf of Council Royal Geographical Society I congratulate you upon your magnificent journey and successful attainment of the South Pole (signed) Curzon, President'. I can tell by the applause that all here present endorse the action of the Council in sending this telegram."

A few months later there was still no news of Scott; but Amundsen was telling the Society how his success had been achieved. His paper, read to a packed meeting on 15th November, 1912, was short, modest and very much to the point, for Amundsen was a man who liked, in everything, to confine himself to essentials. And how easy he made it seem. His winter quarters, he told his audience, were built "in a cozy corner", his supplies were unloaded "at a dizzy speed", the health of his men "remained always excellent", his return journey from the Pole was made "at a great pace... and everybody ate as much as he liked". He made it sound a different world to the purgatory in which Scott and his companions were being starved, frozen and buffeted to death. And this helped to give rise to a myth which has never altogether been nailed: the myth that Amundsen was lucky. This impression was reflected in the comments made by the Society's president, Lord Curzon, who introduced the Norwegian with the words: "Our guest was attended throughout by good fortune upon which we congratulate him: fine weather, sound health, a transport that never broke down, a commissariat that never failed."

But was Curzon justified in attributing Amundsen's success to good fortune? The question is worth asking in view of the fact that the meeting culminated in one of the very rare incidents to mar the Society's relations with an explorer. Let us consider the points that Curzon mentions one by one. First, the weather. Amundsen and Scott set off for the Pole at almost exactly the same time, the former on 19th October, the latter on 23rd October; and they set off from very much the same point of departure, heading for the same objective. It is difficult to support the argument that the one enjoyed good weather and the other bad. It is true that Scott was unlucky in the end to be caught by a blizzard when barely eleven miles from his depot, but it is generally agreed that, even if he had reached this depot, he could never have journeyed the further 165 miles to McMurdo Sound. In other words, it simply is not true that Amundsen was luckier than Scott with the weather; he simply coped with the same weather better.

(Top) *Ponting at work in his darkroom at Scott's base McMurdo Sound.* (Centre) *Evans at the sewing machine.* (Bottom) *Mears at the pianola*

Earl Curzon of Kedleston (1859–1925), the President of the Society whose remarks offended Amundsen. A portrait in oils by J. S. Sargent, R.A., painted in 1914

(On the facing page) *"Shackleton's well-sited hut on the West coast of Ross Island. In the foreground is Pony Lake, in 1908 a place for dumping rubbish, now a place for finding items of historic interest"*

"Inside the hut nothing seems to have changed in 70 years. A leg of ham, still edible, hangs from a hook; Shackleton's home-made "Plasmon" brew, still drinkable, is in the red tins; knee-high felt boots are laid out on the bunks and King Edward VII and Queen Alexandra gaze down from the poorly-insulated walls." Photographs and captions by Jeremy Sutton-Pratt

(Overleaf) *Three original sketches of the Antarctic coast made by Edward Wilson during Scott's expedition of 1901/4*

As regards health, that of both expeditions was basically good – no-one has ever suggested that Scott and his companions failed because of sickness or unfitness. It is possible to argue that the Norwegians had a slight edge over the British because they spent the winter resting rather than working, and because their diet contained rather more fresh meat. This advantage, however, was marginal, and accrued from good planning rather than good fortune – witness Amundsen's remarks: "The winter passed quickly and comfortably, everyone had work to do, but not too much. We had no physician; we didn't need one"; and again: "Before the sun disappeared, several days were spent on a seal hunt. The total amount of the seals killed amounted to 120,000 lbs. Thus we had fresh meat in plenty for ourselves and our dogs." There is nothing especially lucky in this.

Curzon's third point: that Amundsen was lucky to have "transport that never broke down" must have taken the Norwegian aback. For Amundsen's success in travelling by dog-drawn sledge was achieved only as a result of the most meticulous planning, hard work and sacrifice. To quote just one example from his address: "Once ashore, the first thing we did was to give our dogs a shelter. We had brought with us ten very big tents. They were pitched on the barrier, after which the snow under each tent was dug out, 6 feet down, so the ultimate height of these doghouses became 18 feet. The diameter of the floor was 15 feet. Our intention in building these houses so large was to make them as airy as possible, in order to avoid the hoar frost so annoying to dogs. We achieved our object. Even during the most severe period of the winter no frost could be noticed. The tents were always cozy and warm. Each tent had room for twelve dogs, and every man had his own team to look after. Having thus cared for our dogs, the turn came to ourselves." Note the precedence. When Amundsen chose as his watchword "dogs first and last", he meant quite literally that he put the safety and comfort of his dogs before that of himself and his men – a fact which those who infer that Amundsen was callous and unfeeling towards his animals might like to bear in mind.

Lastly the President mentioned "a commissariat which never failed"; and here again Amundsen must have been surprised to hear his success attributed to good fortune. For while it is true that the Norwegians enjoyed what amounted to almost a surfeit of food – on their return from the Pole everyone ate as much as he wanted and they fed their chocolate to the dogs – this happy state of affairs resulted again from meticulous planning and painstaking attention to detail. To quote for the last time from Amundsen's address: "Our business [during the winter] was to improve our equipment and reduce its weight. . . . Of the utmost importance was the packaging of provisions. This was the work of Captain Johansen. It had to be done with care and attention. Of the 42,000 biscuits that were packed, each and every one was turned in the hand before the right place for it was found."

The comments which Curzon made as he introduced Amundsen would probably have been forgotten if he hadn't committed another gaffe as he brought the meeting to a close. His exact words are quoted in the *Journal*: "I will now put the vote of thanks for one of the most absorbing and . . . one of the most modest lectures to which we have ever listened, and I almost wish that in our tribute of admiration we could include those wonderful good-tempered and fascinating dogs, the true friends of man, without whom Captain Amundsen would never have got to the Pole."

It would be idle to pretend that this didn't spark off a furore. For Amundsen, whether rightly or wrongly, felt that the words implied criticism of the way he had used his dogs to reach the Pole and had then killed them for food.

It was rare indeed for the Society to find itself in serious contention with an explorer; and perhaps all that needs to be said is that Curzon was certainly tactless and Amundsen was certainly quick to take offence. In any event the controversy was soon

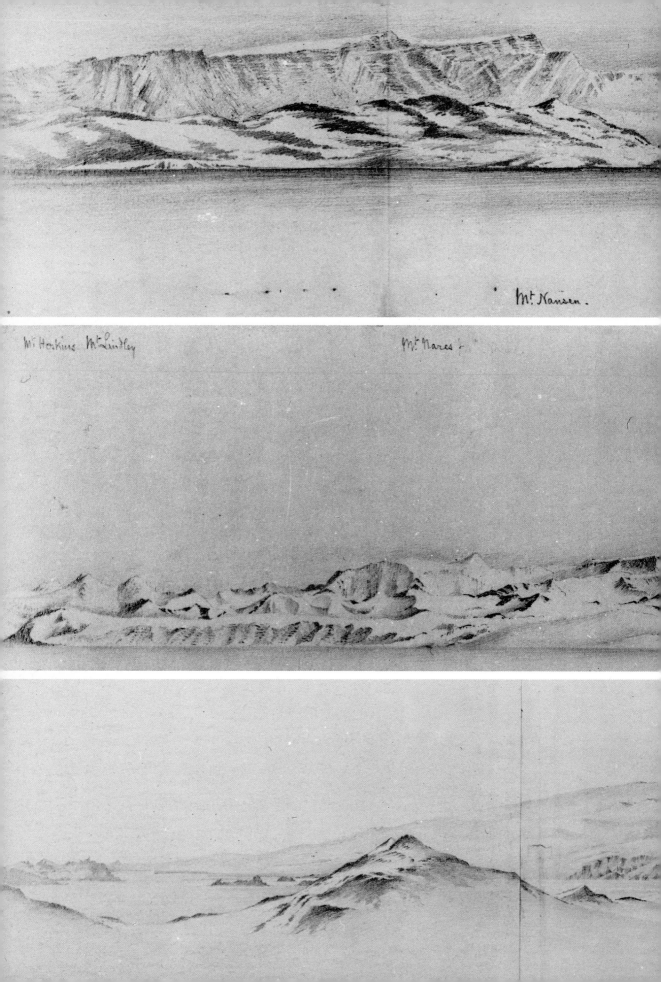

Mt. Nansen.

Mt. Hoskins   Mt. Lindley   Mt. Nares

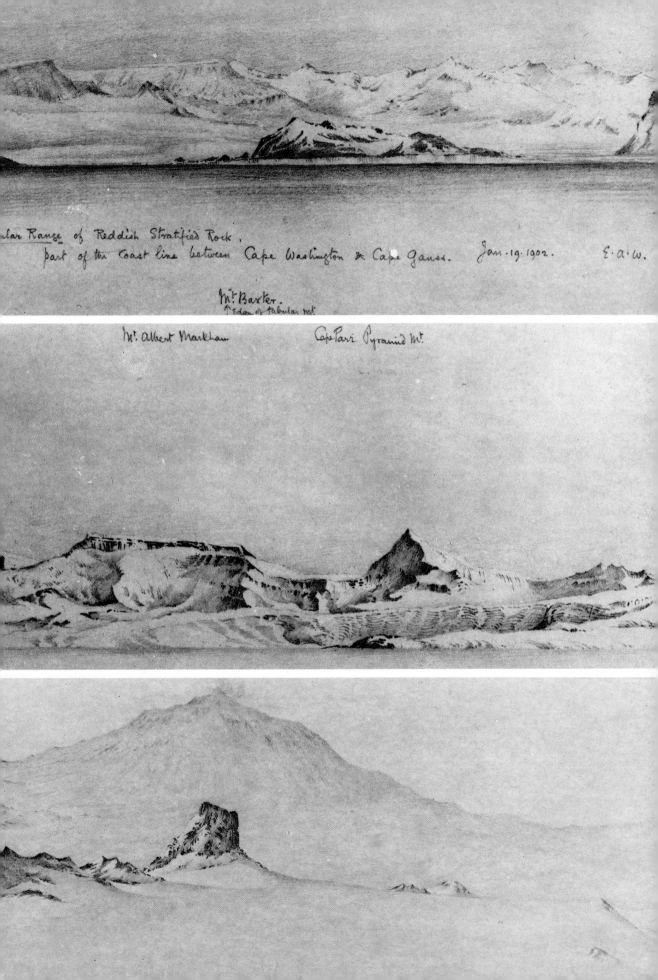

...lar Range of Reddish Stratified Rock,
  part of the coast line between Cape Washington & Cape Gauss. Jan. 19. 1902. E.A.W.

Mt Barker.
↑ Eden or tabular mt

Mt Albert Markham   Cape Tarr Pyramid Mt

eclipsed by the tragedy to come. For a couple of months later the Society heard of Scott's death.

It was so unexpected that the first message was thought to be a hoax; for the public who had applauded Amundsen had never doubted they would soon be applauding Scott. Gradually, however, as details continued to come in by telegraph, the full extent of the disaster was numbly accepted. The *Geographical Journal* for March had the black edges of an obituary; messages of condolence poured in from all over the world; explorers vied with one another in the eloquence of their panegyrics and of all the tributes paid to Scott none was more moving or more discerning than than that of the Society's President. For Curzon this time got his priorities right, and was the first person to make the point that Scott would be remembered best as a man and would achieve immortality not for what he did but for what he was. He wrote:

"As to the men . . . let me try to express what manner of men they were. Captain Scott had shown in his last words and in his last hours, what his whole life had conclusively proved to his friends. Simple-minded, high-souled, earnest, indomitable, a natural leader of men – his main characteristic was his utter disregard of self. His last thoughts were for his comrades, his last praise for them, his dying wish to impute no human blame, but to accept without a murmur the decree of Providence. Can anything be more beautiful than the calm heroism with which he sat down, with death staring him in the eyes, and weighed in the scales the doings of himself and his comrades? The result is that this plain man, who claimed powers neither of speech nor writing, has left a message which will outlive the highest flights of trained eloquence. This explorer, who reached his goal only to find he had been anticipated by another, and who died in the hour of his maimed achievement, will be remembered longer than many winners of an unchallenged prize."

After paying tribute to Wilson, Bowers, Oates and Evans, Curzon goes on to analyze the causes of the disaster. He quite rightly lists as contributory factors the taking of five men to the pole instead of four, the breakdown (apparently through brain damage after a fall) of Petty Officer Evans, and the blizzard which they ran into when only eleven miles from their depot. Then he comes to the heart of the matter: "It does, however, emerge that the Norwegians' equipment of 120 dogs and of men not required to pull, was a superior mechanism for progress. . . . The merits of haulage by dogs are (a) saving of time, (b) relief from the fatigue of human traction, and (c) economy of food supplies, the dogs as they are killed being available as food for the surviving animals and for men."

If only someone had said it earlier! The writing had been on the wall ever since the treks of Rae and McClintock during the search for a North West Passage. The tragedy was that in England it had taken fifty years for the writing to be understood.

One other question Curzon attempted to answer: "the eternal and possibly unanswerable query, was the deed worth the price? What has the world gained by the sacrifice?" He went on to stress the importance of the expedition's scientific research, and to quote, very aptly, the answer which Scott himself had given to this very question only a few days before he sailed: "It is the duty of an explorer to bring back something more than a bare account of his movements; he must take every advantage of his unique opportunity to study natural phenomena, and to add to the edifice of knowledge those stones which can only be quarried in the regions he visits." Scott certainly practised what he preached. For as he struggled back, dying foot by exhausting foot, towards One Ton Depot, he had on his sledge 35 lbs. of rocks and fossils which he had quarried out of the Beardmore Glacier. They were beside the tent that he died in. It is for this – for the bricks he laid in the edifice of knowledge – that he would wish to be remembered.

The mentor did not long survive his pupil. Markham had loved Scott, as he himself said, "as a son", and his death was a grievous blow to the old man. He died soon

(On the facing page) "*Scott's hut at Cape Evans, sited on a beach close to sea level. Mount Erebus 18 miles distant*"

"*Scott's stables where his ponies spent the winter of 1911. In the far right is the iron blubber stove used by Oates and Meares to cook pony food*"

"*Scott's hut was double the size of Shackleton's – approx. 50′ × 25′ and well insulated with seaweed and sackcloth. The fittings are more solid than Shackleton's and the layout more complicated, with different divisions for officers and men.*" Photographs and captions by Jeremy Sutton-Pratt

"*The cavern in the iceberg*". Terra Nova *in distance. Photograph by Ponting, 8th January, 1911*

afterwards. And the manner of his dying was as bound-up with tradition as his life. . . . As a midshipman, more than sixty years earlier, Markham had been accustomed to read in his hammock, a book in one hand and a candle in the other. This tradition he still adhered to. A few weeks after his eighty-sixth birthday the candle dropped, the bed caught fire and Markham died. Those who regard him as ultra-conservative point out wryly that over his bed there hung an unlit electric light bulb. The fact remains, however, that for all his idiosyncrasies, Markham did more to advance the cause of British polar exploration than any other man in the nineteenth or twentieth century. Without him the world would never have heard of Scott of the Antarctic. As a member of the Society put it: "It used to be thought treason to suggest that any President could surpass or even equal Sir Roderick Murchison; [but] I venture to prophesy that when the story of the Society's work comes to be written, the names of Murchison and

The huge ice bastions of Castle Berg. Photograph by Ponting, 11th September, 1911

Markham will be bracketed together as stars of the first magnitude." As indeed they are.

The conquest of the Poles marks the end of what has been termed the heroic age of exploration. By reaching the very farthest ends of the earth Peary and Amundsen to all intents and purposes wrote the last chapter in the story of the exploration of this planet. After them there were few more worlds for explorers to conquer. This is not to say that after 1913 there were no more of the epic old-style journeys – there was Fuchs's crossing of Antarctica, Hunt's conquest of Everest and Herbert's crossing of the Arctic pack-ice, to mention only three which took place under the aegis of the Society – but exploration from now on became increasingly mechanized and increasingly scientific. The crack of the dogwhip and the man shading his eyes to stare at far horizons gave way to the drone of aircraft and the man peering at the slide beneath his microscope.

*Scale model of Everest and
its approaches (in map room
of R.G.S.) shows (above)
the northern route of the
unsuccessful expeditions of
the 1920s and 30s. The
peak behind Everest is
Lhotse, 27,890 ft. high;
though the 1924 and 1933
expeditions climbed as high
as 28,150 ft. they failed to
reach the summit of Everest.
The southern route (below)
up the Khumbu glacier was
pioneered by Eric Shipton in
1951, and followed to the
summit by the expedition led
by John Hunt in 1953.
Everest is the peak on the
left, and Lhotse on the right*

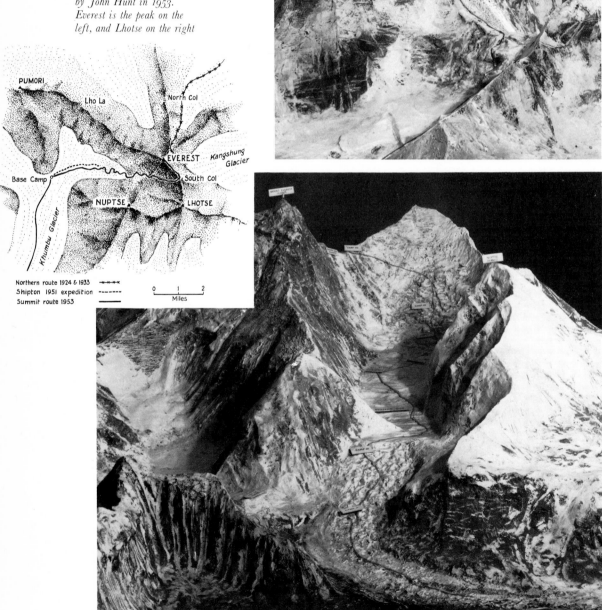

7. The Discovery and Ascent of Everest

THE SHERPAS CALLED THE MOUNTAIN CHONOLUNGMA, GODDESS MOTHER OF THE World. For it was her eternal snows which fed the rivers that watered the valleys that nurtured the plants and animals that gave them life. For half a millennium the Sherpas – a race of Mongol origin who had migrated south from the Tibetan plateau during the fifteenth century – had lived in the shadow of their majestic goddess, unquestioning; a tough, compassionate people, clinging to one of the most remote and physically demanding corners of the earth. Then came men from another continent; and they, unlike the Sherpas, asked questions.

The first Europeans to sight Chonolungma did little more than measure the mountain, place it on their maps and eventually rename it Everest. The fact that it turned out to be the highest mountain in the world did not present an immediate challenge; for mountaineering was a cult which originated only towards the middle of the nineteenth century and was confined initially to the European Alps. However, as the peaks of Europe succumbed one by one to ice-axe and crampon until (in 1865) even the supposedly inviolable Matterhorn had been conquered, mountaineers began to look farther afield. It was inevitable that before long they should find their way to Everest; inevitable too that they should see the Goddess Mother of the World as the ultimate challenge.

And if one asks the usual question – "Why? What was to be gained by climbing the highest mountain on earth?" – no better answer has ever been given than that of Frank Smythe: "The force that drives man towards the summits of the highest hills is the same force that has raised him above the beasts. He is not put into this world merely to exist . . . but to find love and happiness. Some achieve happiness best by seeking out the wildest and most inaccessible corners of the earth, and there subjugating their bodies to discomfort and even peril, in search of an ideal which goes by the simple name 'discovery', discovery not only of physical objects but of themselves."

It was in search of this almost mystical grail that men came, and kept on coming, to Mount Everest.

Sir George Everest (1790–1860): military engineer in charge of the trigonometrical survey of India. Mount Everest is named in his honour

Mountaineers of the nineteenth century were schooled in the European Alps, and the Himalayas seemed to them not only impossibly high, but impossibly remote. And few of their great peaks were remoter than Everest.

We cannot be certain who was the first European to sight the mountain: perhaps one of Alexander's Greeks, stranded far from home in the wake of the campaign on the Indus, but more probably a Jesuit priest. For the Jesuits established missions in the Himalaya in the seventeenth century, and are known to have crossed and recrossed many of the passes connecting India and Tibet. However, the first description we have of the mountain is by the naturalist Joseph Hooker, who in 1848 stood looking westward from the lower slopes of Kangchenjunga. "There was," he wrote, "no continuous snowy chain; indeed the Himalayas seemed suddenly to decline into black and ragged peaks, till in the north-west they rose again in a white mountain mass of stupendous elevation." Just how stupendous this unknown massif was, surveyors were about to discover. For in the same year as Hooker wrote his description, men with great theodolites – many of them so heavy that they had to be carried slung between poles – were struggling to the crest of the hills above Darjeeling. The Great Trigonometrical Survey of India was reaching out to encompass the peaks of the Himalaya.

Few projects have demanded such prolonged and meticulous hard work as the Great Survey of India, begun by William Lambton in the early years of the nineteenth century, expanded to a programme of international significance by Sir George Everest in the 20s and 30s, and completed by Andrew Waugh in the 40s and 50s. Kenneth Mason (himself a surveyor of international repute) describes this great undertaking. "Sir George Everest, with very few assistants, measured the great meridional arc [or great circle] passing from Cape Comorin in the South, through the centre of India, to the Himalaya. This arc forms the foundation on which was calculated the mathematical spheroid which most closely fits the figure of the earth . . . in India. The positions and heights of the Himalayan mountains, indeed of all places in India, are calculated on this spheroid. On the completion of his arc and the network of triangulation associated with it, it became possible to add by observation a framework of triangulation covering the Himalaya, and to fix with accuracy the positions and heights of the summits without actually setting foot on them. No man before or since has done so much for the geography of Asia."

The Society had always shown a keen interest in the work of the Survey, and as Waugh's teams approached the Himalaya their interest is reflected in the pages of the *Journal*. A succession of presidents reported progress. Hamilton (1849): "The trigonometrical Survey of India progresses satisfactorily. . . . The position and elevation of Darjeeling have been properly fixed, and the stupendous altitudes of several great peaks – those of Chamalari and Kauchinginga rearing upwards of 28,000 feet – have been trigonometrically determined." Smythe (1851): "The grand Survey continues, and 40 sheets of the India Atlas have now been published. . . . These operations have been costly; the expenses already incurred amount to more than £360,000 besides all instruments and incidentals; but never was money spent in a better cause." Beechey (1856): "By far the most important work in Asia is that of the Trigonometrical Survey of India. Too much praise can not be bestowed upon this elaborate and important work, carried out with such precision through countries largely unexplored."

During the late 1840s Waugh's survey teams triangulated nearly all the major peaks of the Himalaya; and by 1852 his office was convinced that one of them – the inaccessible massif half-hidden by Kangchenjunga, Peak XV on their tables – would prove to be the highest mountain in the world.

In almost every book written about Mount Everest in the last fifty years, the story is repeated that one day in 1852 an official of the Indian Survey (usually identified as Radharah Sikhdar, the Bengali chief computer) rushed into the office of his superior (Sir Andrew Waugh) exclaiming: "Sir! I have discovered the highest mountain in the world!" It is a good story. But it bears no apparent relation to fact. Neither of the men concerned ever mentioned the incident; nor did anyone else until well into the present century when the story seems first to have appeared in a Bengali nationalist magazine. In any case the "discovery" of Everest was not an isolated incident, but a joint achievement by men in both field and office working together over a number of years; and the last word in finding and naming the mountain can safely be left with Waugh himself. In March 1856 he wrote to the President of the Society:

> "SIR – Computations of the position and elevation of all the principal peaks of the Himalaya have now been completed . . . and I am in possession of the final values for the peak designated XV in the list in the Office of the Surveyor-General. We have for some years known that this mountain is higher than any in India, and most probably the highest in the world.
>
> "I was taught by my predecessor, Colonel Geo. Everest, to assign to every geographical object its true or native appellation. I have always scrupulously adhered to this rule. But here is a mountain without any local name that we can discover*. . . . So the privilege, as well as the duty, devolves on me to assign this lofty pinnacle a name whereby it may be known among geographers and become a household word among nations. In testimony of my affectionate respect for a revered chief, in conformity with the wish of members of the scientific department, and to perpetuate the memory of that illustrious master of geographical research, I have determined to name this noble peak 'Mont Everest'.
>
> "The final values of the co-ordinates of position for this mountain are as follows:—

Sir Andrew Scott Waugh (1810–1879): Surveyor-General of India, completed the work of his predecessor Sir George Everest

Mont Everest, or Himalaya Peak XV

Station of observation	Recorded latitude N.	Recorded longitude E.	Height in ft.
Menai	27°59′17.1″	86°58′6.1″	28,990
Harpoor	27°59′16.5″	86°58′5.7″	29,026
Lodnia	27°59′16.7″	86°58′5.8″	28,999
Janjpati	27°59′16.7″	86°58′6.0″	29,002
Miriapoor	27°59′17.0″	86°58′5.8″	29,005
Jirol	27°59′16.7″	86°58′5.8″	28,992
MEAN.	27°59′16.7″	86°58′5.9″	29,002"

So by 1856 Everest had been accurately placed on the map and its height determined. For many years, however, it proved impossible to approach the mountain, for, following a succession of frontier wars both Nepal and Tibet closed their borders to foreigners.

It could be argued that this was just as well: that mountaineers a hundred and twenty years ago had neither the technique nor the experience of high altitude climbing for an attempt on Everest to end other than in disaster; but at the time the situation for those who wanted to explore the Himalaya was frustrating. Indeed, for the men of the Indian Army, it was more than frustrating, it was intolerable; for their job – the defence of India – demanded a working knowledge of the Himalayan passes. In the western Himalaya the acquiring of such knowledge presented no problem. Kashmir lay open to exploration; and in the second half of the nineteenth century army officers led a number of exploring-cum-surveying expeditions to the Karakoram, that "Roof of the World"

* It seems that the Sherpa name "Chonolungma" was not heard of until many years later when Europeans first reached the base of the mountain.

b

*Some of the earliest
photographs ever taken of
Assam and Sikkim, found in
an album inscribed "To
Agnes from her affectionate
husband on the anniversary
of her birthday, 26th
February, 1869.
Darjeeling". The name of
the photographer is not
known, though he may
perhaps have been Dr. B.
Simpson, a tea planter.
Views (a) and (e) are of
boats on the Brahmaputra
River; view (d) is of the
Governor's house in Bhutan,
photographed in 1863; the
house in view (c)
is unidentified; and view (b)
shows the site of the first
government cinchona
plantation in Sikkim in the
Rujong Valley. It was the
Society's president Sir
Clements Markham who
took the cinchona plant
from South America to
India where it was first used
to produce quinine on a
commercial scale*

a

c

d

e

where in a comparatively small area over sixty great peaks rise to a height of more than 22,000 feet. Mason indicates very clearly the purpose of these expeditions. "Younghusband was sent on a second journey to the Karakoram to search for passes across the main range. There were rumours of an old pass, the Saltoro, which led direct into Baltistan, and though it was realized no large force could attack India over such a pass, there was fear that in the event of a clash between Britain and Russia a diversion here might cause trouble." To many geographers, and in particular to Murchison, the idea of Russian troops attacking India via the Himalaya was ridiculous. But in the aftermath of the Crimean War the Army took it very seriously indeed. They therefore regarded it as part of their duty to dispel the veil of secrecy which hung over Nepal and Tibet. Because of the ban on foreigners, Europeans had little chance of remaining alive in these forbidden territories. But it occurred to Major Montgomerie of the Bengal Engineers that Asians might be more successful.

His idea gave rise to some truly remarkable journeys of exploration, those of the Pundits.

Montgomerie was a brilliant surveyor, a Gold Medallist of the Society, and arguably the man who did more than anyone to open up the Himalaya. He came to India in 1851, was attached to the Trigonometrical Survey, and proved so adept at his work that in 1853 he was offered the important task of completing the survey of Kashmir and the Karakoram. The President of the Society gives a resumé of his work:

"For ten years Montgomerie directed operations in the arduous but interesting field of the Karakoram, an area of some 70,000 square miles of rugged country almost entirely unknown, in which his survey teams were obliged frequently to set up their stations at altitudes of from 15,000 to 20,000 feet. Many important valleys, lofty peaks and gigantic glaciers were discovered, and papers descriptive of these new districts were communicated to the Society. In 1864 the Survey was completed, and Montgomerie came home on sick leave to receive at the hands of Sir Roderick Murchison the Founder's Medal. Returning to India in 1867, Montgomerie gave increased attention to a subject which, previous to his visit to England, had occupied much of his thoughts: the possibility of exploration beyond the Himalaya being carried out by trained natives. . . . The employment of British officers in this work being impracticable, the training of skilled native observers for survey purposes was taken in hand, the plan being to equip these men as traders, and send them with their sextants and compasses concealed, to make route surveys of the unknown regions."

It was arduous and dangerous work: arduous because of the desolation and high altitude of the terrain to be explored, dangerous because the Tibetan and Nepalese authorities imprisoned, tortured and frequently put to death foreigners who were caught in their territory. Montgomerie's Pundits risked their lives every step of their journeys. And how many steps some of them took! A typical journey – Nain Singh's trek up the Brahmaputra from Sikkim to Lhasa – involved walking some 1,580 miles. Nain Singh had been trained to walk at a uniform 2,000 paces to the mile, and every pace he took he counted, dropping a bead from his rosary every hundredth pace. In other words, on his journey to Lhasa he took three million one hundred and sixty thousand steps, each one of which he meticulously made note of. The mind boggles at such devotion to duty.

In a paper read to the Society in 1866 Montgomerie describes his Pundits' equipment, and the subterfuges they adopted to avoid detection.

"I had noticed the frequent use made by Tibetans of the rosary and the prayer wheel, and consequently recommended Pundits to carry both with them, especially

Four more photographs from Agnes's album: (a) Cheboo Lama, a Tibetan of Sikkim, (b) Tibetan of Sikkim holding a small prayer wheel, (c) Tibetan of Sikkim playing a stringed musical instrument, and (d) Buddhist Priest of Bhotan in robe and pointed hat carrying beads

Thomas George Montgomerie (1830–1878): Army officer, surveyor and geographer; initiated the training of the "Pundit" explorers

as it was thought these ritualistic instruments could (with a little adaptation) form useful adjuncts in carrying out a route-survey.

"It was necessary that Pundits should be able to take their compass bearings unobserved, and that when counting their paces they should not be interrupted. Nain Singh found the best way of effecting this was to march separate with his servant, either behind or in front of the rest of the camp. When people did come up to him, the sight of his prayer-wheel was generally sufficient to prevent them from addressing him. For when he saw anyone approaching, he at once began to whirl the wheel round; and as all good Budhists doing this are supposed to be absorbed in religious contemplation, he was seldom disturbed. The prayer-wheel used by Pundits was an ordinary hand one; but inside instead of the usual Buddhist prayer ['*on mani padmi hom*' (Oh, Jewel of the Lotus)], were slips of paper for recording bearings etc.

"The rosary, instead of the usual 108 beads had 100, every tenth bead being larger than the others. The small beads were made of red composition to imitate coral, the large ones were seed of the udras plant. This rosary was carried in the left sleeve; at every hundredth pace a bead was dropped; so each large bead to drop represented 1,000 paces.

"Observations of latitude were difficult. They were usually taken with an Elliot sextant of 6″ radius, reading to ten seconds. Artificial horizons of dark glass were provided; but the use of quicksilver was found more satisfactory. Nain Singh invested in a wooden bowl, such as is carried at the waist by all Bhotiyas for drinking purposes; and he found this answered capitally for his quicksilver, since its deep sides prevented the wind from acting on its surface. Quicksilver is a difficult thing to carry, but he managed to conceal his by putting some in a cocoa-nut and by carrying his reserve in cowrie shells closed with wax."

The Pundits were given careful training. They were taught how to use sextant and compass, how to determine height by boiling water, how to fix positions, and how to take astral observations. They were also given medical training, provided with drugs, and where necessary were taught a trade to provide them with "cover". This training often took several years. They were then infiltrated across the border with orders to explore a specific area. Sometimes they were captured. Sometimes they were tortured. Sometimes they were killed. Often they were away for years at a time. But their observations, without exception, were remarkable for their accuracy; and between them they surveyed pretty well the whole of the Eastern or Nepalese Himalaya and a great deal of the Tibetan plateau which lies to the north.

Several surveys were carried out in the vicinity of Everest, the most important being that of Hari Ram in 1871–2. In a report to the Society, Montgomerie gives details.

"This explorer, on trying to enter Tibet, was as usual stopped and told he would not be allowed to proceed. He was rather in despair, until he was fortunate enough to ingratiate himself with a district official whose wife happened to be ill. I always made my explorers take a supply of medicines with them, and Hari Ram offered to use these to treat the woman if he were allowed to see her. His offer was accepted; and having seen her he searched . . . (his medical book) until he found a disease with the same symptoms; he then boldly prescribed drugs, and awaited the result in not a little trepidation. In a few days the woman became wonderfully better, much to the astonishment of the amateur practitioner, who was from that day treated with marked kindness and hospitality, and was eventually [allowed to] march on, without interruption, except the ordinary delays at custom-houses where his baggage was searched – though fortunately his instruments were so well concealed they were never discovered. . . . On 9th September he reached the hot springs at Tatapani, where he took latitude and thermometer readings, making it 15,000′ above the sea. Four reservoirs had been built to catch the water of these springs, which appeared to be sulphurous and had a high reputation for their curative properties. The place swarmed with Tibetan antelope, which were quite tame, never being disturbed since they were considered to be dedicated to the deity of the springs. . . . He [then] followed the general course of the Bhotia-Kosi River, which he was obliged to cross fifteen times within twenty-five miles. At one place the river ran in a gigantic chasm, the sides of which were so close to one another that a bridge of 24 paces [instead of the usual 60] was sufficient to span it. Near this bridge the precipices were so impracticable, that the path had to be supported on iron pegs let into the face of the rock – the path being formed by bars of iron and slabs of stone stretching from peg to peg and covered with earth. This extraordinary path is in no place more than eighteen inches, and often not more than nine inches in width, and is carried for more than a third of a mile along the face of the cliff, at some 1,500 feet above the river, which could be seen roaring below in its narrow bed. The Pundit, who has seen much difficult ground in the Himalayas, says he never in his life met anything to equal this bit of path. . . . The explorer, it will be seen, in the course of his survey went completely round Mount Everest; but his route was so hemmed in by great mountains that he never got a view of Everest itself; it was invariably hidden by the subordinate peaks which are close to it. Neither the Bhotias nor the Ghurkas seem to have specific names for these great peaks, except in the case of Kanchinjinga." Montgomerie ends his report with a summary of the Pundit's achievements. "This explorer's work has stood all the usual tests satisfactorily. His route-survey was 844 miles in length; he took latitude observations at 11 points and determined his height at 31 points. His journey opened-up the geography of nearly 30,000 square miles of what hitherto had been *terra incognita*, and will, I think, prove a valuable addition to the Trans-Frontier geography of India."

Nain Singh
(c. 1826–1882): village schoolmaster, Gold Medallist of the Society, and most famous of the "Pundit" explorers who, in conditions physically demanding and hazardous, secretly paced out route-surveys of almost the whole of the Eastern Himalayas

It is pleasant to record that the work of the Pundits did not go unrecognized. In 1877 the Society honoured one of the greatest, Nain Singh, with its Gold Medal, "thus publicly marking [their] appreciation of the noble qualities of loyalty, courage and endurance, by the display of which he added . . . so largely to our knowledge of Asia."

It was, however, one thing for a Pundit to circumambulate Everest, and another for a European to get anywhere near it; and throughout the latter part of the nineteenth century there was a marked difference between the pace of exploration in the Punjab (or Western) Himalaya and the pace of exploration in the east. In the former, the British-controlled territory of Kashmir extended deep into the Karakoram; and here roads were pushed into the foothills, and political agents, army patrols, forestry officers, engineers, missionaries and hunters, gradually opened-up this section of the Himalaya. It is true that, to start with, more interest was shown in the passes than the peaks; but towards the end of the century a trickle of mountaineers began coming to the Karakoram to climb for pleasure: people like Conway from England, the Bullock-Workmans from the United States, and the Duke of the Abruzzi from Italy. These climbers found the great peaks a challenge to their prowess as explorers and mountaineers. To quote James Ramsay Ullman: "Year by year the tide of the mountain-invaders swelled, advanced, ascended". In 1892 the Society sponsored the first of its many expeditions to the Himalaya: Martin Conway's ascent of the Crystal Peak (19,400 feet).

Exploration in the east, where Nepal and Tibet continued to deny access to their territory, proceeded at a much slower pace; so that although Everest had been accurately placed on the map by 1852, it remained for more than half a century unvisited and virtually unknown. This deadlock was broken in 1904 by what is usually known as

*Snout of the Rabkar
Glacier; from* Mount
Everest, the
Reconnaissance *by C. K.
Howard-Bury*

Younghusband's diplomatic mission to Lhasa. The word "diplomatic", however, is a bit of a misnomer; for it was a column of troops which Younghusband led over the Himalayan passes, his objective being to extract concessions from the Dalai Lama. He succeeded; and one of the concessions he obtained was that British expeditions should be granted occasional permission to climb in the Tibetan Himalaya – perhaps at the back of his mind was the memory of a talk he had had with Lieutenant (later Brigadier-General) Bruce when they were travelling together in Chitral in 1893 and the idea of climbing Everest had been first mooted.

This could hardly be said to fling the door to Everest wide open, but at least it prised it ajar; and during the decade 1904–1914 a start was made on reconnoitring the mountain's approaches. In the north Rawlings and Ryder surveyed the valley of the Brahmaputra and the Dingri Plain, while in the south Dr. Kellas, who lived a remarkable double-life as London research-chemist and Himalayan explorer-climber, pioneered a route from India, and also began to train the Sherpas as porters-cum-guides. This approach-work culminated in 1913 in Captain Noel's journey to within forty miles of the foot of the mountain – almost certainly the nearest a European had yet penetrated.

All this was valuable reconnaissance; but as Noel himself pointed out: "No explorer had yet approached Everest's glacier valleys. The mountain stood stupendous, seen only through telescopes, its slopes untrodden by human beings." The Society were making plans to launch a big officially-sanctioned expedition, when Europe was plunged into the holocaust of the First World War.

When hostilities were over, the thoughts of mountaineers turned again to Everest. And it was at this point that the Society and the Alpine Club to all intents and purposes took over control of the attempts to climb the mountain. Younghusband, in his book *Everest: the Challenge*, explains how this came about.

"The idea of actually climbing Everest only took shape after the Great War. . . . The moment came at a meeting of the Royal Geographical Society [on 10th March, 1919]. Captain Noel was delivering a lecture on a reconnaissance he had made before the war. In his lecture he made no reference to anything more than approaching the mountain. But in the discussion which followed, Captain Farrar who was President of the Alpine Club spoke of the summit itself. He said that the Alpine Club would view with the keenest interest any attempt to ascend Mount Everest, and that an attempt now commanded chances of success not previously available. He said that the Alpine Club was prepared not only to lend financial aid, but to recommend young mountaineers. . . . This was the spark which set flame to the train. I was sitting beside Farrar as he spoke; and when he had finished I asked the President to let me say a few words. I said that our own Society would be interested in the project, but that this was big business and must be done in a big way: that the first thing we would have to do would be to [enlist the help of] our own Government; but that the Government would be reasonable if they were approached properly by Societies like ours and the Alpine Club. . . . Now it so happened that I was myself about to succeed to the presidency of the RGS, and I determined to make this Everest venture the main feature of my three years' presidency. . . . So when I became President I formed a Mount Everest Committee [composed of] representatives of both the Society and the Club."

Younghusband goes on to make a point which has been much debated among mountaineers from that day to this:

"Theoretically it would have been better for some individual to have initiated and conducted his own expedition, and the method of running Everest expeditions by committee has been severely criticized, among others by R. L. G. Irving in his book

Sherpas played a major role in the climbing of Everest. The lower group shows the "tigers" of an early expedition, the upper the Sardars of 1936. Karma Paul (a) was the interpreter; Ang Tarkey (b) was at that time probably the best Sherpa mountaineer.

The Romance of Mountaineering. Mr. Irving voices the views of many mountaineers, when he objects to the system of selecting climbers – selecting them instead of waiting for them to initiate a climb. For, he argues, however much the selectors endeavour to impress on the men chosen the need for caution, they cannot relieve them of the feeling that they were picked and sent out to accomplish a particular feat, and that failure to accomplish this feat will bring disappointment to others besides themselves. 'By all means,' Mr. Irving writes, 'let us encourage men to go on their own responsibility to climb the Himalaya, but let us not set the ring for them. Our great footballers and cricketers have become public entertainers. But mountaineering is altogether unfitted to follow such a trend.'"

Younghusband seems to have been sympathetic to this point of view. He admits that "there would be more romance to mountaineering if an enterprising individual got together some fellow-mountaineers, collected the necessary funds, and set off to conquer the peaks of the Himalaya." But he goes on to say that in the case of the highest mountain in the world, other methods were called for. "For the peak is situated in the most seclusive country in the world . . . and the prospect of private individuals being permitted to climb it is remote." He also makes the point that so little was known about Everest that two or even three expeditions would be needed, that this would call for "a steady continuity of effort over a number of years, and here was another reason for forming a committee instead of awaiting the sporadic efforts of individuals".

These were valid points in favour of "climbing by committee" in 1920. Whether they were equally valid thirty years later is a matter of opinion.

Throughout the summer and autumn of 1920 the Society conducted negotiations with the British Government, the Indian Government and the Dalai Lama, with the result that in January 1921 permission was obtained both to reconnoitre and attempt to climb Mount Everest; also to survey the surrounding peaks. It was decided to launch a reconnaissance party at once, and, hopefully, to attempt the summit the following year.

These were exciting times for the Society. During the early 1920s almost every issue of the *Journal* – and there were now twelve a year – contained reports from Everest; some volumes included the first photographs ever taken on the mountain; and although the summit was not attained, these early expeditions achieved a quite astonishing degree of success. This is especially true of the 1921 reconnaissance, led by Colonel Howard-Bury, which pioneered the most practicable route up the Tibetan side of the mountain (via the East Rongbuk glacier, North Col and the North-east Ridge), reached a height of more than 23,000 feet, and surveyed an area the size of Switzerland with such accuracy that their maps are still in use today. Howard-Bury, in his report to the Society, sums up these achievements with characteristic succinctness.

"The expedition accomplished what it set out to do. All the approaches to Mount Everest from the north, north-west and east were carefully reconnoitred, and a possible route to the top was found via the north-east ridge; only climatic conditions prevented a much greater height being attained. . . . Some 13,000 square miles of new country was surveyed and mapped, a large number of birds and mammals collected, the geology of the region carefully worked out, and a series of photographs taken of a country quite unknown and containing some of the grandest scenery in the world."

The expedition of 1922, led by Brigadier C. G. Bruce, followed the route which had been pioneered the year before. And it was now that the formidable nature of the mountain, and in particular its last two thousand feet, became for the first time apparent. The climbers established their base camp in good time at the head of the Rongbuk Valley, and managed to reach the lower slopes of the North Col (21,000 feet)

(On facing page) *"The great North East ridge of Everest".* Photograph and caption Captain John Noel

"The first hundred miles of the route from Darjeeling to Everest is through the steep forested valleys of Sikkim – a treasure land of tropical plants, tall trees and rare orchids". Photograph and caption Captain John Noel

(Overleaf) *"Base Camp at the head of the Rongbuk Valley. This is the site used by all expeditions approaching the mountain from the north. It is readily reached by yak transport, and there is sparse grass on which the animals can forage. Everest in the background about 10 miles distant".* Photograph and caption Captain John Noel

without too much difficulty. Then the weather worsened, the monsoon broke several weeks earlier than had been anticipated, and instead of being able to advance and acclimatize slowly as they had hoped, Bruce's party found themselves obliged to make a rushed attempt on the summit. The wonder is not that they failed, but that they got as high as they did. For nearly three weeks a succession of climbers – Mallory, Norton and Somervell, Finch, Bruce and the Gurkha Telgbir Bure – clawed their way painfully across the upper slopes of the mountain. They suffered from altitude sickness, shortage of food, frostbite, winds of frenetic violence, and, above all, from complete and utter physical exhaustion. But they climbed higher than men had ever climbed before – Mallory and Norton to 26,800 feet, Finch and Bruce to 27,300 feet – before bad weather and avalanches (in one of which seven Sherpas lost their lives) drove them off the mountain.

The lessons learned from this courageous and well-led expedition were summarized that autumn in the *Journal*.

"The Committee have concluded that the difficulties and hardships endured by the expedition were understated, and that published accounts give little idea of how formidable the mountain really is. The last 1,700 feet are technically difficult, and an ascent [seems] impossible unless there are 4 consecutive fine days. . . . The idea that the ante-monsoon season would provide the necessary fine weather was too sanguine. The truth probably is that the weather about Mount Everest is nearly always wild, and the greatest obstacle on a mountain already difficult enough. . . . The work of the porters was beyond praise; and the Tibetan authorities and the chief lamas of the monasteries were in every way most friendly and helpful, and apparently much appreciated the scrupulous observation of our undertaking not to shoot [game]."

It may have been partly because Bruce went out of his way to respect Tibetan custom on this latter point – no animal was killed within twenty miles of the Rongbuk monastery – that permission was given for a further attempt on the mountain in 1924.

It has been claimed that this third expedition was "over-organized"; certainly it was the largest ever to approach the mountain, no fewer than 350 porters were needed to carry its equipment through Tibet. Bruce, once again, was in command; but unhappily for him he suffered a bout of malaria in the hills above Darjeeling, and was obliged to hand over to Colonel E. F. Norton. Norton came within a hairsbreadth of success; indeed some people claim that he *did* succeed, arguing that Mallory and Irvine might in fact have reached the summit before they fell to their death. Be that as it may, the 1924 expedition and in particular its tragic climax have become part of mountaineering history: a story which has been told and retold, but never more evocatively than in Norton's *Despatches to the Royal Geographical Society*, published in the *Journal* only a couple of weeks after being dictated by the expedition's snow-blind leader at the foot of the mountain.

"We reached Base Camp on April 29th, exactly according to plan, and the way seemed clear for a possible assault on the mountain somewhere about May 17th. . . . On May 7th we arrived at Camp II, but that evening it became clear all was far from well. For who were these weary crippled men, staggering and straggling down, through the seracs of the glacier from the direction of Camp III? They are porters, who have encountered such low temperatures and head winds that they have been clear driven out of their camp by exposure and exhaustion. . . . That night there began a blizzard lasting continuously for 48 hours. We woke on the morning of the 10th to find the tents full of fine powder snow, the temperature minus 22° Fahrenheit (10 degrees lower than anything recorded in 1922). . . . There was nothing for it but

(On facing page)
Photograph taken by Howard Somervell, showing Norton climbing the rocks of the North Face at a height of about 27,000 feet – at that time the highest point ever attained

Captain John Noel and his camera at North Col Camp, 23,000 feet, the highest altitude at which a .35 cine camera has ever been used. The camera was specially designed and built for the Society by the late Mr. Newman. It took 400 ft. magazines of .35mm Panchromatic film, and was fitted with a 20" Taylor Hobson telephoto lens with a six-power view finder directional telescope; it was of duralumin construction and weighed only 40 lbs. It is now held by the Science Museum, London

176

Some of the mountaineers who did most to make possible the climbing of Everest: (a) *Dr. A. M. Kellas,* (b) *Brigadier-General C. G. Bruce,* (c) *Brigadier E. F. Norton,* (d) *George Leigh Mallory,* (e) *Eric Shipton,* (f) *Bill Tilman,* (g) *Lord Hunt, and* (h) *Sir Edmund Hillary and Norkay Tenzing*

retreat. . . . So the end of Round One finds us discomforted but far from defeated. We have one man with seriously frostbitten feet, one with a broken leg, two severe cases of bronchitis, and worst of all, Lancenaik Shamsherpun of the 6th Gurkhas suffering from haemorrhage of the brain. But tomorrow we hope to get the sick men and the expedition as a whole blessed by the Head Lama at Rongbuk Monastery."

The ascent was renewed on 17th May, but almost at once snow and high wind made climbing virtually impossible, the thermometer recorded 56° of frost, and the climbers were forced to retreat. Towards the end of May, however, there was a brief spell of fine weather; and although by now both Europeans and Sherpas were close to the limit of their endurance, two attempts were made on the summit. Somervell describes the first.

[On 4th June] "we got up full of hope just as dawn was breaking. There was an early delay because the Thermos had shed its cork during the night, and we had to waste nearly an hour melting snow to make more liquid. But we got going about 6.45, and trudged slowly up a rocky shoulder slanting in the direction of the summit. Our side of the shoulder was in shadow and very cold; but at length, panting, puffing and sometimes slipping back on the scree and compelled to stop and regain our breath, we attained the sunlight and soon began to get warm. We crossed a patch of snow, with Norton chipping steps, and reached the band of yellow rock which is such a conspicuous feature in distant views of the mountain. This rock has weathered into horizontal ledges some 10 or more feet wide, and provides a safe and easy route towards the summit-ridge. So up these ledges we went, pulling ourselves with heavy breathing from one to another, and occasionally walking along them for respite, but always heading up and to the right to avoid loose-looking rock on the north-east ridge.
"But the altitude was beginning to tell on us. At about 27,500 feet there was an almost sudden change. Lower down we had been able to walk almost comfortably, taking three or four breaths for each step; but now eight or even ten complete respirations were needed for every step forward. And even at this slow rate of progress we had to rest every 20 or 30 yards. We were coming to the limit of endurance. At about 28,000 feet I told Norton I could only hinder him and his chances of reaching the summit. I suggested he should go on alone, and settled down on a sunny ledge to watch him. But Norton too was not far from the end of his tether. I watched him move slowly, but oh how slowly, upwards. After an hour I doubt if he had risen more than 8 feet above my level . . . and after a while he returned. We agreed reluctantly that the game was up. . . . So with heavy hearts, beating over 180 to the minute, we retraced our steps. The view was beyond words for its magnificence. Gyachang Kang and Chouyo (among the highest mountains of the world) were over 1,000 feet beneath us. Around them lay a perfect sea of peaks, all giants among mountains, but all as dwarfs below us."

The two men struggled back to Camp IV, Norton snow-blind and virtually unable to see, Somervell with a constricted throat and quite unable to speak.

"We are both rather done in," the latter wrote, "but we have no complaints . . . no excuses . . . we have been beaten in a fair fight; beaten by the height of the mountain and our own shortness of breath. But the fight was worth it. . . . We now await news of Mallory and Irvine, who today are making another attempt with oxygen. May the Genie of the Steel Bottle aid them! All of us are hoping he may, for nobody deserves the summit more than Mallory."

The weather on 8th June was as good as could have been hoped for, with a light wind drifting layers of mist-cum-cloud across the upper slopes of Everest. Mallory and Irvine had been expected to set out from Camp VI at dawn; and later that morning, in the hope of spotting them as they neared the summit, Odell struggled up towards the camp where the two climbers had spent the night. And spot them he did. A little after 12.30 the clouds for a moment lifted, and Odell saw two figures on the lower of the "steps" which led to the summit-ridge; he reckoned they were no more than 600 yards from where he was standing, at a height of about 27,950 feet. Then the clouds closed in, and Mallory and Irvine vanished. They were never seen again. The only clue to what might have happened was that nine years later a climber on the 1933 expedition to Everest found an ice-axe (which must have belonged to one of them) on the snow-slopes at 27,600 feet immediately below the second step.

Now it is theoretically possible that Mallory and Irvine climbed up from where Odell spotted them; that they reached the summit of Mount Everest, but were unable to get back to their camp before dark, and died of exposure somewhere on the upper thousand-feet of the mountain. Possible, but not at all probable. And bearing in mind the position, height and time at which they were last seen, by far the most likely explanation is that they had been for some reason unable to negotiate the second of the "steps" (either because of exhaustion or because of the failure of their oxygen); that when Odell saw them they were on their way *down*, returning to Camp VI, and that shortly after the clouds closed in, one of them slipped and both climbers fell to their death.

So the 1924 assault ended in tragedy. Indeed on each of the early expeditions the mountain had taken toll of its challengers: in 1921 Dr. Kellas; in 1922 the Sherpas Dorje, Nurbu, Pasang, Pema, Sange and Temba; in 1924 the Gurkha Shamsher, the Sherpa Manbahadur, and Mallory and Irvine. Perhaps these deaths weighed with the Tibetan authorities in their refusal over the next eight years to sanction another expedition.

Unable for the time being to continue their assault on Everest, mountaineers turned their attention to other parts of the Himalaya; and the late 20s and early 30s saw a number of major peaks either reconnoitred or climbed: 1927 saw Ruttledge's exploration of the Nanda Devi ring, 1929 saw Bauer's reconnaissance of Kangchenjunga, 1930 Dyhrenfurth's further reconnaissance of Kangchenjunga and the first ascent of Jongsong; in 1931 Smythe made the first ascent of Kamet, and 1932 saw the first German expedition to Nanga Parbat. Then, in response to pressure from the Society and the recently formed Himalayan Club, the Dalai Lama relented.

During the 1930s the Society sponsored four more attempts on the summit. These were all directed up the north (or Tibetan) face of the mountain; for Nepal still remained forbidden territory, its government refusing every request to approach the mountain from the south.

The 1933 expedition was led by Hugh Ruttledge, and consisted of fourteen climbers, any one of whom was considered capable of taking part in the final assault on the summit. Extracts from Ruttledge's report, read that autumn to the Society, describe their progress.

"The Tibetan plateau can be terribly bleak and cold in the early spring. Under the shadow of Chomolhari we had 36°F of frost, followed by a long march through a blizzard. . . . On April 16th, after marching up a stony and desolate valley which appeared to lead nowhere, we suddenly turned a corner and found the great Rongbuk Monastery, outlined against a grim background of wind-torn mist behind which we knew was Everest. A bitter wind was blowing off the mountain, and we lost no time in pitching camp. Fortunately the head Lama was willing to bless the expedition. He did so next morning with full ceremony, to the infinite satisfaction of

Lt.-Col. C. K. Howard-
Bury: members of the 1921
expedition outside the
Everest Hotel, Darjeeling:
and a wooden bridge on
their route through the
Himalayan foothills

the porters. . . . The keynote of our strategy was a slow and methodical advance, to enable all climbers to acclimatize; and we decided that each successive camp should be thoroughly stocked and held for at least four days prior to a further advance. . . . [This methodical plan was frustrated by bad weather] Camp III was established on May 2nd, when the advance party experienced blizzards similar to those which drove out the party of 1924. The approach to North Col was via a tremendous ice wall. It was arranged that parties should work on the wall in shifts, each man cutting steps for 20 minutes at a time, while his companions drove in pitons and fixed ropes for the porters. The brunt of this work fell on Shipton, Smythe, Harris, Wager, Greene and Boustead. Bad weather persisted, so that it took from May 6th to May 15th to make the route up to North Col. . . . Meanwhile news was received from Calcutta that the monsoon had appeared early off Ceylon. It was evident no time must be lost. By May 29th Camp VI had been established, about halfway up the great 'yellow band', 600 feet higher than the Camp VI of 1924. But shortly after the single tent had been pitched, one of the many blizzards rushed up from the west without warning, and within seconds it was impossible to see more than a few yards ahead."

Next day Harris and Wager made an attempt on the summit. They managed to get to about 28,100, but found the second "step" leading to the North-West Ridge "impossible"; and it was they who found the ice-axe which must have belonged to Mallory or Irvine. A couple of days later Shipton and Smythe made another attempt. They tried to avoid the step by traversing the steeply shelving slabs which led to the summit-ridge; but fresh snow made the slabs unclimbable, and at much the same height as Harris and Wager they were forced to give up.

That night the monsoon broke in its full fury; on retreating to Camp V several of the climbers were found to have seriously dilated hearts, and to quote Ruttledge: "There was nothing for it but to take the party down. . . . We stayed a week at Camp III, watching Everest get steadily whiter and whiter. [I] then reported matters to the Mount Everest Committee [telling them] that various members were prepared to stay on at Base Camp and observe weather conditions, and that the few remaining fit men had volunteered to make another assault should opportunity offer. The Committee, however, very wisely recalled the expedition."

A couple of years later the Dalai Lama gave permission for further attempts on the mountain, to take place between June 1935 and June 1936. News of this, however, didn't reach the Everest Committee until early in '35, by which time it was too late to organize a large expedition for that year. It was therefore decided to send out a small reconnaissance party under Shipton at once, and to follow this with a full-scale expedition under Ruttledge the following spring.

It has been suggested that Shipton's party spent too much time reconnoitring the approaches to Everest, and not enough time on the mountain itself; and it is certainly true that the summer of 1935 was exceptionally fine in the Himalayas, and had the climbers arrived at the foot of Everest early in May, they might perhaps have mounted a successful assault on the summit. This, however, was not their brief. Their brief had been carefully laid down by the Himalayan Committee, which, from its room in the Society's headquarters in London, liked to exercise firm control over the expeditions it was responsible for launching. Their brief was:

1. To collect data about monsoon snow conditions at high altitude, and investigate the possibility of a monsoon or post-monsoon attempt.
2. To examine the possibility of alternative routes from the west: in particular the North-West Ridge and the Western Cwm.
3. To report on ice conditions on the approaches to the North Col.

Everest is not the most spectacular of the Himalayan peaks. There are several candidates for that accolade, among them (a) Makalu and Kangchenjunga, (b) Ama Dablam, (c) Tawche, and (d) the unnamed ice peak photographed by Gregory in 1953

4. To try out new men as possible candidates for the main expedition.
5. To try out new tents and other equipment.
6. To carry out a stereo-photogrammetric examination of the north face and approaches to Everest.

These objectives were fulfilled with that lack of ostentation which was to characterize all Shipton's expeditions. His party spent more than three months on and around Everest, first establishing camps on the North Col, where they found the monsoon snow liable any moment to avalanche; then attempting to reconnoitre the Western Cwm, which was subsequently found to be the key to the summit; and finally, in Shipton's own words, "indulging in a veritable orgy of mountain climbing in which we reached the summit of 26 peaks all over 20,000 feet in height."

On his return to England, Shipton read the usual expedition leader's paper to the Society, and at the end of it Ruttledge commented: "I wonder if all of us have realized, when listening to Mr. Shipton quietly describing his adventures, exactly what has been done; because his achievement is one of the most remarkable in Himalayan annals." To which Dr. Longstaff added: "I don't know if he made it sufficiently evident that by climbing 26 peaks of over 20,000 feet, this is more than have been climbed (altogether) since the days of Adam!"

It was hoped that this successful reconnaissance would be followed by an equally successful assault. But the 1936 expedition ended again in failure.

Shipton felt that his success in 1935 might have convinced the Committee of the advantages of a small, light and mobile party. But in this he was disappointed. The 1936 expedition was planned on a massive scale – 12 climbers, 165 porters, and sufficient equipment and provisions to lay the mountain under seige. The omens were propitious, both the expedition's meteorologist and the chief Lama of Rongbuk prophesying good

Summit of Everest emerging from behind the Nuptse ridge. Photograph by Sir Edmund Hillary, taken about 15 miles from Thyangboche

weather. But it was not to be. Before the climbers had reached North Col the monsoon broke – more than a month early – and they could reach only 23,000 feet: no higher than was attained by the first reconnaissance party of 1921.

One more assault was made on Everest before Europe was again plunged into war. This was Tilman's "cut-price" expedition of 1938.

The failure of the 1936 attempt led to something of a reaction against the large and highly-organized expeditions which over the years had achieved comparatively little at such a high price, and the idea of a smaller and more informal approach appealed particularly to men like Shipton, Smythe and Odell whose love of mountaineering was basically individualistic. Bill Tilman was the ideal leader for such an expedition – a tough solitary figure who regarded tinned food as a "luxury" and lived (and expected everyone else to live) off none-too-fresh eggs and pemmican. His small team of highly skilled and experienced climbers arrived early in the Rongbuk Valley, and Camp III was established by 20th April. The weather, however, was even more hostile than usual – high winds and temperatures down to $-30°F$; soon almost everyone was suffering from colds and sore throats, and the climbers were obliged to retreat to a "recuperation camp" near the foot of the mountain. Then, unexpectedly and a month earlier than usual, it started to snow. In spite of appalling conditions the assault was resumed; Camp V was established at 25,800 feet and Camp VI at 27,200 and Shipton and Smythe prepared to make a bid for the summit if the weather improved. Instead it worsened. Snow continued to fall. And to quote Tilman: "When they [Shipton and Smythe] finally left the scree-patch on which their tent was pitched, they found themselves almost at once in thigh-deep powder snow. The futility of persevering was only too plain; so they returned to their tent and thence down to Camp V." It seemed that the Goddess Mother of the World would yield neither to the massed cohorts nor to the dedicated individualists.

When, after a gap of ten years, mountaineers were able to return to the Himalaya, they found that two things in particular had changed. The war had brought about great technical improvements in equipment, and especially in oxygen equipment; and Nepal had opened its territory to foreigners, so that for the first time since Everest had been triangulated, its southern approaches were open to exploration.

Immediately after the war the Himalayan Committee many times petitioned Nepal to allow an expedition to approach the mountain from the south, but without success; for, as Shipton said, "the Nepalese believed that money and Western civilization could do nothing for them but promote unhappiness." However, a breakthrough was eventually achieved by the Americans Oscar and Charles Houston. They, early in 1950, were unexpectedly given permission to visit the Khumbu Glacier, which winds up the southwestern flank of the Everest-Nuptse massif. The Houstons were joined by the experienced Bill Tilman, and these three men between them pioneered what was later to become a well-trodden approach route: from the railhead at Jogbani, to the superbly-sited monastery at Thyangboche and thence up the Khumbu Glacier to the Western Cwm. On this first reconnaissance, which lasted only five weeks, Houston and Tilman did not even sight the cwm, let alone set foot in it. They did, however, point out a possible way to approach it, and on this foundation-stone the Committee were to pyramid a succession of expeditions which eventually achieved success.

The most important of these expeditions was that led by Shipton in 1951; for it was Shipton who discovered and pioneered the route by which the summit was eventually attained.

Prior to 1950 mountaineers had concentrated, of necessity, on the north face of the mountain, their eyes ever on the gentle-looking rise of the north-east ridge, which appeared to offer a not impossible route to the final peak. This northern approach, however, was found by bitter experience to have disadvantages. Above 23,000 feet it was

exposed to the full force of the north-west gales which lash the summit on four days out of five; the northerly tip of the rock-strata meant that there were few footholds and virtually no level ledges on which to pitch a tent; the lack of sun precluded an early start to the day's climbing; and, above all, the most difficult climbing problems were found in the last 1,700 feet, at an altitude at which mountaineers were least able to cope with them. A southern approach looked, at first sight, to present even more impossible problems; for the south face of Everest consists of stupendous cliffs and sheer beautifully-fluted walls of ice. In the south-west, however, a broad and relatively gentle ridge rises from the col between Everest and the neighbouring peak of Lhotse; and if only this ridge could be reached, the final 1,500 feet to the summit looked to be a great deal easier than the final 1,500 feet from the north. The main task of Shipton's expedition of 1951 was to see if a route to this ridge could be pioneered; and in particular to reconnoitre a mysterious cwm (or depression) which was believed to nestle at the foot of the ridge, but which had never been properly seen – let alone properly studied – from the mountain itself.

Here is Hillary's description of how a new route was discovered.

"The next fortnight was one of the most exciting I have ever spent. . . . Shipton and I descended into a paradise of blazing colour. In our ten days up the Khumbu [glacier] every leaf, branch and twig had assumed its autumn coat. To my eye, accustomed to the evergreen forests of New Zealand, it was unbelievable. It was like being in a new world: a world of crimson and gold, and above it the white purity of soaring ice and the deep dark blue of the sky. For ten days we climbed and explored in country that men had never seen. We crossed difficult passes and visited great glaciers. But at the end of it, it wasn't so much our achievements I remembered, exciting as they had been, but the character of Eric Shipton: his ability to be calm and comfortable in any circumstances; his insatiable curiosity to know what lay over the next hill or round the next corner; and, above all, his remarkable power to transform the discomfort, pain and misery of high-altitude life into a great adventure. . . . On the morning of September 30th it was fine and clear, and Shipton wanted to climb to a position where we could get a look into the Western Cwm. . . . We scrambled onto the bottom of a ridge which came down off Pumori. We were both fairly fit and climbed steadily. But eventually the height started taking its toll. In the rarified air our lungs were working overtime and rapid movement was impossible. At 19,000 feet we stopped for a short rest and admired the wonderful views that were opening up around us. Then we pushed on up the last pitches. We scrambled up a steep bluff, chipped a few steps over some firm snow, and collapsed with relief on a little ledge at about 20,000 feet.

"Almost casually I looked towards the Western Cwm, although I didn't expect to see much of it from here. To my astonishment the whole valley lay revealed to our eyes. A long, narrow, snowy trough swept from the top of the ice-fall and climbed steeply up the face of Lhotse to the head of the Cwm. And even as the same thought was simmering in my own mind, Shipton said, 'There's a route there!' And I could hear the note of disbelief in his voice. For from the floor of the Cwm it looked possible to climb the Lhotse glacier – steep and crevassed though it appeared – and from there a long steep traverse led to a saddle at 26,000 feet – the South Col. Certainly it looked a difficult route, but a route it was. In excited voices we discussed our find. We had neither the equipment nor the men to take advantage of our discovery, but at least we could try to find a route up the ice-fall, and then return next year and attack the mountain in force."

The ice-fall turned out to be a formidable obstacle: a frozen near-vertical cataract,

A line of porters in the Western Cwm, photographed by George Lowe

some 2,000 feet in height, guarding the approaches to the cwm. For several days Shipton and his team picked their way through a maze of seracs and crevasses, menaced all the time by a great wall of hanging and unstable glaciers. On the evening of 4th October they had an exceedingly narrow escape when Pasang, Riddiford, Hillary and Shipton himself were very nearly swept into a crevasse when the snow they were traversing broke away. They decided to retreat for a fortnight, then try again in the hope that ice-conditions would have improved.

When they returned to renew the assault in mid-October, they made good progress to start with; then, in the upper reaches of the ice-fall, they met an unexpected obstacle. For here, to quote from Shipton's report to the Society, they found that

"a tremendous change had taken place. Over a wide area the cliffs and towers that had been there before had been shattered as by an earthquake, and now lay in a tumbled ruin. This had evidently been caused by a sudden movement of the main mass of the glacier which had occurred sometime during the last fortnight. It was impossible to avoid the sober reflection that if we had persisted and if a party had happened to be in the area at the time, it was doubtful whether any of them would have survived. Moreover the same thing might happen on other parts of the ice-fall. With regard to our immediate problem, however, we hoped that the collapse of the ice had left the new surface with a solid foundation, although it was so broken and alarming in appearance. Very gingerly, prodding with our ice-axes at every step, and with 100 feet of rope between each man, we ventured across the shattered area. The whole thing felt very unsound, but it was difficult to tell whether the instability was localized around the place one was treading or whether it applied to the area as a whole. Hillary was ahead, chopping his way through the ice blocks, when one of these fell into a void below. There was a prolonged roar and the surface on which we stood began to shudder violently. I thought it was about to collapse, and the Sherpas, somewhat irrationally perhaps, flung themselves to the ground. In spite of this alarming experience it was not so much the shattered area that worried us as the parts beyond, where the cliffs and seracs were riven by innumerable new cracks which threatened a further collapse. We retreated to the sound ice below and attempted to find a less dangerous route. Any movement to the left would have brought us under fire from the hanging glaciers. We explored to the right, but here we found that the area of devastation was far more extensive: it was moreover overhung by a line of extremely unstable seracs."

In spite of these hazards Shipton and Bourdillon managed to reach the top of the ice-fall, and stood looking beyond it along the gently sloping glacier which flowed between the vast walls of Everest and Nupste from the cwm at its head.

It was, they were able to confirm, a practicable route to the summit.

At the moment, however, the glacier was split by formidable crevasses. These, Shipton judged, could only be crossed with the aid of special equipment and after the carrying up of supplies. The problem was that to carry up supplies through the unstable autumn ice would have endangered the lives of the porters; and after consulting the other members of the team and the Sherpas' leaders, Shipton decided the risk was too great. He withdrew. He had, it is worth pointing out, not only carried out his brief but had far exceeded it. To have pushed on would have been to court disaster.

Back in England satisfaction that a route had been found was tempered by disappointment that the Nepalese government were willing to authorize only one Everest expedition per year, and that next year (1952) had been given to the Swiss. There was some talk of a joint Anglo-Swiss expedition with Shipton and Dittert as co-leaders on the mountain, but this fell through, and in the end the Swiss concentrated their undivided attention on Everest, while the British sent out a training expedition to another part of the Himalaya. In his paper read to the Society in the summer of 1953 Shipton explains the background to this expedition.

"A proposal to launch an Anglo-Swiss expedition under joint leadership was thought by the Himalayan Committee to be impracticable, and it was therefore decided to defer the British attempt [on Everest] until 1953. I put forward a suggestion that the 1952 season might profitably be used by sending an expedition to attempt the ascent of Cho Oyu, a 26,800 foot mountain 20 miles west of Everest. Apart from the interest of the ascent itself, the expedition would serve several important purposes: to test the ability of a number of mountaineers to climb to great heights, to provide a nucleus of men with experience of working at high altitudes for an Everest team, to carry out experiments in the use of oxygen apparatus, to study physiological problems of high altitude climbing, such as acclimatization, diet and liquid consumption, and to test clothing and equipment. The Committee accepted this proposal."

It was said by some people at the time that the Swiss in 1952 failed gloriously on Everest while the British failed ingloriously on Cho Oyu. Certainly the Swiss, to quote the president of the Alpine Club, "pushed their effort to the very limit of human endeavour". Following Shipton's route up the Khumbu glacier and into the Western Cwm, they made two most determined assaults on the summit, and Lambert and Tenzing reached 28,200 feet. This, however, was not as close to success as perhaps it sounds, for Lambert and Tenzing only achieved 28,200 after almost superhuman efforts, having themselves prepared three consecutive high-altitude camps in the last of which they spent the night with neither food, oxygen nor sleeping bags; the wonder is not that they didn't climb higher but that they survived. Meanwhile the British on Cho Oyu were

Gyangka Range from Chushar

having a disappointing time. The mountain proved far more difficult technically than had been expected, the climbers suffered from ill-health, and although a great deal of valuable work was done in testing equipment – and in particular oxygen equipment – the party returned that summer to England with nothing spectacular and little concrete to show for their three months among the great peaks.

Nevertheless, as had been widely expected, the Himalayan Committee appointed Shipton to lead the forthcoming (1953) British expedition to Everest; and it must have seemed to the public that the assault on the mountain was building up to a logical climax, when it was unexpectedly announced that Eric Shipton had resigned and had been replaced as leader by John Hunt.

When people asked why they met a wall of silence. There are times when silence is golden, but this was not one of them. For many people were puzzled and hurt by what had happened, and their feelings have not been assuaged by the veil of secrecy with which the episode has remained shrouded. In fairness to all concerned, it is time the veil was lifted.

Both Eric Shipton and John Hunt give, in their autobiographies, a very fair resumé of the affair as they saw it. The essence of what Shipton says is that when the Himalayan Committee met (in July) to choose a leader for the coming attempt on Everest, he expressed doubts about his own capabilities, but that in spite of this the Committee "reached the unanimous decision that I should be asked to lead". He accepted, and asked that Charles Evans be appointed as deputy-leader, and to this the Committee agreed. However, at the next meeting of the Committee (in September) its members went back on their original decision and proposed that Shipton and Hunt be appointed co-leaders, with the latter in charge from Base Camp onwards. This proposal Shipton felt unable to accept – partly because he was already committed to Evans as deputy-leader. He therefore offered his resignation, and it was accepted. . . . The essence of what Hunt says is that in July, while serving with the 1st British Corps in Germany, he was invited by letter to join the forthcoming expedition to Everest as organizing secretary and climber. "I nearly," he wrote, "jumped over the moon!" His excitement increased when, shortly afterwards, he received a letter from Claude Elliott (the chairman of the Himalayan Committee) "inviting me, prematurely as it later transpired, to be deputy leader to Eric." He came to London in great excitement and with high hopes, but had a sadly "disillusioning" meeting with Shipton; he then returned to Germany, "in very low spirits", believing there would be no role for him to play in the coming expedition. Shortly afterwards, however, he was told that Shipton had resigned and that he had been appointed leader.

Those who know Shipton and Hunt will not need to be told that their accounts are scrupulously fair and unequivocal. However, neither of them was privy to the deliberations of the Himalayan Committee, so with the best will in the world they cannot tell the whole story. To unravel what really happened we need access to the minutes of the meetings of the Committee, and to a Memorandum on the Everest Leadership by T. S. Blakeney, Assistant Secretary of the Alpine Club.

In Blakeney's opinion the July meeting of the Himalayan Committee held the key to all that took place subsequently. Here is his account of what happened. "When Shipton was confronted with the leadership question for 1953 he expressed doubts about himself for the job, suggested that newer blood was needed, and admitted that he preferred small parties. In the face of all this it was a gross mistake that he should have been talked into accepting the leadership. . . . Most of the blame must be attributed to Claude Elliott, [who was] indecisive and hesitant and too easily swayed by anyone who held firm opinions." Blakeney also castigates the Committee for its next decision. "Shipton then asked that a deputy-leader should be appointed, and said he would wish to appoint R. C. Evans. Lamentably, the Committee agreed to this, but with reservations which were not made clear at the time, least of all to Shipton. For the underlying intention of the

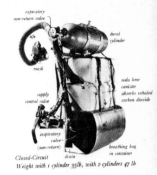

expiratory
non-return valve
dural
cylinder
mask
soda lime
canister
absorbs exhaled
carbon dioxide
supply
control valve
inspiratory
valve
(non-return)
breathing bag
in container
Closed-Circuit
drain
Weight with 1 cylinder 35lb, with 2 cylinders 47 lb

pressure
reducing
valve
dural
cylinders
mask
flow rate
manifold
economiser
reservoir
trip valve
opened at
inspiration
Open-Circuit
Weight with 3 cylinders 41lb, with 1 cylinder 18 lb

*The first climbing of
Everest depended on the use
of oxygen. The use of
oxygen depended on Sherpa
porters. The conquest of the
mountain was therefore very
much a joint enterprise*

John Hunt with radio at Camp IV, after the first ascent

Committee was to have Hunt as deputy-leader and to endeavour to get spheres of command laid down for Shipton and Hunt. Furthermore, though Evans had been named as potential deputy-leader, the Committee (or an inner core of them) were determined to get Hunt.'' There was, it need hardly be said, nothing wrong with such an intention; indeed, as was subsequently proved, Hunt was in every way the ideal man for the job; but one cannot help wishing that his supporters had aired their views openly at this early stage.

Matters came to a head at the next meeting of the Himalayan Committee; this was on 11th September. As Blakeney points out, some of Shipton's staunchest supporters were unable to attend, whereas Hunt's were there in force. Shipton, much to his surprise, was asked to leave the room while the question of deputy-leadership was discussed. Several members then expressed belated doubts as to whether his style of leadership would be what was needed; it was suggested that he was "altogether too gentle and too vague in matters of organization . . . that what was needed was 'a tiger', of a man of more forceful and dynamic personality." To quote Blakeney again:

> "The unfortunate Elliott wavered; he disliked revoking the decision of the Committee which had been reached in July, but accepted the current views that Hunt must be brought into the leadership. A long discussion followed, and it was agreed to put to Shipton the proposition: 'That the Himalayan Committee felt it was necessary to recognize that the Everest expedition was of national importance and it was therefore necessary to strengthen the party by associating a man of dynamic personality, drive and enthusiasm with the leadership.' They therefore proposed that Shipton be co-leader with Hunt up to Base Camp, and Hunt be sole leader thence forward."

(On the facing page) Expeditions to Everest enjoy not only some of the most spectacular mountain scenery in the world, but also, on their way through the foothills of Sikkim, some of the most beautiful flora

Hillary and Tenzing back at Camp IV after their first ascent of Everest: 30th May, 1953

When "this unpalatable draught", as Blakeney calls it, was put to Shipton he felt unable to accept it. To cut a long story short, he offered the Committee his resignation, and this was accepted.

So Shipton withdrew from Everest with the same quiet dignity and lack of ostentation with which he had pioneered a route to its summit. He made no fuss; although, to quote his autobiography, "the chagrin I felt at my sudden dismissal was a cathartic experience." So cathartic that for almost five years Shipton retreated from the world, being employed first as warden of an Outward Bound Mountain School in Eskdale then as a casual labourer on a forestry estate in Shropshire. It was only in the last decade of his life that he returned again to "that untravelled world" of mountain peaks and far horizons – this time in Patagonia – which for most of his career had brought him so much happiness. Meanwhile, as is well-known, Hunt went on to climb Mount Everest, thereby confirming in many people's minds that the Committee had made the right decision. Maybe they had. But they certainly made it the wrong way.

It is a relief to turn from the vacillations of the Committee to the exploits of the mountaineers. One feels in a fresher, more invigorating world.

Hunt's immediate concern was to win first the co-operation and then the loyalty of those climbers who had already agreed to serve under Shipton. This was no easy task. The reaction of Edmund Hillary when he was asked by Hunt if he would join him was typical. "I already knew and disapproved," Hillary subsequently wrote, "of the Himalayan Committee's decision to change leaders in mid-stream, and felt a tremendous disappointment that Shipton was being superseded. 'Everest without Shipton won't be the same' was my thought; 'and anyway, who is this chap Hunt? I wonder if he's any good?'. . . . Evidence of Hunt's calibre was not long in appearing, for the post brought a series of detailed plans which I reluctantly had to admit seemed to hit the nail on the head every time . . . it was obvious that organization was going ahead at

(On the facing page) Two scenes well remembered by expeditions to Everest: the beauty of the approach, and the grandeur of the wind-torn summit

(Overleaf) Thyangboche Monastery has perhaps the most magnificent setting of any building in the world. Photograph A. Gregory

great speed and with great efficiency." In the end, Hunt got every one of the climbers he wanted – George Band, Tom Bourdillon, Charles Evans, the two New Zealanders Edmund Hillary and George Lowe, Michael Ward, Michael Westmacott and Charles Wylie; also James Morris (*The Times* correspondent), Wilfred Pugh (the physiologist) and Tom Stobart (the photographer); Tenzing joined the party subsequently as climber and sirdar. In his battle with Everest, Hunt had won the first round.

It was, however, one thing to assemble a number of first-class mountaineers, and another to weld them into a first-class team; and the fact that Hunt was able to do this so quickly and effectively was not the least of his achievements. To quote his auto-biography: "Soon we were becoming a united and contented party. . . . This blending process took place while we were walking to Everest, and continued during the three weeks when we divided into groups after arriving at the monastery of Thyangboche and went off to train with our Sherpas. By the time we reached Base Camp on 18th April we were not only very fit, we were very confident about our equipment and our plans, and we were very good friends. . . . This harmony, I believe, was all important." It must have been a particularly satisfying moment for Hunt when Tom Bourdillon – the man who had championed Shipton's cause more vehemently than anyone – said to him one evening: "What a very happy party you've got going." This *esprit de corps* was soon to be tested to the full by the demands and hazards of the ascent.

Hunt's conquest of Everest has been described so often that it is difficult to say anything new about it. However, since it is sometimes easier for an event to be viewed in perspective by someone not actually involved in it, the account by the German mountaineer Gunter Dyhrenfürth is of more than usual interest:

> "The British expedition was prepared with meticulous attention to detail. Its leader, John Hunt, was a Colonel at the Staff College; so he was accustomed to military precision – which he also expected of his colleagues. He got together a large and strong team of climbers, most of whom had considerable experience of the Himalaya. . . . The expedition was particularly well-equipped, the most important items being: an aluminium ladder made up in sections for bridging large crevasses, special rope ladders, a 2-inch mortar for shooting down avalanches, radio sets, greatly improved protective clothing, primus cookers for use at high altitude, and two types of oxygen apparatus: closed-circuit cylinders (excluding the outside air, with the oxygen exhaled by the wearer being used again), and open circuit cylinders (with the outside air being drawn in, mixed with oxygen and then expelled). Hunt considered it of paramount importance that sufficient time was set aside for thorough training, acclimatization and practice with the different types of oxygen sets; so during the approach to the mountain not only 5,000-metre peaks were climbed but also those of 6,000 metres. The Sherpas also practised with the use of oxygen."

Dyhrenfürth goes on to explain the basic reason why the British succeeded whereas the Swiss the previous year had failed. The two expeditions established camps at very much the same places and along the same route – up the Khumbu glacier, on either side of the ice-fall, along the Lhotse glacier and finally in the south col – but whereas the Swiss managed to set up only temporary and often unstocked tents, the British made each camp a permanent holding-point, well supplied with food, sleeping-bags and oxygen. This involved stockpiling supplies at high altitude on an unprecedented scale. Again to quote Dyhrenfürth: "Nine of the eleven British climbers reached the South Col, three of them on two occasions. Out of twenty-five porters, nineteen carried loads of between 30 and 40 lbs. up to the Col; six of them went there twice. It was a resounding success for Hunt's programme of training and acclimatization – and for the oxygen."

Dyhrenfürth was right to stress the importance of oxygen, a point reiterated by the Society's president James Wordie in his address for 1953.

Everest: the south summit

"This year's expedition differed in one vital respect from those of former years. The intention of the earlier expeditions, from that led by General Bruce in 1922 onwards, was to try and reach the summit without the use of oxygen, and if this should not prove possible to turn to oxygen only when absolutely necessary. As a result no climbers above about 26,000 feet were in prime physical condition; and it seemed that some form of artificial aid was required, not only for the last thousand feet, but at medium levels as well. The Himalayan Committee therefore took the view that oxygen was needed on a much bigger scale than formerly, that it was in fact the secret of success. . . . This involved a very heavy lift for the Sherpa porters right up to South Col. And the amount of oxygen which had to be carried decided the size of the party. There could be no doubt about this. A small party was out of the question; a large party was essential. . . . Col. Hunt's plan, as laid before the Committee last October was that the climbers were all to become accustomed to the use of oxygen on the training climbs, that the three couples intended for the final assaults were to use oxygen from the base in the West Cwm at about 23,000 feet, that oxygen was to be used while sleeping at and above the South Col, and that it was to be used for all climbing above the South Col. This plan was adhered to. Indeed in the event oxygen was used by some climbers at heights below 20,000 feet."

So the British managed to establish half-a-dozen fit climbers, well provided with supplies, only a couple of thousand feet below the summit. All that could have thwarted them now was the weather. And the weather held. At almost exactly 11.30 a.m. on 29th May, 1953, Hillary and Tenzing levered themselves cautiously onto the roof of the world: "A few more whacks of the ice-axe," to quote the laconic New Zealander, "a few very weary steps, and we were on the summit of Everest."

And it is perhaps worth pointing out that the ascent was only achieved, in the final analysis, as a result of the most remarkable physical effort. All the planning, all the training, all the oxygen in the world would have been useless without the mountaineering skill and the sheer physical guts of the climbers. Hillary and Tenzing were not only well-endowed with these qualities, they personified them. So it is perhaps only right to close the story of Everest with a tribute to their courage, endurance, strength and mountaineering skill.

That, and a paragraph from Hunt's autobiography. . . . "Among the many messages [of congratulation that we received on the mountain] was a generous tribute from Eric Shipton. In gratitude for all he had done to make our success possible, we drank his health in the expedition's rum." A message and a tribute that say more about mountaineers and mountaineering than many a high-flown panegyric.

*The Society's first home was
3 Waterloo Place which it
occupied from 1839 to 1854.
After a brief spell in
Whitehall Place (adjacent
to caption) it moved to 1
Savile Row (below). Here,
the men who were to wipe
"unexplored" from the maps
of the world were trained
for their work. By 1913
Savile Row had become too
small to cope with the
Society's ever-expanding
business, and it moved to its
present site in Kensington
Gore (opposite page):
further additions to the Gore
building were made in 1930
as part of the centenary
celebrations*

8. The Educational Role of the Society

THE SOCIETY HAS SOMETIMES BEEN ACCUSED OF UNDUE TRADITIONALISM AND of favouring exploration at the expense of other branches of geography. There is an element of truth in this. It should, however, be borne in mind that throughout the greater part of the nineteenth century exploration was a most urgent need, for the world had to be mapped before it could be studied. It might therefore be truer to say that the Society has tended, at any given time, to champion whichever facet of its discipline has been currently in fashion – exploration in the nineteenth century, scientific investigation in the twentieth, perhaps it will be conservation of the environment in the twenty-first? The Society has been the mirror of its discipline rather than the arbiter.

In one respect, however, the RGS can claim to have been a pioneer – in geographical education.

When the Society was founded in 1830, one of its declared objectives was "to advance geography so that it might attain the rank of a science" – a rank it had already achieved on the Continent, thanks to the work of such men as Humboldt and Ritter, but was very far from achieving in England. One might have thought that because the nineteenth-century British were such dedicated explorers, they might also have been dedicated geographers. This, however, was not the case. The subject was seldom taught at either schools or universities; and to quote a report in 1833 from the University of London, "geography seems not yet to be regarded as a part of general education". When the Society appointed its Secretary, Captain Maconochie, to the newly-founded and short-lived chair of geography at University College London, the experiment was not a success. Maconochie found himself a pastor without a flock; his lectures were poorly attended, and when, at the end of three years he retired, no successor was appointed. For thirty years academic geography in England was neglected; then, towards the end of Murchison's presidency, it found an able, if somewhat idiosyncratic, champion.

Francis Galton, a cousin of Charles Darwin, is a difficult man to pass judgment on. The usually accepted assessment of him is that he was "an able scholar with wide interests". This, however, does less than justice to his versatility; for he was a distinguished meteorologist, a resourceful inventor, a lithographer, a psychologist and a pioneer in research into breeding and heredity. It is true that in all these fields he was a gifted amateur rather than a dedicated professional; but the diversity of his accomplishments, combined with the power of his oratory and the extent of his wealth, ensured him an audience. In the 1860s he decided to champion what he describes as "a new concept of geography". . . . "We are beginning," he told the British Association, "to look at our heritage, the earth, much as a youth might look at an ancestral possession, long allowed to run waste, visited recently by him for the first time, whose boundaries he is learning and whose capabilities he is beginning to appreciate. The career of the explorer will soon inevitably be coming to an end. The geographical work of the future will be to obtain a truer knowledge of the world. We will want to know all that constitutes the individuality, so to speak, of every geographical region." It seemed to Galton that the explorers of the future would need to do more than hack their way through the jungle; they would need to survive in it, study it and bring back detailed information about it. Explorers would need, in other words, to understand the rudiments of geography. Galton tried to bring this about firstly by writing his own *Art of Travel* and by editing what can best be described as an explorers' handbook, the well-known *Hints to Travellers*, and secondly by setting geographical examination papers at selected schools and awarding annual medals to the most promising pupils. The first idea took root and prospered, the second withered and died.

The Art of Travel and *Hints to Travellers* have both been highly successful publications. It is true that the former may today make comic reading, for it contains advice on such bizarre subjects as how to mount an ox, how to roll up one's sleeves ("by turning the cuffs not inside-out but outside-in"), and (alarming thought!) how to use gunpowder in water as an emetic. *Hints to Travellers*, however, includes practical advice on matters of more substance – mapping, route-surveying, astronomy, photography, the collecting of *fauna* and the use of instruments. Towards the end of the century, the demand for instruction in these subjects became so great that the Society took to providing not only books on them, but lectures. These lectures gave many famous explorers an introduction to their calling; they also attracted widespread interest among the general public, and from that day to this they have been attended annually by many hundreds of people from all over the world. *Hints to Travellers*, meanwhile, grew from a flimsy first edition of 31 pages to a handsome 1938 eleventh edition of 921 pages, a volume packed with valuable information on subjects such as health and disease and the use of instruments for field astronomy; it has now been re-issued as a series of pamphlets (each covering a specialized subject) much used by polytechnics and universities.

Galton's other scheme, the school medals, was not so successful. He had hoped that if the major schools could be encouraged to take an interest in geography, this interest would spread to the universities, the teaching profession and eventually to the public. So each year the Society set papers on physical and political geography; and each year it presented school medals simultaneously with its gold medals. This was fine in theory. In practice, however, two schools, Liverpool and Dulwich, invariably carried off the bulk of the awards – maybe the fact that Galton's brother-in-law was headmaster of Liverpool had something to do with this. The other schools lost heart; eventually they ceased to enter candidates, and after fifteen years the medals scheme was discontinued.

However, in the same year as the last school medal was presented, 1884, the RGS became involved in another and more important venture. Thanks largely to the perseverance of its Honorary Secretary, Douglas Freshfield, the Society decided to appoint "an Inspector of Geographical Education", whose brief would be to look into the whole question of how the subject could be better taught. The man chosen was John Scott Keltie, himself subsequently a Secretary of the Society for many years. For eighteen months Keltie toured Europe, collecting an enormous library of text books and a bizarre collection of teaching aids. He then compiled his report, and set off on a lecture tour of schools. To quote Mill, "the stimulus of his criticism roused teachers in Britain to demand better text books and maps . . . and this was the dawn of a new era in the school teaching of Geography."

This was a step in the right direction; and even as Keltie was delivering his lectures, the Society was throwing its weight behind another and equally important project: the establishing of geographical appointments at the universities.

In England in the 1870s and 1880s there was enormous interest if not in geography *per se* then at least in its fruits; the careers of explorers like Livingstone and Stanley, for example, were followed with the avidity nowadays reserved for soccer and pop stars. Academically, however, the subject was nebulous and ill-defined. No one seemed able to say whether it was one discipline or several; whether it was an art (an adjunct of history and politics) or a science (an adjunct of geology and botany). This confusion was about to be ended by the man who is regarded by some as the greatest of British academic geographers.

Halford John Mackinder was born in Lincolnshire in 1861. His career started brilliantly: he obtained an honours degree at Oxford in both Natural Sciences and History, was President of the Union before he was twenty-two and was called to the Bar before he was twenty-three. On leaving the University in 1885, he embarked on a lecture tour during which, to quote a contemporary, "he preached what he termed the new geography with all the missionary zeal of a Wesley". His lectures soon attracted the attention of Freshfield and Galton, and Mackinder was invited to address the Society. His paper *On the Scope and Methods of Geography* (read on 31st January 1887) determined not only his own future but that of his subject. His first few sentences show both the breadth of his vision and the clarity of his exposition.

"What is geography? This seems a strange question to address to a Geographical Society, yet there are at least two reasons why it should be answered and answered now. In the first place geographers have been active of late in pressing the claims of their science to a more honoured place in the curriculum of our schools and universities. The world, and especially the teaching world, replies with the question, 'What is geography?' There is a touch of irony in the tone, and the educational battle now being fought will turn on the answer which we can give to this question. . . . In the second place, for half a century several Societies, and most of all our own, have been active in promoting the exploration of the world. The result is that we are now near the end of the roll of great discoveries. The Polar regions are the only large blanks remaining on our maps. A Stanley can never again reveal a Congo to the delighted world. And as tales of adventure grow fewer and fewer, as their place is more and more taken by the details of Ordnance Surveys, even Fellows of Geographical Societies may despondently ask 'What is Geography?'"

Mackinder's answer was that the discipline must not be divided, as was the present trend, into separate branches, the one scientific and the other historical; but that its scope must embrace both "the science of tracing the arrangement of things in general on the earth's surface", and also "the science of tracing the interaction of man in society and his environment".

There are two ways of looking at this. Mackinder's admirers point out that the views he expressed were, to his audience, revolutionary and that to expound them at the age of twenty-six to so traditionalist a body as the RGS required considerable courage. His detractors point out that the draft of his paper had already been read and approved by influential members of the Society, and that although his views may have seemed revolutionary in England they represented little more than contemporary thinking on the Continent. The truth, I suggest, is that Mackinder was both able and courageous; but he was also lucky – lucky to appear on the scene at the very moment the Society was needing a revitalized image of geography to "sell" to the universities. This image Mackinder provided. And the upshot of his address was that a readership in geography was established at Oxford, half the stipend being paid by the Society and half by the university; and Mackinder, at the age of twenty-six, became its first occupant.

Where Oxford led, other universities were soon to follow. The seed sown by the Society took root, and to quote the learned if somewhat long-winded Mill, writing in 1930, "The Society worked long and hard to secure the full recognition of the dignity and value of Geography as a branch of University education, and its reward has been considerable. To its courage in tackling, at the outset, the most difficult task of securing a lodgment in the ancient seats of learning and backing its appeal by an annual grant, is due the widespread acceptance of Geography as a University subject. There is now a Geographical Department in every British University where forty years ago there was none."

One might have thought that, once the Society had become so involved in academic affairs, it would have continued actively to champion the teaching of its subject. In a way it did. For the next forty years it provided financial aid to further the teaching of geography not only at Oxford and Cambridge, but also at the Universities of Manchester, Edinburgh and Wales; in addition, it gave annual grants to the nautical training establishments *Worcester* and *Conway*. However, in 1893 a group of teachers led by Dickinson and Mackinder were encouraged by the Society to break away from their parent body and to form the Geographical Association, an organization devoted almost exclusively to advancing geographical teaching and thought. From that day to this, the two Societies have worked in harness – most, if not all, of the time in harmony – for the advancement of what they both hold to be "that most important and entertaining branch of knowledge".

The Society made an equally important contribution towards the teaching of geography by its dissemination of knowledge: that is to say, by the publication of its *Journal*, and by the facilities provided by its library and map room.

It would be hard to overestimate the importance of the *Journal* in helping both to popularize geography and to provide data upon which geographers of different disciplines could subsequently and continuously build. The *Journal*, in other words, was a fountain-head: a source continually being replenished by the research work of its contributors, and continually feeding new ideas and facts into the stream of geographical development.

It is interesting to see how, during the 150 years of its life, it has grown with its subject. In its early years, the *Journal* (originally entitled *The Journal of the Royal Geographical Society*) reflected the amateur, and, dare it be said, not very efficient management of the Society. It came out sometimes twice a year, sometimes three times; varied in size between 200 and 500 pages; and, to quote Mill, was "often many months behind schedule". These early volumes consisted mainly of first-hand accounts by explorers, serving officers or government officials, describing their travels in some little-known part of the world. Some academics tend to belittle these "and-so-we-climbed-to-the-top-of-the-hill" reminiscences; such trivia, they say, are not geography. The truth is, however, that usefulness (like beauty) lies mainly in the eye of the beholder, and many of these early travelogues not only have an ingenuous charm but contain information which may seem platitudinous today, but was both interesting and novel at the time it was written; they are also extremely valuable as a primary research source. There was nothing so frivolous as an illustration in these *Journals* of the 1830s, 40s and 50s, but each issue usually contained two or three folding maps of exceptionally fine quality. As one of the Society's former librarians has said: "Skilled labour was cheap in those days, great parts of the world were still unmapped, and almost every traveller brought back route-traverses of unknown country, which were worked up into maps by the Society's draughtsmen; these maps were distinguished by their magnificent hill-shading and rock-drawing."

Towards the end of Murchison's regime, a number of Fellows – Freshfield, Galton and Markham in particular – voiced the opinion that the *Journal* was "imperfect, dull and over-formal", and they initiated a campaign for regular and prompt publication, a livelier style, a more scientific content and, above all, a more popular method of presentation, including the use of illustrations. These suggestions were rejected by the Council, who regarded it as beneath the Society's dignity to court popularity. Markham, however, was not to be denied; and it seems that the man who in his later life was often dubbed a reactionary must, in his youth, have been quite a firebrand (if not a revolutionary!), for he launched a magazine of his own, *Ocean Highways*, in direct competition to the *Journal*. This achieved such success that the Society was eventually obliged to buy him out and to incorporate the more progressive features of his magazine in their own, insisting, however, on the dignified but ponderous title *The Proceedings of the Royal Geographical Society and the Monthly Record of Geography*. This was in 1878 and we can see, in the compromise between old and new, the tactful hand of the Society's Secretary, Henry Walter Bates.

Few men have worked more selflessly for the advance of their chosen subject than "dear old Bates", who was Secretary to the Society from 1864 until his death in 1892. He was a great man on at least two counts. In the early part of his life he spent eleven years in the Amazon basin, observing and collecting insects; returning to England, he wrote *The Naturalist on the River Amazons*, "one of the best narratives of scientific travel ever written, and generally regarded as ranking with Humboldt's *Journal* and Darwin's *Voyage of the Beagle*". In the latter part of his life, though plagued by ill-health, he brought to the affairs of the Society the same clear-sighted devotion to his subject which had distinguished his work in the Amazon. His biographer, H. P. Moon, tells us:

"In 1864, Bates applied for the post of Secretary and was successful. This was a most important event, not only for Bates but for the whole field of geographical studies. There was some trepidation about his appointment, since the very brilliance of *The Naturalist on the River Amazons* made the Committee wonder whether a man of his calibre would take kindly to the post. . . ." [But the doubters need not have worried.] "Bates served the Society faithfully for 27 years, being Secretary throughout one of the greatest periods in its history, when it led the world in

Three of the Society's distinguished and long-serving Secretaries: Henry Walter Bates (1825–1892), Sir John Scott Keltie (1840–1927) and Sir Laurence Kirwan (1907–)

exploration and geographical research. He was editor of publications, and his good literary style brought these to a very high standard. He was unobtrusive and rarely spoke in Council unless appealed to by the President; but when he did speak 'it was like an oracle'. His tact and discretion with officials was exceptional, and he was, Mill tells us, 'an artist at directing energies in the right direction'. His great experience in travel and exploration was generously given to all who sought it, and he won the affection of everybody."

It is rare to find a great man who was so universally not only respected but loved. The improvement that took place in the *Journal* during his years in office was typical of the useful but unspectacular work he did for the Society. For unobtrusively and with offence to no one, he raised it from an amateur somewhat dull series of travelogues to a handsome volume totalling nearly a thousand pages a year, full of valuable and often highly technical reports which were of interest throughout the world and were properly illustrated with both maps and lithographs. It would be hard to overestimate the debt which the Society – and geography – owe to this talented, unassuming and wholly delightful man.

When he died the Society was lucky to be able to appoint in his place another of its gifted Fellows who also devoted the greater part of his life to the service of geography: Sir John Scott Keltie. Keltie had been the Inspector of Education whose report had set in motion the Society's campaign for improving the teaching of geography in schools. In 1885 he was appointed the Society's Librarian, a position which, as Mill wrote, "brought him into closer and closer co-operation with Bates until he became his right-hand man in all that concerned the working of the Society. When Bates died, he was his natural successor. . . . His first important task was to continue the re-organization of the Society's publications. The *Monthly Proceedings* had, under Bates's editorship, gradually come to assume many of the features of a magazine, collecting material from sources other than the Society's meetings. It was felt by the more progressive members of the Council that geographical intelligence should be presented in a form more popular than hitherto, and a battle raged in particular around the retention, in the title, of the word Proceedings. It was, in fact, some time before the Committee would agree to the more attractive wording in use today: but the first number of *The Geographical Journal* appeared in 1893, and its success under Keltie's judicious and skilful direction was both immediate and permanent." Highlights of Keltie's years in office were his work for the Sixth International Geographical Congress, held in London in 1895 under the auspices of the Society, and his organization of the Society's move from Savile Row to its present headquarters in Kensington Gore. It would be idle to pretend that he was as distinguished academically as Bates, but he was clear-sighted and a good organizer; he also had a happy knack of befriending explorers and preserving a harmonious atmosphere in the Society.

As Keltie had been Bates's natural successor, so Arthur Hinks stepped naturally into Keltie's shoes. He took over as Secretary in 1915 and as Editor of Publications in 1917. His span of office was even longer than Bates's – thirty years – and he brought to the affairs of the Society academic distinction as both an astronomer and a cartographer, and a painstaking if idiosyncratic attention to detail. As regards the *Journal*, he introduced two important changes, both technical. He inaugurated the transfer from hand-set type to machine-set monotype, and he modernized the techniques of the draughtsmen responsible for the Society's maps. Both the beginning and the end of his Secretaryship were made difficult by war; but, like his predecessor, Hinks was never too busy to help an explorer, especially if he could offer technical advice on subjects such as geodetic triangulation or photographic surveying in which he was one of the leading authorities in the world. To quote his obituary: "Whether it was an Everest expedition or a less grandiose piece of original work, nothing was ever too much trouble for him. He kept in close touch with explorers both during their travels and after, and so built up a store of knowledge and sound advice which he was ever ready to pass on."

Hinks was succeeded by Sir Laurence Kirwan, whose term of office was equally long and equally difficult but undoubtedly of even greater benefit to the Society; for Kirwan had a better-balanced understanding than Hinks of geography as a whole, and the Society in general and the *Journal* in particular prospered under his efficient and clear-sighted regime. His work was especially valuable in three ways. First, as an eminent archaeologist he revived interest in an aspect of geography which the Society had recently tended to neglect. Second, he had a quite remarkable record in successfully conducting important negotiations, and in advocating policies which nearly always turned out to be right. And last, he raised the *Journal* to a position of undisputed preeminence in the field of geographical literature. The tribute paid to him on his retirement was, if anything, an understatement:

"After 33 years as Editor of the *Journal*, all but three of them while he was also Director and Secretary, Sir Laurence retired in June this year (1978). He will be greatly missed and very difficult to follow. Throughout his editorship, his aim has been to produce a *Journal* covering geographical and allied fields of study and research, diverse in content, topical when the occasion demands, but always with the maintenance of high scientific standards as his first care. His editorship coincided with a difficult time in the *Journal's* history, when costs have mounted and high-grade printers qualified to produce a learned journal have found it increasingly hard to take on work not financially profitable. Despite these problems, Sir Laurence has preserved the world-wide prestige of the *Journal*, and has achieved outstanding success in maintaining its high standard."

It is perhaps worth noting that the last four Secretaries of the Society (and Editors of the *Journal*) have held office respectively for 28, 23, 30 and 30 years. There cannot be many organizations which have had only four Secretaries in 111 years. Some people might regard this as evidence of the Society's innate conservatism. Others, more perspicacious, regard it as evidence of the Secretaries' ability and of their whole-hearted commitment to their work.

The Society has also helped to advance the cause of geographical education by the facilities it has provided through its library and map room.

Presidents with a particular interest in mountaineering: Douglas Freshfield (1845–1934) and Sir Francis Younghusband (1863–1942)

When the founder-members first met in the Raleigh Club in the summer of 1830, one of their declared objectives had been "to accumulate gradually a library of the best books on geography . . . as well as such documents and materials as may convey the best information to persons intending to visit foreign countries". To start with this was little more than a pious hope, since the Society had neither the funds with which to buy books, nor a home in which to display them. In 1839, however, the Society quit the Hall of the Horticultural Society – "that great unfurnished barn" in which it had held its earliest meetings – and acquired a lease of 3, Waterloo Place. The new premises were extensive, and included a gallery, part of which was partitioned off and lined with shelves to form the Society's first library. By 1850 the collection of books included 4,000 bound volumes and about 1,000 pamphlets; most of the former having been presented by Fellows or Government departments, and most of the latter being the publications of foreign Societies received in exchange for the *Journal*. A part-time librarian was appointed, and the collection indexed.

In 1854 the Society was obliged to move again, this time to 15, Whitehall Place, on the site of the present War Office. The new building seems to have been something of a white elephant. When the Society tried to enlarge the windows they found their excavations

Presidents with a particular interest in economic geography: Lord Rennell of Rodd (1858–1941) and Professor Sir Dudley Stamp (1898–1966)

blocked by flues, when they applied for permission to build a new entrance their request was refused by the local council, and the ventilation of the ballroom, where they had hoped to hold their meetings, proved so bad that they were obliged to hire a hall in another part of London. There were, however, two back rooms which were converted into a library; and in these somewhat austere surroundings, volumes gradually accumulated, the emphasis shifting imperceptibly from personal travelogues to more scientific studies of a particular region.

It was not, however, until 1871, when the Society moved to Savile Row, that the library began to assume something of the reputation and importance it enjoys today. 1 Savile Row was a spacious and elegant Regency building, a fitting home for the Society which was now beginning to lead the world, not only in exploration but also in scientific research. Mill describes the library: "The back room on the first floor was the main library: its bookcases were surmounted by a frieze of oil paintings of Africa and Australia from the brush of Thomas Baines. Doors led to the gallery round the map room in which shelves and cross-cases held works of travel, arranged in the order of the continents. A large central table displayed the most recent books. The Librarian sat at a small table in one corner, his assistant at a small table in another. . . . Savile Row became the Mecca of all true geographers, the home port of every traveller. Here the men who were to wipe 'Unexplored' from the maps were trained for their labours; and here on their return their records were tested and used to confirm or correct the maps of the region they had traversed." Mill adds that the building also became something of "a shrine to foreign geographers"; and this was especially true after Livingstone's body had lain there in state before being taken to Westminster Abbey.

In 1885 Scott Keltie was appointed Librarian. In his seven years of office he carried out many improvements, including the introduction of "the new electric light"; and by the time he moved from the librarian's table to the secretary's office, the book collection had grown to over 30,000 volumes and was overflowing its allotted space. The new Librarian, Dr. Mill, in his own words, "came [to Savile Row] in the innocent belief that he would find a unique opportunity of acquiring a knowledge of all that was known in Geography when in charge of the finest collection of geographical books in the world; but he soon discovered that the days were over when the Library of the RGS was a comfortable study in which the Librarian was free to read all day." The work had been extended and speeded up. What with editing *The Geographical Journal* and the need for starting a Subject Catalogue and preparing a new Authors' Catalogue, there was little leisure. Mill was succeeded after a short interval by Heawood, who was Librarian for the unprecedented span of 33 years, and saw the number of books on his shelves rise from 50,000 in 1901 to well over 80,000 when he retired in 1934.

It was during Heawood's term of office that the Society made its most recent move, to Kensington Gore. By 1912 it was obvious that the premises at Savile Row were too small to meet the Society's requirements, and the President, Lord Curzon, arranged for the purchase of a new home. This was Lowther Lodge, a building facing Kensington Gardens, designed by the architect, Norman Shaw; and when this in turn became too small, the present lecture-hall, council room and library were added as an extension in 1930 as part of the centenary celebrations. To quote George Dugdale, the Librarian:

"The Library now contains more than 100,000 books, including about 35,000 volumes of periodicals. The main subjects covered are geography in all its aspects, cartography, surveying and travel and exploration. New books acquired during the year average at about 650, the great majority being sent by publishers as free copies for review in the *Journal*. About 850 periodicals are currently taken, and the Library has roughly the same number which are no longer current. A large proportion of the periodicals are acquired through exchange agreements whereby the Society sends

The Geographical Journal in return for the equivalent journals of other geographical societies or institutions.

"The Library's extensive resources for research make it one of the most important world centres of geographical information. It has a detailed and extensive subject catalogue on cards, containing over 300,000 entries; articles and pamphlets as well as books are included. The alphabetical author catalogue of books and pamphlets is in two parts – older books published prior to 1910, and modern books published after 1910. There is a separate author catalogue for the numerous periodical articles. Readers are free to consult these catalogues as they wish. . . . Brief mention should be made of some of the notable special collections which have over the years been donated or bequeathed. These all bear the donor's name, and include the Fordham Collection of road books, the Hotz Collection on Iran and the Orient, the Gunther Collection on Southern Italy, the Feilden Collection on the Polar Regions, and the Rennell Collection of books on geography and travel in Asia and Africa. Each of these collections comprises several hundred volumes, and includes many rare and valuable items."

It is worth mentioning that the library is run with such unostentatious efficiency that the reader today is able quickly to obtain a mass of detailed and often highly technical data on whatever subject he is interested in.

The map room, like the library, was conceived at the meeting of founder-members in the Raleigh Club, one of the declared objectives of the embryo Society being "to accumulate a complete collection of maps and charts from the earliest period of rude geographical delineations to the most improved of the present time". For some years lack of premises and shortage of funds were serious stumbling blocks. It is true that in 1837 the collection was catalogued, and that during the next decade useful contributions to it were made by the Ordnance Survey, the Admiralty, the French Government and the King of Bavaria; but by 1850 the number of maps and charts still amounted to under 10,000. Better things, however, were in the offing. In the words of a former librarian, G. R. Crone:

"The decade 1850–1860 was critical in the development of the map collection. Events were stimulating an interest in maps and the Society was beginning, through its association with the great era of African discovery then opening, to catch the public eye. In the early 1850s it was recorded that the map room was 'visited daily by intelligent strangers as well as by members'; and this public interest was of great assistance at a time when the Society was making requests to the Government for help in securing suitable accommodation. Finally, in 1854, the Government agreed to make an annual Treasury grant to the Society of £500 to provide an apartment 'in which the Society's valuable collection of maps and charts may be rendered available for general reference'. The grant has been continued to the present day, and in return the map room has been kept open to the public."

As soon as it had attained permanent status, the map room flourished; and over the next few years the work of Murchison as President, and Trelawney Saunders as Curator, brought about a vast increase in its collection – in 1857 for example, it acquired 6,225 maps and charts, almost as many as it had accumulated during the first twenty years of its existence. In the 1860s the foundations were laid for a continuing influx of maps from specialized sources. In 1863, the Admiralty agreed to supply the Society with all its hydrographic charts as soon as they were published, an arrangement which has continued to this day. Next year the War Office, the India Office and the Ordnance Survey undertook to do the same, and this led subsequently to maps also being donated

The Society's map room has been open to the public every day except holidays since 1854. Its staff have the reputation of being able to produce any one of its three-quarters of a million maps, charts or atlases within five minutes of it being asked for

on a regular basis by the Air Ministry and the Map Section of the US Army. By the time the Society moved into the new premises in Savile Row, its collection had grown to substantially over 30,000 maps and charts and nearly 500 atlases. These were now housed for the first time in fitting surroundings: "a courtyard was covered in with a glass roof and converted into a commodious map-room, with a wide dais where the Map Curator sat overlooking his domain . . . along one wall were a number of valuable globes and a remarkable model of the Victoria Falls constructed by Thomas Baines." The map room also contained a number of Baines' original paintings. For it was now that the Curator began in earnest to amass that collection of explorers' maps, charts, diaries, letters, reports, sketches, paintings and photographs which today (to quote a recent report on the Society) "form part of our national heritage".

That was a hundred years ago. The Society has since moved to new premises, and 1 Savile Row is now the home of Hawkes and Gieves the tailors, who today cut their cloth where maps used to be spread and Livingstone's body lay in state. As for the map room, it has continued steadily to accumulate and bring up to date its invaluable collection. Successive Curators and Librarians have directed their energies to acquiring material in a particular field; Edward Heawood, for example, who was Librarian from 1901–1934, specialized in collecting early atlases, and it is due largely to his enthusiasm and expertise that the Society now holds a magnificent collection of over 4,000 atlases, many of them signed editions. As a result of this specialization, the cover provided tends to be somewhat uneven. Nonetheless, the collection is probably the largest and undoubtedly the finest under private ownership in Europe and provides a unique source of material for research. To quote Brigadier Gardiner, a recent Curator (or Keeper, as the head of the map room is now designated), "It contains over 600,000 map-sheets, providing world-wide coverage at scales of interest to geographers. . . . The object of the Society has always been 'the advancement of geographical science', and the map collection has been built up with this in mind. It is arranged on a geographical basis, continents, oceans and countries forming the primary divisions, further subdivided into districts and special maps. The map room has been open to the public during working hours since 1854, and 95% of its visitors today are members of the public. Maps are not available for loan. Service, however, is quick; almost any map requested can be provided within five minutes, and copying of maps can be done at short notice." The story goes that Hammond Innes once wanted to put this claim of speedy service to the test, and asked for the three most obscure maps and charts he could think of. They arrived with ten seconds to spare!

The map room also has responsibility for pictures and photographs. For more than a hundred years the Society has encouraged explorers to deposit a pictorial record of their travels with them; as a result it has built up a collection which contains over 3,000 sketches, watercolours, oil paintings and prints, together with more than 100,000 photographs, negatives and slides. These include illustrations of many of the expeditions reported on in the *Journal*, contributions from travellers and residents in all parts of the world, and some outstanding examples of the work of early professional photographers. Much of this material is of considerable historic interest.

Mention should also be made of the archives. These include the Council's committee and minute books from 1830 to the present day, correspondence files, administrative records, manuscripts and letters associated with the *Journal*, and a large number of explorers' letters, diaries and log-books. The last named in particular provide a rich field for research, for they contain material from such explorers as Ross, Sturt, Eyre, Back, Wallace, Darwin, Livingstone, Stanley and Scott. The cataloguing of this material has been carried out by Christine Kelly, with the aid of a grant from the Pilgrim Trust.

It has not been difficult to make what looks like a tidy analysis of the educational work of the Society. But when this has been done a great deal more remains. For the Society helps to advance the cause of geography in a great many other unobtrusive ways: by its lectures, its exhibitions, its symposia, its awards, its liaison with other learned Societies, its association with organizations such as The Royal Institute of Navigation, The Young Explorers Trust and Survival International, by its participation in international projects and congresses, its monographs (research memoirs on specialized subjects), its publication of maps (a whole volume could be devoted to this important branch of its activities), and above all by the work of many of its Fellows who serve on a multitude of committees advancing a multitude of causes. To give just one example of this latter work: Sir Laurence Kirwan wasn't only the Society's Director and Secretary, he was (and still is) President of the British Institute in Eastern Africa, and the man responsible for saving the archaeological treasures of the Nile Valley when they were threatened by flooding after the building of the Aswan Dam; he also did valuable work on the Chile/Argentina Border Commission.

All of which goes to show that those who regard the Society as an old-fashioned Explorers' Club are very wide of the mark. For behind the spectacular façade of its expeditions it carries out an enormous amount of valuable work devoted to the less popular, but by no means less important aspects of its discipline. There are more ways of advancing geography than by tracing the course of an unknown river or being first to set foot on the summit of some unclimbed peak.

9. "Something more than Scientific Investigation"

I T HAS BEEN SAID THAT THE HEROIC AGE OF EXPLORATION DIED WITH MARKHAM; and certainly those arduous treks by man-hauled sledge which Markham championed with such enthusiasm have little in common with expeditions supported by the Society today. These, to quote one of their leaders, "set [their] face firmly against heroics; [their] function is to collect, to photograph, to observe and to record". However in the post-war period some of the Society's expeditions have also had another function, have been involved in something more than scientific investigation. In recent years the work of several teams sent out by the Society has been given an added urgency by the involvement of conservationists – men and women who are appalled at the way the natural resources of the earth are being depleted and in many instances destroyed. Three expeditions in particular illustrate the growth of this ecological/conservationist involvement: Iain Bishop's Mato Grosso expedition to Brazil (1967–9), Norman Falcon's Musandam expedition to the valleys of Northern Oman (1971–2), and Robin Hanbury-Tenison's expedition to Mulu in Sarawak (1977–8).

These expeditions also highlight another development of the post-war years: the diminution of the role of expedition leader. Throughout the nineteenth and early twentieth centuries expeditions were frequently built-up around personalities – notable examples being those led by Shackleton. In recent years, however, projects involving exploration and scientific study have tended more and more to be inaugurated, planned and at least partially controlled by the Society from its headquarters in London. Certainly the expeditions to Brazil, North Oman and Sarawak fall into this category. They were conceived, nurtured and carried out by the painstaking work of committees. They, like so many of today's lesser-known expeditions, were very much the children of the Society.

The expeditions to Brazil, North Oman and Sarawak form only a small proportion of those planned and organized by the Society since the war, and before describing them in detail some of the Society's other important ventures ought to be mentioned.

From 1949–52 a joint Norwegian-British-Swedish expedition led by John Giaever carried out valuable scientific research on the coast of Queen Maud Land in Antarctica. This expedition was sponsored jointly by the Norwegian Government, the Society and the Scott Polar Research Institute. Its principal work was in the fields of glaciology, meteorology and surveying, and its technical reports on these subjects are still in the process of being published. However, to quote the Norwegian Ambassador: "While there is no doubt about the importance of the scientific work achieved, it seems to me more important still that the expedition has been an example of what can be done by international co-operation . . . and it is to be hoped it will serve as a precedent for further international work in the Antarctic" – a hope which was soon to be fulfilled during the International Geophysical Year.

(On the facing page)
Three stages in the spoliation of a rain forest: cutting down and burning the trees; irrigating a ranch; and driving in the cattle which are now taking over the world of the Indians

(Overleaf): *The changing face of the Mato Grosso.* Inset: *Yesterday: Indian village.* Double-page spread: *Today: a herd of Melori cattle being driven over the land which is being prepared for them*

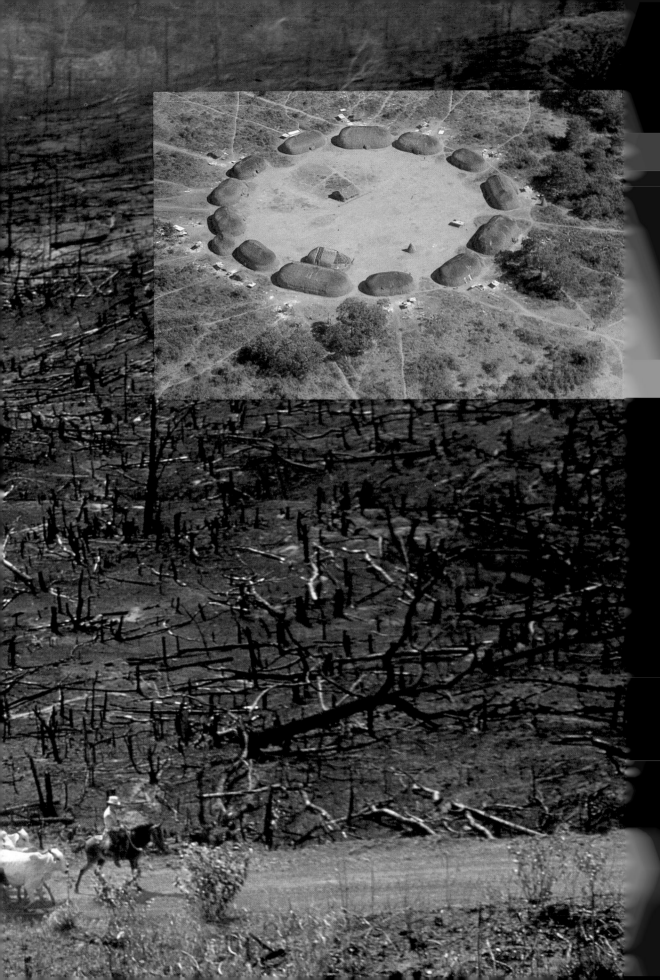

From 1952 to 1954 the largest British polar expedition for 40 years, led by Commander C. J. W. Simpson, carried out a detailed survey of Northern Greenland. Simpson's expedition, like Giaever's, made extensive use of aerial reconnaissance, and many of their flights over the Greenland ice cap were not only valuable but hazardous. This expedition was very much the brain child of the Society's president, James Wordie, and was only made possible by the co-operation, on a massive scale, of the Royal Navy and the Royal Air Force.

The first crossing of Antarctica, in 1957–8, was by a team led by Sir Vivian Fuchs. The president in his address to the Society paid tribute to this magnificent achievement: "Our meeting today is a momentous and historic one. The first overland crossing of the Antarctic continent has been accomplished by a British Commonwealth expedition – an expedition sponsored and supported by our Society, organized, administered and financed by a Committee of Management drawn largely from our Council, and led by one of our Fellows. Your Council has decided to award to Sir Vivian Fuchs a Special Gold Medal in order to commemorate an achievement which is outstanding in the history of polar exploration." As well as being a great journey in the old-fashioned sense – that is to say in being first to traverse an unknown part of the world – Fuchs's expedition had a serious scientific purpose, that of making a seismic traverse of the continent, a task it fulfilled meticulously in spite of appalling and often hazardous conditions.

In 1968–70, the Society sent a very different expedition to a very different part of the world – a party of scientists who carried out a detailed ecological survey of the South Turkana area of Kenya. The area covered was some 9,500 square kilometres lying south-west of Lake Rudolf. The *Journal* reported: "The Society felt there was a very great need for more research in the semi-desert of the biological tropics, and South Turkana was ideally situated for semi-desert productivity studies. It was also a little known area geographically, and one peopled by nomadic Turkana, an obscure tribe whose pastoral skill enables them to live under very harsh environmental conditions. These consider-ations offered excellent prospects for an integrated research programme, one it was hoped in which East Africans themselves would take part, revolving round the theme of biological productivity and including studies of the land, its fauna and flora, and its people." This expedition pioneered a new ecological approach, and its system of detailed observation and recording has since been used all over the world.

MATO GROSSO

The Society's 1967–9 expedition to the Mato Grosso was also primarily concerned with ecology; and it is because this expedition helped to initiate a somewhat new approach that it is described in detail.

The Society's links with South America have been comparatively few; but those which have been forged have been both important and durable. The 1830s saw the surveys of Schomburgk in Guiana and Fitzroy in the Argentine and Chile, the former setting a pattern (and a standard) for systematic investigation, the latter charting more than 5,000 miles of unknown coast with meticulous accuracy, The 1860s saw Chandless's careful plotting of the southern tributaries of the Amazon, a task made doubly difficult by the hostility of the Indians. Also in the 1860s were Markham's journeys to the Amazon and the Andes: journeys which, among other things, added greatly to our knowledge of the Incas, and led to the introduction of the chinchona plant to India and the consequent marketing of quinine. The turn of the century saw a number of useful but comparatively lightweight expeditions such as Pratt's to the Amazon and Whymper's to the Andes; it was not, however, until the 1920s that the Society became involved with

(On the facing page)
Some of the flowers, plants and insects of the Mato Grosso. Deforestation today leads to the extinction of one species of flora and fauna every day. Within five years, at the present rate of destruction, one species will be obliterated every hour

another major project in South America, and this, alas, proved more notorious than meritorious.

In 1924 Colonel Fawcett disappeared into the interior of Brazil in search of those legendary cities which, he claimed, "would provide the answer to the enigma of the prehistoric world". He found no Machu Picchu: only the Kalapalo Indians who clubbed him and his companions to death on the bank of the Culiseu River. His disappearance and the failure of the expeditions which followed to find any trace of him underlined the fact that at the centre of the Brazilian provinces of Mato Grosso, Pará and Amazonas (an area almost the size of Europe) lay a vast and unexplored area of natural jungle, about the last blank space on the map of the world which could still truly be labelled *terra incognita*. And *terra incognita* this jungle might still be today were it not for two facts. In the early 1960s the Brazilian government shifted its capital from Rio de Janeiro to Brasilia, and at much the same time the aeroplane and the jungle airstrip began to overcome both the enormous distances of the Mato Grosso and the hostility of the Indians. The resiting of the Brazilian capital could be seen as symbolic of the nation's *volte-face* from dependence on its coast to dependence on its interior, and it wasn't long before a great highway was being driven from Brasilia north-west to Manaus on the Amazon. This highway was a harbinger of change, a path into the future, whose purpose was to open up what from time immemorial had been virgin territory. The jungle was to be obliterated: to be metamorphosed to pastureland for cattle.

The Brazilian authorities realized that their new highway would mark the end of an era. They therefore invited scientists from all over the world to come to the Mato Grosso, and to take note and record for posterity a way of life which was drawing inevitably to a close.

This invitation the RGS gratefully accepted. In April 1966 they and the Royal Society sent a reconnaissance party to the Mato Grosso to select a camp-site and co-ordinate plans with the Brazilian authorities; and a year later scientists began to arrive at the base which had been chosen – a spot at the junction of forest and *cerrado*, midway between the Rio Xingu and the Rio das Mortes and a little over a mile from the advancing highway. What followed was an innovation in the technique of exploration. To quote the Society's president:

> "The situation demanded something different from the traditional expedition. In order to carry out scientific investigation in depth, the Base Camp became a small temporary field research station in the midst of a large area that was very poorly known from the scientific point of view and hardly disturbed by man and his animals. Some work was also done much farther afield, along the Suiá Missu and Xingu rivers, a refuge of the dwindling Indian tribes who once overran the Mato Grosso. The careful study of the undeveloped natural environment, by scientists of many disciplines, can provide much information which is essential when the time comes to develop. Indeed, if the kind of scientific information which the expedition obtained is not available to the developers, or is not heeded by them, disaster may befall not only the natural environment but also the people concerned."

The work of the scientists fell roughly into four disciplines: geomorphology (with particular emphasis on soil study), botany, zoology and medical research. In each field the expedition carried out a great deal of patient, unspectacular research.

The geomorphologists' article *Soil Landscapes in the North Eastern Mato Grosso* (published in the *Journal* in June 1970) gives in its concluding summary a good idea of the scope and importance of the work undertaken.

> "Agricultural development in the Mato Grosso must take account of the absence of centres of population and of mineral raw materials. It is an area where labour is scarce, local marketing outlets are non-existent, and where the transportation of

The Aripuana highway: symbol of Brazil's determination to develop the resources of her interior

The expedition made its base midway between the Xingu and the das Mortes, only a mile from the new highway from Brasilia to Manaus

produce to outside markets is difficult. The low inherent chemical fertility of the predominant dystrophic soil is a limiting factor to agricultural development. Not only is the reserve of nutrients low, but it is concentrated in the organic fraction of the soils. Agricultural use generally requires the felling and burning of the vegetation, which allows a brief period in which crops can be sustained by the released nutrients. However, the rapid mineralization of soil humus following clearing will result in a sharp fall in the capacity of the soil to retain nutrient ions, and the leaching of nutrients released by mineralization and from the ash will result in extremely low nutrient levels within one or two years of the burn. Continued crop production would be impossible without the use of fertilizers, and their cost in the Mato Grosso would be prohibitive. So, despite the favourable climate and the attributes of the soils for arable farming, it would seem that cattle ranching is the most likely form of pioneer land use. . . . Northern Mato Grosso has survived into the latter part of this century as one of the most extensive areas in the world of tropical wilderness. It is not for this article to present the case for conservation, but it would seem that the difficulty of intensive agriculture and the difficulty of maintaining the precarious balance of fertility on a dystrophic soil are valid reasons for the preservation of substantial parts

To botanists the Mato Grosso was an Eden. Several major plant collections were made, resulting in the classification of nearly 8,000 numbers. A number is not necessarily a new species, it may only *look* like one and in fact be an already classified plant in an unfamiliar stage of development; nevertheless the assembling of 8,000 numbers was a veritable labour of Hercules, especially since ten samples of each had to be found, pressed, dried and tabulated, in order to meet the requirement of institutions throughout the world – to give an idea of the richness and variety of the Mato Grosso's plant life, an English county would yield fewer than 1,300 numbers. The botanists reckoned that it would take ten years for their findings to be classified, and that several hundred new species would be discovered. Of equal importance, and perhaps even greater interest, was their observation and recording of many rare and hitherto unknown botanical phenomena.

Zoologists too had a field day. South America, in contrast to South Africa, has no large herbivores, no herds of grazers and few carnivores; to paraphrase the expedition's report, a man can walk all day through its forests without seeing or even hearing a single mammal; one is far more likely to fall foul of vicious vegetation than vicious predators. It is therefore hardly surprising that the zoologists managed to trap no more than 40 species of mammal. Those who specialized in termites, fish or birds, on the other hand, found they had not too little to study but too much.

No creatures can be said to rule the Mato Grosso, but without doubt the most numerous and influential group are the termites; to quote the expedition's report: "it was impossible to dig up a trowelful of earth from anywhere without finding termites in it; their omnipotence in the Mato Grosso world cannot be overstated." As well as classifying nearly 4,000 different varieties of termite, the expedition made some fascinating individual studies, discovering a number of bizarre behaviour-patterns – like the worker ants who, when attacked, rupture themselves on one side and pour out a mass of sticky material. This procedure is, of course, lethal to the ruptured workers, but the glue ensnares their attackers.

Rosemary McConnell studied fish. In a couple of months she collected some hundred species, nearly half of which were previously unknown. Her report is graphic.

"I did a lot of fishing by night. With a good torch one can bail out the sleeping fishes with a dip net and take the nocturnal fishes more easily. Their gleaming eyes, red, orange and silvery-yellow, catch the torchlight and give their presence away. The

The building of a jungle airstrip is often the first step in developing a new area of pasture

The camp set up by the Society's expedition

freshwater prawns also have gleaming eyes, as do the innumerable spiders, some of which used to run on the water-surface at night while others lined the river bank with eyes glinting like diamonds.... Of course one was wet through from chest downwards every day and almost every night. It was hard work physically as one had to improvise and even set gill nets by swimming (in the absence of a boat) and with circumspection, since I was well aware what electric eels and piranha can do!"

As for birds, the ornithologists netted and observed a greater number in eight weeks than they would have found in the British Isles in a lifetime: 263 different species, many of which had never before been classified. This discipline, perhaps more than any other, demonstrated the Mato Grosso's richness and diversity in little-known life.

The principal medical work involved the study and treatment of the Xinguano Indians. It is now widely appreciated that when an isolated primitive community is brought for the first time into contact with people from the outside world, an embrace can be as lethal as a bullet. What is not so widely known is that, even today, little can be done to arrest the rampant infections which result from such a meeting. It was the hope of expedition doctors to be present at the first contact with such a community – "If only," as one of the doctors put it, "we could collect blood from such an isolated fragment of humanity, we could then have it analysed. The vital ingredients missing, such as the antibodies providing immunity against viral attacks, would be noted, and future missions could arm themselves beforehand with the boosts essential to survival." This was important work. Of equal importance was the expedition's research into leishmaniasis.

Leishmaniasis is one of the more unpleasant tropical diseases, with affinities to leprosy. The disease first appears as a small painless but persistent pimple, which slowly enlarges and eventually ulcerates. The resulting ulcers are harmless in themselves, but a

"The forest is going. There seems to be no room for such a luxury in a world ever hungry for land".
Photograph and caption
Douglas Botting

forerunner of disfigurement to come. For the parasite in the infected area lies dormant for anything up to twenty years, then produces secondary lesions of the nose and palate. These are hideously destructive, eating away flesh and cartilage until nose and mouth are virtually destroyed and the patient dies. It was discovered in the early 1960s that forest rodents are the primary hosts of leishmaniasis, but it was Iain Bishop and his team who discovered the vector by which the disease is transmitted from rodent to man: the sandfly *lutzomyia*. However, as is the case with malaria, not every sandfly is a carrier, only females of the species *lutzomyia flaviscutellata*. In five weeks of concentrated research the expedition trapped 107 rodents, 21 of which were found to have positive lesions; they also trapped and dissected 3,280 sandflies – since *lutzomyia* can fly *through* the mesh of mosquito-netting, the finicky nature of this research can be imagined. It will be several years before the full pattern of host-vector-secondary host is finally established; but there is now hope that leishmaniasis, like malaria, may one day be brought under at least partial control.

In addition to their research work, the expedition doctors lent a hand with day-to-day medical problems. To quote their report: "This work emphasized the overwhelming lack of general practice in the area. The camp's *Casa médica* was the best equipped surgery for hundreds of miles in any direction. Even Aragarças Hospital, suddenly in need of morphine, had to send a vehicle to our camp for this essential drug, a round trip of 500 difficult miles. . . . To invade the Mato Grosso has its complications, and these are inevitably exacerbated by the medical hazards of a tropical environment, rich in disease and a long way from professional care." Members of the expedition noticed that whenever they asked an isolated family "What is your greatest need?" the reply was always the same. "Good health."

At the end of a couple of years the scientists sent out by the Society packed up their notes and their specimens and flew home to universities and research establishments all

A young settler near the Araguaia River. Today she can wander into the wilderness that surrounds her home and pick orchids; it seems unlikely the orchids will survive her adolescence.

He told the expedition he had once been rich; but the developers took away his land and used him to help them cut down the forest

over the world; their camp was left deserted, and the layman was left wondering exactly how valuable their incredibly detailed research programme had been. Certainly an enormous amount of specialized information had been collected. It is, however, doubtful if much of this information will ever be seen (let alone understood and used) by those who are actually developing the Mato Grosso. Except therefore for the work of the doctors and the soil-scientists, one is left with the slightly uneasy – and probably wholly unworthy – suspicion that the exercise may have been more esoteric than practical. What, for example, one cannot help asking, was the use of Rosemary McConnell discovering some fifty new species of fish, when every one of them is about to be made extinct by the obliteration of its environment? A specimen on slide and an erudite life-history on tape is a poor substitute for the living creature making its contribution to the

Some of the 8,000 numbers (i.e. possible new species) collected by the Society's expedition to the Mato Grosso

complex pattern of life on earth. One cannot therefore help wishing that the scientists had seen it as their function not only to "collect, to photograph, to observe and to record", but also to conserve.

It must in fairness be said that some of Iain Bishop's team were committed to conservation, and that some of the work they did will help greatly with the management of the Parque Indigena do Xingu (one of the largest Indian Parks in Brazil). Others, however, clearly agreed with the report of the geomorphologists: "that it was not [their] purpose to present the case for conservation". And this, I think, was a pity. Because if those who have the ability and the privilege to study the last of the earth's wild places at first hand do not speak up for their preservation, who will?

In 1970 the Society sent a very different expedition to a very different place.

MUSANDAM

The Musandam peninsula lies at the tip of Northern Oman, jutting out like the stump of a tooth into the mouth of the Persian Gulf. It is barren territory – bare rock, little rain, violent wind – and its inhabitants live the sort of life one would expect to find in a bronze age village. Yet every tanker to leave the ports of the Arab Emirates, Bahrain, Kuwait or the oil terminals of Iran passes within sight of its rocky promontories. It is the Gibraltar of the Gulf.

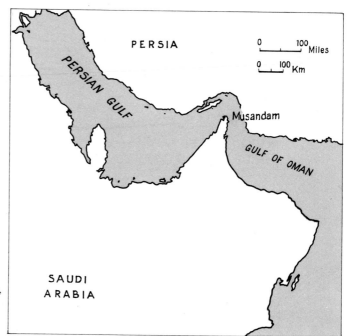

The Musandam peninsula, with its forbidding coastline, is on a busy trade route – yet until recently was little known to the outside world.

Until recently the peninsula was thought to be of little interest to geographers: a belief encouraged by the rulers of Oman, who preserved a sturdy independence and declared their territory "politically inaccessible". In 1970, however, H.M. Sultan Qaboos agreed to the Society's request to send a small expedition to the area, ostensibly to study its remarkable drowned valleys. In the event, the expedition carried out important work in several fields – geology, hydrography, biology and archaeology – as well as compiling the first detailed survey of an area which had not been properly mapped for a hundred years. However, perhaps the most important thing about the expedition was that it went at all: that it established contact with an area which is both politically sensitive and strategically vulnerable.

The team which the Society brought together consisted of six full-time members: a marine biologist, a hydrographer, a sedimentologist, a geophysicist and two geologists, one of whom was the leader, Norman Falcon. Its basic equipment was a pair of motorized dhows, the *Nasser* and *Tarak*, the larger of which served as a mobile camp. Provisions were bought in Dubai, and supplemented by local fish. Water was brought to whichever part of the coast the team were working on by inflatable RAF dinghies, the most frequently-used source being the fresh-water well in Khasab Bay.

The expedition arrived off the peninsula in November 1971, and its first task was to establish friendly relations with the inhabitants. Indeed it might be said that this was its most important task, since further study of the area would have been impossible without the goodwill of those who lived there. They soon discovered that the inhabitants, the Shihuh, fell into two quite separate groups: the mountain-dwellers of the interior, and the fishermen of the coast.

The mountain-dwellers are fanatical isolationists. To quote the *The Geographical*

Entrance to Elphinstone Inlet, named after one of the founder-members of the Society. A Biblical landscape. the Shihuh say "it all depends on God. If He sends no rain, we die". The Society's expedition, less fatalistic, investigated the possibility of tapping water believed to exist in the detritus in the bed of the larger wadis

Magazine, they "lead a way of life reminiscent of Bronze Age villagers. Housed in stone huts with a sunken floor, they are dependent on goats and the cultivation of small man-made fields in dammed wadi courses, the fields being surrounded by stone walls to keep off the goats and the wind. Many Westerners would regard their way of life as little more than a survival technique; but the mountaineers guard it jealously . . . and their isolationist tendencies have long been the cause of the political inaccessibility of the promontory." The fishermen, in contrast, have made contact with the outside world, and often welcome strangers as the potential bringers of material benefits. Again to quote *The Geographical Magazine*: "Salt water, rocks and fish are their only natural resources. Dhows and small craft are the tools of their livelihood. The fish they catch can be bartered or sold, and thereby changed into clothing etc. Until the development of the oilfields hastened the motorization of dhows, fish-marketing was difficult, since fish had to be dried before it could be exported; now, however, many craft have engines, and motorized dhows with ice boxes ply from ports on both sides of the Gulf, doing the rounds of the coastal villages to collect fish." It is a hard life. The lack of fresh water is a constant anxiety, and storms arise with great suddenness, often driving vessels to destruction against the undercut cliffs of the peninsula. The expedition had been forewarned of the local inhabitants' reputation for unfriendliness. In the event, however, Falcon tells us that they "found friendliness everywhere, especially among the cheerful hard-working crews of the dhows, who often kept a friendly watch over our instruments". As soon as the Shihuhs' co-operation had been assured the expedition began its studies.

Its main objective – at least on the theoretical side – was to collect data bearing on the geographical history of the Gulf during the Pleistocene Ice Age. Falcon told the Society in his address:

Fishing boats on the beach at Sibi

The Geographical Journal February 1973

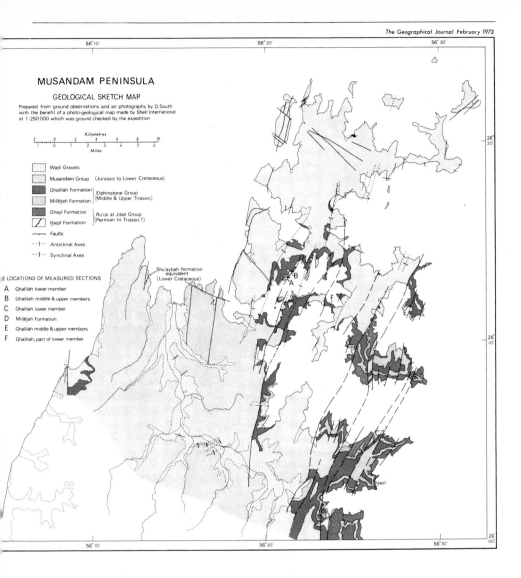

MUSANDAM PENINSULA

GEOLOGICAL SKETCH MAP

Prepared from ground observations and air photographs by D. South
with the benefit of a photo-geological map made by Shell International
at 1:250 000 which was ground checked by the expedition

Kilometres

Miles

Wadi Gravels

Musandam Group (Jurassic to Lower Cretaceous)

Ghalilah Formation } Elphinstone Group
Milàḥah Formation } (Middle & Upper Triassic)

Ghayl Formation } Ru'ûs al Jibal Group
Haqil Formation } (Permian to Triassic?)

Faults

Anticlinal Axes

Synclinal Axes

Shu'aybah formation
equivalent
(Lower Cretaceous)

LOCATIONS OF MEASURED SECTIONS

A Ghalilah lower member
B Ghalilah middle & upper members
C Ghalilah lower member
D Milàḥah Formation
E Ghalilah middle & upper members
F Ghalilah, part of lower member

Haqil

"The drowned valleys of Musandam are of special interest because of their bearing on the Quaternary history of the Gulf, about which little is known. The falls and rises of the sea-level during the Pleistocene, as ice caps formed and melted, clearly had a profound effect on the Gulf's geography and climate. A fall in sea level of a hundred metres would have made it mostly dry land, except for an estuary in the Strait of Hormuz, receiving the waters of a major river contributed by the Tigris, Euphrates and Karun. In the Gulf itself, most sedimentary evidence will have been swept away during the marine transgressions which heralded the inter glacial period. The Musandam peninsula, on the other hand, may have preserved some Pleistocene clues in its inlets. . . . It is only about 20,000 years since the ice sheets began their retreat. About 8,000 years ago the Sumerians were leading a civilized life in lower Mesopotamia; it would be especially interesting to know what was happening in the Gulf during the intervening millennia."

A further spur to exploration, Falcon explains, was provided by the geological situation of the area.

"Reconstructions of Pangaea, the Palaeozoic super-continent thought to have existed before Gondwanaland and Laurasia drifted apart, usually show Oman in the same situation as today, facing an ocean – a surprise, considering the geological events known to have taken place in the interval! The magnificently exposed rocks of Musandam display the calcareous successions of the Arabian shield. Farther east [in Iran] this succession is represented as clastic sediments. The geology of the sea floor in between has been an outstanding problem for years, the question being whether the Oman range continues below the sea to join up with the ranges of Iran, or whether the link has been broken by horizontal movements. It seemed useful to have a fresh look at the rocks of Musandam in the light of new concepts of ocean development which could have a bearing on the history of the north Arabian Sea, now known to be an area of recent subsidence."

So for the better part of three months Falcon and his team worked their way by dhow round the forbidding coastline of the Musandam peninsula. "Reconnaissance mapping was carried out from the dhow *Tarak* by inshore cruising at slow speed around almost the entire coastline from Bukha in the west to Dawhat Qabal in the east. Landings were made at numerous localities to check observations made from the dhow and to investigate areas of special geological and geomorphological interest. Excursions were made on foot up the Wadi al Ayn and its tributaries. . . . Nine trigonometrical points were established; also five bench-marks related to mean sea level and tied to trigonometrical control."

The hydrographers, meanwhile, were surveying the sea approaches in general and the approaches to the Al Maksar isthmus in particular; for one of the objectives of the expedition was to study the feasibility of cutting a canal through Al Maksar, at a spot where the waters of the Indian Ocean and the waters of the Arabian Gulf are separated by a ridge less than 300 metres wide. Tide poles and automatic gauges were installed, and six weeks of continuous observation were carried out. Soundings were made by echo-meter, mounted in one of the RAF Gemini; and a geophysical (sparker) survey was made in several of the inlets. This sparker survey was perhaps the most interesting work carried out, its objective being to define the bedrock topography of the submerged valleys, and to determine the extent to which they were filled with detritus and sediment. For sonar-readings proved what hitherto had been only surmised: that the valleys contained horizontal sediments averaging 40 to 50 metres in thickness, increasing in places to over 100 metres. Falcon writes:

Arab fort at the approaches to Khasab

Shihuh fishing boat. Most boats today have a diesel engine and ice-boxes, so that the catch, instead of having to be dried and salted, can be sold fresh at the oil ports

"If it is assumed that the fall of sea level during the last glacial maximum was about 90 metres, then the floor of these inlets would have been between 30 and 60 metres above sea level. But their real position must depend on the thickness of sediment which has since accumulated. When the inlets were out of water their floors were probably flattish areas consisting chiefly of sand. During the subsequent marine transgression these continental deposits would have been reworked and redeposited until the water was deep enough to take them below wave action. Since then they would have been covered by marine deposits of the type now forming. Much of the flat-lying sediment revealed by the sparker survey is marine and post glacial. If we assume that the marine transgression entered the inlets about 15,000 years ago (some people would put it later) and that subsequently marine sediment accumulated at the rate of 2.5 mm a year, thirty-eight metres could have been deposited since then. The sparker record often showed 50 metres. . . . It seems possible therefore that a considerable part of the sediment providing reflections in the sparker records is contemporary with Sumerian and post-Sumerian man. Core holes will determine the facts and should also give important sedimentological and climatic evidence."

If any of those listening to Falcon's address now expected the announcement of some major discovery or break-through in the extension of knowledge, they were disappointed. For this is not the style of expeditions today, whose members advance their discipline not by spectacular leaps and bounds, but inch by cautiously-qualified inch. All Falcon claimed for his survey was that it provided a platform from which future study could be profitably extended.

However, on a more practical level the expedition carried out work which might have immediate and far-reaching consequences. Part of its brief had been to keep a lookout for viable ways of assisting the local inhabitants to ameliorate their lot; and two

Building a Barasti hut

possibilities in particular were looked into – the feasibility of cutting through the Al Maksar isthmus, and the practicability of improving supplies of fresh water.

The Musandam peninsula is joined to the mainland by the Magalab isthmus, which at its narrowest point (Al Maksar) is less than 900 feet wide and 300 feet high. On either side of it lie basins of comparatively deep and sheltered water, one facing south into the Indian Ocean, the other north into the Arabian Gulf. The isthmus at Al Maksar consists of soft rock: interbedded limestone, sandstone and shale, which it would not be difficult to excavate. To quote Falcon: "The expedition analysed in depth the feasibility and economic rationality of cutting through this isthmus so that dhow traffic could move easily in sheltered waters from the Gulf of Oman to the Arabian Gulf without entering the Strait of Hormuz, with its strong tidal currents, storm hazards, and competition with the ever increasing tanker and freighter traffic. The distance saved would be about 64 kilometres on a round trip." Such a cutting would do much to help the Shihuh fishermen; and, as a bonus, the archaeological fruits of excavation might be considerable.

Fresh water is a more complex and intransigent problem.

Falcon holds the view – and he is undoubtedly right – that "water is the Achilles heel of the Shihuh . . . for rainfall is uncertain, and when as frequently happens the winter rains fail, the rock cisterns dry up, and water has to be fetched by sea or people must move." Two factors bring about this chronic shortage of water: the rare but violent rainfall, and the rocky nature of the terrain. To quote *The Geographical Magazine*:

"There are no permanent springs or streams in the mountains [of Musandam], where the rare precipitation tends to be torrential and the run-off catastrophic. The rain drains rapidly down to the coast, only very occasionally reaching the sea above ground, and normally sinking into the coarse rock detritus of the wadis, then following an underground path to the sea. One might expect good water to be common in the coastal area, but unfortunately few wadis contain enough detritus to hold important supplies. . . . The barren rocks of the coastline are split with fissures and cracks; in these circumstances sea water can penetrate the rocks, and any fresh water which sinks into the land will come to rest on the salt water. Only in wadis containing a fill of alluvial detritus is there likely to be enough pore space to hold water in quantity. Hand-dug wells have been made in most places on the detritus at valley mouths. After good winter rains these yield fresh water, but they turn saline in years of drought. The only alternative supply [to these wells] is from rock cisterns, or through fetching water by sea. Some cisterns, probably several hundred years old, are like small empty swimming baths, others mere crevices in the rock dammed by masonry."

(On the facing page)
An aerial view of the Musandam Peninsula showing its strategic importance at the entrance to the Persian Gulf. The terrain has a Biblical simplicity. Its inhabitants ask God for only one thing: water

(Overleaf)
A typical "drowned" valley of the Musandam Peninsula. It is thought that the beds of these valleys were above sea-level some 10,000 years ago and may well provide valuable clues on pre-Sumerian history

Falcon goes on to suggest a remedy: that the Wadi al Ayn holds the key to the area's water problem.

"This broad wadi has a relatively flat surface of alluvial detritus which rises from sea level at Khasab to about 152 metres above sea level 24 kilometres to the south-east near Rubat. Numerous tributary wadis enter the main valley carrying coarse detritus in their lower reaches. The total volume of detritus in this valley system is not known because the shape of the valley bottom beneath it is not known; but it should be adequate to retain a large proportion of the fresh water which sinks into it after rains have fallen in the catchment area. Its sub-surface water is now tapped only at

Khasab, where in wells one kilometre from the sea the fresh water is close to high tide level. But this fresh water table must rise gradually up the valley and may be high enough at its head to give prospects of a piped supply,. If water can be found near Rubat, only three kilometres of pipe and a pump would be required to establish a water point on the east coast, and this would help considerably in solving the fresh-water problem of the coastal villages."

Falcon recommends an investigation of the wadi by drilling: and adds that wells, irrigation and goat-proof fences could make an area now used only occasionally after rain "blossom as the rose".

After three months the expedition left Musandam, very conscious of the fact that it had done little more than scratch the surface of a virgin field. It was, however, an important expedition on three counts. First, it mapped accurately and in detail an area which hitherto had been mapped only sketchily. Second, it carried out valuable preliminary research work in geomorphology, hydrology, and to a lesser extent in biology and archaeology. And third, it put forward viable suggestions for improving the lot of the peninsula's inhabitants.

This last aspect of its work is of particular interest.

Explorers through the ages – with a few exceptions like Stanley – have a pretty good record in their relations with the people whose lands they have visited; it has not, generally speaking, been *their* fault that exploration has been followed so often by exploitation. All the same, the idea of explorers going out of their way deliberately to help such people to improve the texture of their lives is comparatively new. It heralds a fresh and very welcome approach to exploration: an approach in which explorers not only take but give, not only seek but find, not only learn from but pass on their knowledge to.

This new approach was very much to the fore in the latest and one of the greatest of the Society's expeditions: a multi disciplinary study in depth of the Mulu rain forest in Borneo, led by Robin Hanbury-Tenison.

MULU EXPEDITION

The Society's links with Borneo go back to the 1850s, when one of its Fellows, Spenser St. John, was British consul on the island. As well as contributing articles to the *Journal*, St. John wrote what was for many years the definitive book on Borneo, *Life in the Forests of the Far East*. This was a work very much in the old style: erudite, full of hair-raising anecdotes, and illustrated with beautiful but stylized lithographs. A more modern approach was that of Alfred Russel Wallace who (also in the 1850s), was not only collecting butterflies, weevils and beetles in the Borneo rain forest, but was putting forward the then revolutionary view that "different species had arisen not from separate acts of divine creation as postulated by theologians, but by natural and developing variability". It is interesting to note that the research work on which this theory was based was carried out several years *before* Darwin read his historic paper to the Linnaean Society in 1858. The rain forest of Borneo has therefore as good a claim as the islands of the Galápagos to be regarded as the fulcrum which set in motion the theory of evolution.

(Overleaf)
Rear view of the Mulu (Sarawak) expedition's native-style longhouse in heavy rain. Although built some ten feet above ground level, during flooding water often rose to within inches of the floor

(On facing page)
An entomologist collecting specimens in the rain forest of Gunung Mulu

The last years of the nineteenth century saw valuable work done in Borneo by the naturalist Charles Hose and the ornithologist John Whitehead. It was not, however, until well into the twentieth century that the Society became involved with another large-scale project in the island. This was Tom Harrisson's Oxford University Expedition to Sarawak in 1932. Harrisson's team, the *Journal* reported, "spent three months in a detailed ecological investigation of the Mount Dulit area in central Borneo, studying in particular mountain and habitat zonations. Incidental to this work, they obtained [specimens of] some 1,000 birds, 350 mammals, 50 reptiles, 20,000 insects, 4,000 other invertebrates and 2,500 plants. Many mountain ranges and peaks were surveyed for the first time. . . . Shackleton climbed Mulu, Sarawak's highest mountain; Banks and Moore climbed Kalulong, which can probably claim to be the island's most inaccessible mountain; many observations were made on the social life of various tribes. . . . The plan of work proved a success; health was good; and every member of the expedition was reluctant to leave when the time came to do so." Indeed, Harrisson himself so fell in love with the island that he spent most of the rest of his life there, working tirelessly for the preservation of the creatures – in particular the orang-utans – which he cared for so deeply. His expedition, both in the work they did and the spirit in which they did it, was a precursor of Hanbury-Tenison's.

Robin Hanbury-Tensison's recent visit to the Mulu rain forest was very much the brain-child of the Society, being conceived at a meeting between Tom Harrisson and the Society's Director, John Hemming. When the expedition returned to England in 1978, after fifteen months in the field, it was hailed as "the Society's largest-ever undertaking, involving even more personnel in the field than the famous explorations of Livingstone, Shackleton or Scott". Yet it had relatively modest beginnings. In 1974 a group of scientists decided to make a strictly limited study of the rain forest which covered the lower slopes of Gunung Mulu – the mountain Shackleton had climbed some

Expeditions today rely heavily on the support of commerce and industry. The photograph shows some of the food donated to the Society's expedition to Mulu – an expedition to which more than 300 firms gave valuable aid

*The island of Borneo is
divided into the two
Malaysian states of
Sarawak and Sabah, Brunei
and Indonesian Kalimantan*

forty years earlier. They were motivated partly by the fact that the Mulu forest is uniquely rich in *flora* and *fauna*, and partly by the fact that it was threatened by spoliation at the hands of the timber and pulp industries. In Hanbury-Tenison's words: "Tropical rain forests are disappearing at a terrifying rate before the mechanized onslaught of modern logging methods. Nearly half the rain forests of the world have been destroyed already, and at the present rate of exploitation the rest will vanish in twenty-five years – most of the ecologically richer lowland areas will be gone in ten years. It has been calculated that modern logging techniques in these forests now cause the extinction of one species of *flora* or *fauna* every day, and that in a few more years they will cause the loss of a species every hour." There were, in other words, similarities between the Society's expedition to the Mato Grosso and their expedition to Mulu; both went to study an area threatened with obliteration. But, as well as similarities, there was an all-important difference, for the latter expedition regarded it as part of its brief not only "to collect, to photograph, to observe and to record", but also to conserve.

    And here they had two strokes of good fortune. First, at about the time they were planning their expedition a number of organizations throughout the world, including the Society, decided to throw their weight firmly behind the growing campaign for conservation. Secondly, the Government of Sarawak decided to make the area around Mulu a National Park, and, perhaps even more important, asked the expedition if they would draw up a plan for its development and management. From the moment this request was acceded to, Sarawak threw its weight whole-heartedly behind the expedition, which in fact soon developed into an enterprise run jointly by the Society and the

Sarawak Government; to emphasize the latter's commitment, over a third of the expedition's doctors and scientists came from Malaysian universities or research establishments. The Park, in other words, might be described as a catalyst that brought East and West together. It might also be described as a pointer to the future . . . to quote Hanbury-Tenison again:

> "The [proposed] Park is uniquely diverse, containing forest types ranging from lowland alluvial at 150 feet above sea level, to mist-forests on the mountain peaks up

Gunung Mulu: the site of Sarawak's largest National Park. The nearby hills have some of the most extensive cave formations in the world – home of more than a million bats, which (inset) emerge each evening.

to nearly 8,000 feet. Moreover, these forests grow on the contrasting but adjacent shale and sandstone of Gunung Mulu itself, and the rugged limestone cliffs of Gunung Api. Each terrain creates its own habitat, and the resultant rich mixture makes the area one of the most scientifically important rain forests in the world.

"It is vital it should be preserved.

"But to protect and preserve a forest it is essential to know and understand what is there. Our main task was to gather this information in order to prepare for the Sarawak Government the most detailed management plan ever made of a tropical

The Tutuh River at Long Terawan. The boat is a Chinese launch, used for trading up and down the river. The water buffalo will be taken (upside-down in the towed canoe) to the nearest town, Marudi, for slaughter

rain forest. Today no single country has enough experts to cover every field of research; and it is only through international co-operation that some of the many secrets still hidden in the rain forests can be unlocked."

So, from modest beginnings, the expedition mushroomed into a crusade for conservation, a crusade drawing support and personnel from all over the world. In the end no fewer than 115 scientists (several of them the world's leading authorities in their discipline) came to study Mulu. Between them they represented thirty universities and eight nationalities, and over a period of fifteen months they carried out more than ten thousand man-days of highly meaningful research.

The task of organizing so large an expedition, of transporting it to a remote area, and of arranging its accommodation and food and the vast amount of scientific equipment it needed, presented a considerable problem: a problem which fell largely on the shoulders of the RGS. It says much for the Society's administrative and logistic expertise that the movement of personnel and supplies was carried out with such efficiency that within six days of leaving England a scientist could be working on his project in the field. What helped perhaps more than anything to bring this about was the establishing of a new style of base camp. To quote the *Journal*:

"In order to leave the scientists free to concentrate on research it was decided that a small team of volunteers should be recruited who would be responsible for the daily running of the camp and for all administrative detail. So doctors, nurses, cooks, mechanics and secretaries joined the expedition in the field; and [the local inhabitants] were also recruited as porters, boatmen, guides, cooks and washerwomen. As a result the Base Camp became quite a comfortable place to live in, and far more scientific work was accomplished there than had been believed possible during the planning stage. . . . Another new concept was that everyone, scientists and administrators alike, contributed an average of £5 per day towards costs. This accounted for more than half the expedition's budget, and, more importantly, gave everyone a strong sense of identity with the expedition and a determination for it to succeed."

It is not perhaps too fanciful to regard the making of this financial contribution as symbolic, tangible evidence of the wish of explorers today to give as well as to take. Be that as it may, the idea had beneficial results. For in spite of its size and complexity, the Society's expedition to Mulu was a singularly happy affair – as its leader said: "There was not a single serious row or personality clash . . . everyone was too interested and excited by what they were doing."

Before the scientists arrived at Mulu in force, a great deal of preliminary work and reconnaissance had to be carried out.

Mulu lies in the north-east corner of Sarawak, about 150 miles from the coast and rather less than half that distance from the border with Brunei. The area designated as a National Park consists of 210 square miles, most of it virgin forest, and includes both the sandstone peak of Gunung Mulu (7,796 feet) and the adjacent and unclimbed limestone peaks of Gunung Api and Benarat. The scenery is magnificent, with mountainous vistas, bizarre limestone pinnacles, mist-forest wreathed in orchids and pitcher plants, and caves which are not only the largest in the world but among the most spectacular.

There are no roads to Mulu. To get there the expedition had to move personnel and stores along more than 180 miles of jungle track and river. Their first job was to establish a base camp. The site chosen was close to the perimeter of the Park, "on the banks of the clean, cool and attractive Melinau River"; and here they cleared a helipad, so that the Royal Malaysian Air Force could fly in supplies and material for building the longhouse which was to be their headquarters for the next fifteen months. This longhouse, which could sleep forty and was built in traditional native style, was erected with the help of local tribesmen in an astonishing ten days. It was a building of some sophistication, and included storeroom, kitchen, dining-area, dormitories, a bamboo-floored verandah, latrines, a shower and electricity; all of which represented, to quote one of the many appreciative scientists, "undreamed-of luxury".

The expedition's next task was to establish sub-camps, three with adjoining helipads, at strategic points in the Park, and to cut trails between them. Six such camps were eventually created, the main ones being at the foot of Gunung Mulu; close to the summit of Gunung Mulu – "a cool and refreshing site with superb views"; in the Melinau gorge, where the river cut through the limestone ridge of Gunung Api, and inside "the Hidden Valley, at the spot where the river disappeared underground". "Thus," to quote the *Journal*, "efficient logistic support was provided for the scientists at an early stage."

These scientists began to arrive in large numbers in July 1977. Each had his or her individual and highly specialized subject to carry out research in, yet each had to dovetail this research into the overall plan which was being prepared for the Government of Sarawak. And this brought about another exceedingly happy aspect of the expedition: that its members had the feeling their research was going to be important not only in theory but also in practice. The work they carried out covered a vast number of disciplines; but for the sake of simplicity, it can be considered under four headings: geomorphology, speleology, *flora* studies and *fauna* studies.

The geomorphologists had to start very nearly from scratch. The Park had, it is true, been surveyed and its general geological structure determined. However, no wholly satisfactory study had been made of its principal feature, the karren, the spectacular limestone pinnacles which leapt spearlike to heights of over 150 feet out of the valleys of

It will take more than a handshake to solve the problems of the Penan, the shy nomadic hunter-gatherers whose existence is threatened by deforestation. But at least the Society's expedition has brought their predicament to the notice of the world, as well as providing useful medical help – for example Dr. Mitton, who used to work with Christiaan Barnard, found that the child wearing a bead necklace to its examination had a hole in the heart

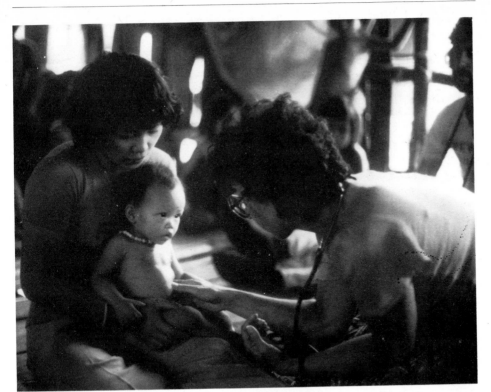

Gunung Api; and virtually nothing was known of its hydrology. The *Journal* explains what was discovered about these very different subjects.

One of the most spectacular features in the area is the limestone pinnacles on the slope of Gunung Api, some 1,000 metres above the Melinau gorge. These are large-scale karren, more than fifty metres high in parts, and extremely difficult to explore and measure. Similar pinnacles also occur on other nearby limestone mountains, notably on Gunung Benarat. Dr. R. G. Ley gave attention to their morphometry and is of the opinion that structural factors, especially jointing, control their disposition. . . . The overall limestone relief reflects the generally high dips and the very uniform and tough rock, interspersed with well-developed jointing. Because of the high dips, closed depressions are steep-sided. Their slopes are controlled by the dip on one hand and by the almost vertical jointing on the other. More often than not the limestones form inaccessible ridges with little development of closed depressions. . . . As a result of high rainfall and the abundant vegetation, joints and bedding planes on the rock are enlarged into deep fissures; and solution of the rock gives rise to knife-like and razor-sharp ridges and pinnacles. . . . The rivers flowing west off the Mulu massif encounter the limestones; some of these end in very fine blind valleys – such as the Hidden Valley – others pass through the limestone ridge by means of gorges. Underground drainage has given rise to some of the finest river caves anywhere in the world."

In their study of the rivers and rainfall of Mulu the work of the geomorphologists was less spectacular but not less important. "Several hydrological projects were set up," the co-ordinator of studies, Marjorie Sweeting, tells us, "but because of the lack of basic data a priority was the establishment of a meteorological station at base camp and of rain gauges up Gunung Mulu and in the Melinau gorge. This was done by R. P. D. Walsh in August

Half the rain forests in the world have already been destroyed. At the present rate of exploitation, the rest will have vanished within 25 years

59

Base camp: a longhouse erected for the expedition by local people using traditional building techniques and materials

1977, and records have been kept for the whole year. Annual rainfall in the lowlands was found to be about 197 inches; this increases slowly in relation to altitude to reach a maximum of 264 inches at 1,517 metres, then decreases slowly until at the summit of Mulu it is only 182 inches. . . . The hydrological characteristics of the Melinau have been monitored during the year; variations in flow were found to be very rapid, and the river resembles a tidal creek in its behaviour. Relationships between discharge and solute load and suspended sediment have been determined; and calcium and magnesium hardness and solute concentrates of different waters have been obtained throughout the year. . . . Other experiments gauged the relative rates of erosion on the Mulu sandstone and the Melinau limestone." To say that Marjorie Sweeting and her geomorphologists added very considerably both to our knowledge and to our understanding of the Park would be an understatement.

The speleologists were led by Dr. Anthony Waltham of Trent Polytechnic. His account (taken from *The Geographical Magazine*) is both informative and graphic.

"It was known that caves existed in the limestone hills, and when the Royal Geographical Society planned its massive expedition to Mulu, a team of speleologists was added to the long list of scientific personnel who went to work in the Park. The result was a revelation. The six cavers who made up our team spent nearly three months exploring and mapping a series of caves which exceeded even the wildest ideas that had emerged in the expedition's planning stage. More than fifty kilometres of cave passages were discovered and surveyed, but it has to be admitted that these comprise only a fraction of the caves believed to exist there. Mulu must now rank as one of the world's great cave regions – a claim founded at least in part on the sheer size of many of the underground passages. . . . Our first visit to Hidden Valley was a disappointment. The river sank into boulders, and to this day nobody has managed

Canoes dwarfed by the precipitous and overhanging limestone cliffs of Gunung Api. The limestone turned out to be honeycombed with caves.

The present passage in Green Cave (Lobung Hijan) was once filled with water, and the wave-shaped walls are a curious feature

to follow its water underground. So the search for caves spread to the valley walls, and soon an entrance was found. This led to a series of fossil caves which again were disappointing in that they did not lead down to the underground river. However, 500 metres of energetic rift passage led to a series of massive chambers, remarkable for their variety of decorations. One of these we named *Gua Ajaib* – Wonder Cave. Massive flowstone walls and towering stalagmites vied with sparkling crystal floors and screens of stalactites to make the most splendid scene. The smaller formations include beautiful gypsum flowers and tangled calcite spirals up to a metre in length. In addition the Moulin Rouge chamber contains a hitherto unknown type of cave deposit. Delicate calcite fans, each the size of a cupped hand, appear to be formed by water splashing and spraying down from the cave roof, and occur in great tiered banks. Lying in the very heart of Gunung Api, Wonder Cave is the jewel of the Mulu Park."

Pure white cockroach found living in the cave

If Wonder Cave was beautiful, the Deer Cave was impressive, principally on account of its size. It is thought to be the largest cave-passage in the world.

"The kilometre-long through tunnel of Deer Cave . . . is so vast that it defies comprehension. At its downstream end it is 170 metres wide and 120 metres high, and at few points is it less than 100 metres in diameter. Mountainous rubble piles and soaring black holes in its roof add to its grandeur. Everything about it is on a magnificent scale. Its bat population approaches a million. The bat-roosts are mostly out of sight on the roof; but the evening bat flight when they all emerge for a night's feeding on insects is one of the great sights of the Park. Sharing the cave with the bats are thousands of cave swiftlets, and between them bats and swiftlets have accumulated vast amounts of guano, beyond the flood levels of the river. This guano supports an enormous population of smaller cave animals – beetles, giant earwigs, millipedes and white crabs. And these in turn support a population of predators, mainly huge hunting spiders, but also long-legged fast and highly poisonous centipedes; there are also cave snakes, many of them more than a metre long. This entire suite of animals is specially adapted for cave life, and its amazing abundance provided us with one of our most vivid memories of Deer Cave. But the cave does not only provide the spectacle of a highly-developed subterranean *fauna*; it provides more lasting and more thought-provoking memories, revealing new insights into the extent of horizontal development in tropical caves, and adding new dimensions to speleology."

Interesting and exciting work was certainly done in Mulu by geomorphologists and speleologists; but no less important was the work of the expedition's botanists. Their research was directed firstly at finding out precisely what was in the rain forest, and secondly at determining the role of what they found in the forest's ecology. J. A. R. Anderson of the Forestry Department of Sarawak was in charge of making a map of the different forest types seen in the Park. This may have been a labour of love, but it was also a labour of Hercules, for the Mulu rain forest was found to be "one of the richest – in some instances *the* richest – in the world in the variety of its vegetation". In one test plot of roughly an acre Anderson found 268 individual trees, representing no fewer than 136 different species: a dramatic contrast with what would be found in an acre of temperate forest, where the yield would almost certainly be only fifteen or at the most twenty species. And trees were probably the easiest of Mulu's *flora* to take stock of. When it came to epiphytes, mosses, fungi and lichens, the botanists found themselves dealing not in hundreds but thousands. In the case of flowering plants, for example, over 2,000 different species were collected, many of them new to science. As for fungi, over 4,000 species were

Limestone pinnacles, known as karren, many of them quite unclimable, rise spearlike some hundred feet above the forest canopy

collected; incredible as it sounds, nearly half were previously unknown. In all, twenty major plant collections were painstakingly compiled; and it is pleasant to record that the first or master set of each will be lodged in Sarawak's forest herbarium at Kuching.

Perhaps of special significance to the long-term future of the Park was the work of John Proctor and his team, who for a full year carried out basic research into the forest's system of nutrient recycling.

Laymen who gaze in awe at the enormous trees and riotous vegetation of a rain forest, often imagine that so much growth must spring from a rich inherently fertile soil. This is not so. The soils which support the great rain forests of the earth are in almost every instance too weak for agriculture. They generate growth by a complex and delicately-balanced system of recycling: a system in which leaf and twig fall, precipitation, and the action of soil animals, termites and invertebrates all play their part in continually decomposing material and making it again available as nutrients. It is a system all too vulnerable to disruption by man, and for this reason there is a very real danger that the magnificent rain forests – "the richest environment on earth for *flora* and *fauna*" – will be obliterated before they can be understood. To quote the *Journal*: "[Proctor's] studies will help to build up a picture of the nutrient turnover in different types of rain forest . . . and will establish baselines which will be of vital importance in emphasizing the dangers of deforestation."

It was soon found that the Park was as rich in *fauna* as in *flora*. There was, alas, no evidence of orang-utans, nor of the Sumatran rhinoceros, although the latter is known to have hunted in Mulu less than forty years ago. However, sixty species of mammals were recorded, including the rare Bornean gibbon, the slow loris and the flying lemur; also the smallest (and one of the rarest) mammals in the world, the pigmy shrew (*Suncus etruscus*). Ornithologists netted, identified and ringed more than 260 different types of bird, including the spectacular hornbills and the even more spectacular Argus or dancing pheasant. But it was the insects and other invertebrates which most showed most clearly the diversity of life in Mulu. Specialists who worked on ants, bugs, beetles, centipedes, millipedes, aphids, woodlice, moths, butterflies, termites and spiders were amazed at their number and diversity. To quote the expedition's leader: "In most of these genera new species were discovered almost daily; and to give just one example of the scale of the scientists' findings, it now seems likely that there are as many species of ants in the Mulu rain forest as in the whole of the North American Continent." All of these insects have a vital role to play in the life of the rain forest, and the knowledge that has been gained of them and of their behaviour will help to ensure both their own preservation and that of their environment.

The scientists also made contact with one other inhabitant of the rain forest: Man.

The Park is sparsely populated, and the Penan Indians who live in and around it might be described as perfect tenants; for they are hunter-gatherers; that is to say they don't practise cultivation, but roam the area in small family groups, living mainly on wild sago, cabbage-palm and animals such as pigs, deer and monkeys, which they shoot with their blow-pipes. This is not the romantic idyllic life that one might imagine if one has never been there. In Mulu – as in the Amazon, the Congo and every other rain forest in the world – food is scarce, survival is difficult, and life is frequently brutal and at times homicidal; though the Penan have never practised some of the more extreme customs that used to be found in the jungles of both the Amazon and Borneo. As Robin Hanbury-Tenison says, there are extremely good reasons why "It is to be hoped that the management plan, when finalized, can present a formula which will accommodate the Penan in their own forest."

The first reason for hoping this is ethical. As Hanbury-Tenison points out, it *is* the Penan's forest. In the bad old days whole ethnic groups such as the Australian

The Penan are devoted to their children. One can only hope that contact with the outside world will not preclude the children of today inheriting their parents' traditional knowledge and skills

Aborigines and the North American Indians were dispossessed of their land and hounded to virtual extermination. Today thinking people know how wrong this was. Of course the world being what it is, commercial greed may still lead to dispossession; but at least the Penan won't be driven out of the Borneo forest as a matter of course and without protest. It is recognized, at least in theory, that they have their rights.

The second reason is self-interest. For the Penan have much to teach us. On the purely practical level they can teach us a great deal about the forest they live in. As Nigel Winser, the expedition's Deputy Field Director, writes: "It is important to consider the wealth of information on which the Penan subconsciously rely to survive. Their knowledge of the medical, nutritional and poisonous qualities of the Park *flora* is immense, and their hunting techniques must be among the most effective in the world. This wealth of information is passed on from generation to generation. Let us hope that their hunting grounds are not so diminished that this knowledge is lost forever."

It could of course be argued that few of us are ever likely to find ourselves in a tropical rain forest, and that the lessons the Penan have to teach us are therefore of little value. But I wonder if this is so? People today are beginning more and more to question the validity of many of the beliefs by which we have been living for the last 150 years. In particular they are questioning the philosophy of limitless economic expansion and the obsession with material possessions which were engendered by the industrial revolution. Have we, people are beginning to wonder, been worshipping false gods? Do we really today lead happier lives than the people of those so-called primitive societies whom our fathers and grandfathers believed it their Christian duty to subjugate? It is perhaps significant that explorers and scientists who have recently been in contact with such people nearly always want to return: that they feel most strongly *they* can learn something from *them*.

So it is surely not only morally right but to our material advantage to see that such people are not wiped off the face of the earth – as is happening for example in the Mato Grosso. In Brazil, to quote Tom Sterling and the editors of *Time-Life*, "the Indians are being driven from their tribal lands, displaced and harassed" – not to put too fine a point upon it, they are being systematically shot, poisoned, raped and burned out of their forest-home, which is being reduced by fire to pastureland for cattle. And that is one solution. In Mulu, the Society's expedition looked into the possibility of another solution, and one which they hope will serve as a blue-print for the future: that of trying to conserve both the natural environment and the people who live in it.

You can make your choice.

The Society, happily, has made its. To quote the Society's President, Lord Hunt:

> "In the conservation of nature the Royal Geographical Society has an important part to play. Of course it still remains essential to our *raison d'être* to promote field research; we have too a duty to encourage youthful exploration. There can, however, be no question but that we should also join with all those others who stand up and fight to save the virgin lands, to prevent pollution, to protect wild life, and to husband the resources of nature for the continuing benefit of man's spiritual, quite apart from his physical needs."

It is good to see the RGS on its hundred-and-fiftieth anniversary at last directing and not merely reflecting the advance of geography; and one can only hope that thinking and caring people throughout the world will follow the lead which the Society's President has so unequivocally given.

(On the facing page)
Karren and rainbow

(Overleaf) *Karren,
wreathed in mist, rising out
of the forest*

10. The Society Today

THE SOCIETY HAS EVERY REASON TO BE PROUD OF ITS PAST. AT THE TIME IT WAS founded, in 1830, man had neither seen nor set foot on large areas of his planet, and it has been the explorers sent out by the Society who, more than anyone, have wiped "unexplored" off the maps of the world, and who have followed up their discoveries with scientific investigation. It has moreover been the knowledge disseminated by the Society which has so greatly helped to bring about the world-wide acceptance of geography as an academic subject. It could, however, be argued that a distinguished past does not necessarily guarantee a useful present. What, one might reasonably ask, does the Society do today? And – perhaps more important – what will it be doing tomorrow?

The Society nowadays has two main functions. In the first place it carries out a great deal of routine work in helping to promote the cause for which it was established, "the advancement of geographical knowledge". In the second place, it acts as a catalyst, fusing and making more meaningful a vast amount of information derived from many different and highly specialized disciplines.

The scope, diversity and value of its routine work becomes apparent if one follows its activities month by month throughout a typical year remembering always that the events described resemble only that part of an iceberg which can be seen at a glance, and that a great deal more goes on than is immediately apparent. Let us examine the year 1977.

In January the Society promoted a sixth-form lecturer, *Transport Policy and the Road and Rail Controversy*, the speakers being Sir Colin Buchanan, a leading town-planner, and David Bowick, the Chief Executive of British Rail. This was open to all sixth-formers and their teachers in the country, and the Society's lecture-hall (which seats 750) was so full that the audience overflowed into gangways and stairs.

March saw the publication of the first of the four-monthly issues of the *Journal*; this included articles on such very different topics as *Prospect of the Falkland Islands* (a study in depth of the Islands' future) by Lord Shackleton; *Caves and Karst in the Hindenburg Mountains* (a detailed analysis of the geomorphology of the West Sepik province in Papua) by David Brook; *The Work of the Field Station in the Tibesti Mountains* (Chad) by Dieter Jakel, and *The RGS Archives* by Christine Kelly.

Also in March the Council announced which expeditions it had decided to support during the coming year. And nothing demonstrates the prestige of the RGS more clearly than the very large number of expeditions – sometimes almost a hundred – which now apply to it each year for recognition and support. Clearly, with its limited funds, the Society cannot help them all, but such is its reputation that as soon as it gives an expedition the seal of its approval, financial aid is nearly always forthcoming from outside sources. And this perhaps is the right time to pay tribute to the many organizations (in particular oil companies, banks, airlines, food manufacturers and makers of scientific and expedition equipment) without whose generous backing the majority of expeditions would never get off the ground. In 1977, to give some idea of the Society's commitments, it approved no fewer than 53 expeditions: fifteen to Asia, fourteen to North, South or Central America, nine to Europe, seven to the Arctic, six to Africa and two to the Pacific. And the objectives of these expeditions was as diverse as their locale –

(On the facing page) The Society's expedition to Mulu discovered some of the largest and most beautiful caves in the world. (Above) Stalactites and stalagmites adorn the main tunnel in Clearwater Cave (Lobang Air Jerneh). (Below) Flowstone blocks the end of Wonder Cave (Lobang Ajaib)

"Cambridge Pathology Expedition to Kenya. Collection of animal materials for parasitic, virological and taxonomic research. Leader J. P. Weaver.... Bristol University Expedition to the Indus Valley. Study social and economic relations between monasteries and local people. Leader Dr. J. H. Cook. . . . British North Polar Expedition, First circumnavigation of Greenland. Leader Wally Herbert. . . . New Hebrides Expedition. Detailed study of Halcyon kingfishers. Leader J. G. Robertson. . . . Expedition to Cabo Frio, Brazil. Qualitative and quantitative underwater survey of the *flora* and *fauna* in ocean upswelling using SCUBA gear. Leader Martin Whittle.... Field Research Project on environmental history of the Near East; upper Khabour basin, Syria. Study of environmental change during late Pleistocene and Holocene times. Leader C. N. Roberts." Supplying such expeditions with information, advice, instruments and aid is one of the Society's more important functions; and indeed without the behind-the-scenes work of its committees (such as the Expeditions Committee, the Research Committee, the Survey and Instruments Committee and the Young Members Committee, few of today's explorers would get their projects off the ground. This would be a loss to everyone. For not only do these expeditions advance the work of those who take part in them, they add in many small but not insignificant ways to our knowledge of the world we live in.

Another event to take place in March 1977 – and one very much associated with these expeditions – was the presentation of the annual Mick Burke Award. "The Mick Burke Award," to quote the Society's press release, "is named after the BBC cameraman who died filming on Everest, and was set up to encourage expeditions to make films of their trips to remote parts of the world. Last year 300 expeditions applied to take part. Six were chosen and provided with cameras and film and sound equipment to make a short film. These were subsequently judged by a panel from the BBC and the RGS; and Pelham Aldridge Blake, the cameraman with the Bristol University expedition to Ladakh, was chosen as the winner. In a special BBC2 'World About Us' programme, he was presented with the trophy by the Prince of Wales."

In May the Society conceived and organized an important Technical Meeting on the ecology of the Sahel – the arid zone between the Sahara Desert to the north and the more fertile savanna to the south. This area has suffered a succession of droughts throughout the 1970s, the grazing lands have deteriorated and the largely nomadic population has suffered great hardship and considerable mortality. On 15th May experts from all over the world met at the Society's headquarters and papers were read suggesting possible ways of restoring the area to its former habitability; these included irrigation schemes, reafforestation projects, and the introduction of cash crops such as guayule (a rubber-producer) or jojoba (a substitute for wax). This meeting bears witness not only to the international status of the Society, but also to its cosmopolitan outlook and its determination to relate geographical research to human needs.

The next event was, for the Society, a sad one: a memorial meeting for Eric Shipton, who, to quote his obituary, "had been a distinguished and loyal Fellow of the Society for fifty years and was outstanding as a mountaineer and an explorer *par excellence*". June also saw the election of a new President, Lord Hunt, and the presentation of the Society's annual medals and awards. And it is interesting to note how numerous these awards have now become, and for what a diversity of work they are given: the Founder's Medal to Michael Wise "for contributions to international understanding in geographical teaching", the Patron's Medal to Kenneth Hare "for discoveries in Arctic geography", and the Victoria Medal to Emrys Jones "for contributions to urban geography". Other awards went to André Guilcher "for studies in oceanography", to Harold Fullard "for contributions to educational cartography", to R. U. Cook "for geomorphological studies", to David Brook "for speleological exploration", to Denys Brunsden "for geomorphological field-work", to Lt.-Colonel Streather "for leadership of the Army's Mount Everest Expedition", to Jeffrey Boswall "for helping to create the wildlife sound

Lord Hunt lecturing

*The Society's Director and
Secretary, John Hemming*

*The entrance hall and
reading room of the Society.*

library", while essay awards and travelling scholarships were awarded to Miss Belinda Fuchs "for her study of the social organization of the Markhon in Pakistan" and to David Bradshaw "for his study of the relationship between settled and nomadic groups in Iran".

Another important event in June was the Queen's Silver Jubilee Lectures. The Society's press release reads: "June 20th will mark the beginning of ten days which will see the greatest gathering of explorers and travellers in Great Britain since the war. For the Society has organized a series of five Jubilee lecture-evenings with the theme EXPLORATION DURING THE QUEEN'S REIGN. This series of lectures by great explorers, climbers, sailors, naturalists and travellers is unique. Each evening will be devoted to a special topic, and the chairman will introduce the speakers and indicate the scientific advances made in exploration as a result of their achievements; the speakers will then all give a twenty-minute talk illustrated with slides and film." The topics chosen were: Mountaineering (Chairman Lord Hunt), Ocean and Sailing (Chairman Rear Admiral Irving), Polar (Chairman Sir Vivian Fuchs); Tropical Forest (Chairman Anthony Smith) and Desert (Chairman Sir Duncan Cumming); and among those invited to speak were George Lowe, Sir Alec Rose, Sir Peter Scott, Wally Herbert, Oria Douglas-Hamilton, Bill Tilman and Freya Stark. Not surprisingly, all seats were sold in advance, and the Society's lecture-theatre was filled for each of the five lectures.

The second half of the year was less eventful. July saw another issue of the *Journal*, with articles on The Seismicity of Kuhistan, Iran, The RGS and the British Arctic Expedition of 1875–76, Late Pleistocene and Recent Climatic Changes in the Egyptian Sahara, Biological Collecting for the Small Expedition and Deep Drill Holes in the Ocean Floor: a diversity which again illustrates the many different branches which combine to form the mighty tree of geography.

In September the Society held a reception organized by the Christian Council of Zambia. This was to honour the memory not only of David Livingstone but also of his followers who, in one of the most remarkable journeys ever made, brought his body 1,500 miles from Chipundu to the coast. Commemorative plaques were presented to the Zambian High Commissioner in London.

In October Educational Corporate Members attended a Sixth Form Symposium on *North Sea Resources*. There were talks by T. F. Gaskell, the Secretary of the Oil Industry Forum on oil and gas supplies, and by Dr. Pawson on fish stocks in British coastal waters; these were followed by group discussion. Next month saw the final issue for 1977 of the *Journal*; this included several historical papers, the President's address, and two technical studies – *Coastal Conservation in France* by Guilcher and Moign, and *Soil Survey and Land Evaluation in Malawi* by Young and Goldsmith. And towards the end of November the Society joined the Watt Committee on Energy, a gathering of representatives from learned societies concerned with all aspects of energy use and conservation.

Finally, on 21st December, there was a one-day symposium on *Careers for Geographers*, introduced by the President. A number of speakers, each an expert in his particular field, explained what openings were available to students of geography in different professions – civil engineering, surveying, cartography, publishing, banking, teaching, government service, etc. And it is interesting to note that this decidedly academic meeting was opened by the man who, some twenty years earlier, had found fame on the ice walls of Everest.

Such a chronological survey of the Society's work by necessity fails to mention many of its activities which go on continuously throughout the year – the routine work of its library and map room for example, and the deliberations of its Council. It also omits many of those long-term projects so dear to its heart. Two of these in particular are worthy of mention; its drive for increased membership and its encouragement of youth. The size of the Society's membership has, over the years, been a pretty accurate indicator of its prosperity. During its period of near-bankruptcy for example in the 1840s membership dropped to under 500; during Murchison's presidency it rose to 2,500, and during Markham's to 4,500. In the period after the First World War it suffered a decline; since then it has increased slowly but surely, the rate of increase being stepped up considerably in the last few years, so that it now stands at a record 7,000, about 1,300 of whom are resident overseas and about 1,200 involved in geographical teaching. As for young members, the recently appointed Director John Hemming has, among other innovations, inaugurated a special and highly successful campaign to attract young explorers and geographers to the Society. There is now a Young Members Committee to look after their interests, and a definite rapport is being established between what used to be regarded as a traditionalist institution and those young field-workers, researchers and teachers who will determine the path geography is to take in the future.

This day-to-day work of the Society can be easily understood. What is not so easy to understand is how the Society helps to draw together the strands of many disciplines and weave them into the one great geographical web.

Today is the day of the specialist, and it is perhaps inevitable that the more one studies geography the more one is confronted by technical data in a specialized field. For most of the twentieth century geographers have been primarily concerned with amassing this technical data; and it is of course true that their research has given us a far greater knowledge of the world we live in. Knowledge, however, is not quite the same as understanding. Nor is it at all the same as wisdom. . . . The point I am trying to make is that the amassing of technical data ought not to be an end in itself. What really matters is the use we make of such data. And it is here that the Society is beginning to play an important role. . . . Geographical research has become so specialized there is a risk of the subject fragmenting into a number of separate disciplines. This would be a tragedy, for the study of the earth as a whole is a far nobler and more rewarding subject than the study of its individual parts. It is here that the Society helps to preserve both unity and continuity. For by integrating the various specialist studies and relating them to the study of geography as a whole, the Society is not only holding its subject together, but is actually adding to the importance of its component disciplines.

One reason for wishing to preserve geography as a single discipline is that it makes it far easier this way to relate it to man. And that, surely, is what the subject is all about; it is, to go back to Mackinder's hundred-year-old definition, "the science of tracing the interaction of man in society and his environment".

The RGS supports this concept that man is an essential – indeed *the* essential – element in geographical progress. And by throwing its weight behind this human aspect of geography the Society is now blazing a trail into the future, a future in which scientists and explorers not only seek out new facts and new horizons, but try specifically to relate their discoveries to the needs of man.

Appendix I

Presents of the Society

Frederick John Robinson, Viscount Goderich (subsequently 1st Earl of Ripon) 1782–1859. The Society's first president

1830–1833	Viscount Goderich (Earl of Ripon)
1833–1835	General Sir George Murray
1835–1837	Sir John Barrow
1837–1839	W. R. Hamilton
1839–1841	G. B. Greenough
1841–1843	W. R. Hamilton
1843–1845	R. I. Murchison
1845–1847	Admiral Lord Colchester
1847–1849	W. R. Hamilton
1849–1851	Captain W. H. Smyth
1851–1853	Sir Roderick Murchison
1853–1855	The Earl of Ellesmere
1855–1856	Admiral F. W. Beechey
1856–1859	Sir Roderick Murchison
1859–1860	Earl de Grey and Ripon
1860–1862	Lord Ashburton
1862–1871	Sir Roderick Murchison
1871–1873	Major-General Sir Henry Rawlinson
1873–1874	Sir H. Bartle Frere
1874–1876	Major-General Sir Henry Rawlinson
1876–1878	Sir Rutherford Alcock
1878–1879	The Earl of Dufferin
1879–1880	The Earl of Northbrook
1880–1885	Lord Aberdare
1885–1886	The Marquess of Lorne
1886–1887	Lord Aberdare
1887–1889	General Sir Richard Strachey
1889–1893	Sir Grant Duff
1893–1905	Sir Clements Markham
1905–1908	Sir George Goldie
1908–1911	Major Leonard Darwin
1911–1914	Earl Curzon of Kedleston
1914–1917	Douglas Freshfield
1917–1919	Col. Sir Thomas Holdich

1919–1922	Sir Francis Younghusband
1922–1925	The Earl of Ronaldshay
1925–1927	Dr. David Hogarth
1927–1930	Sir Charles Close
1930–1933	Admiral Sir William Goodenough
1933–1936	Sir Percy Cox
1936–1938	Prof. Henry Balfour
1938–1941	Sir Philip Chetwode
1941–1945	Sir George Clerk
1945–1948	Lord Rennell of Rodd
1948–1951	Sir Harry Lindsay
1951–1954	J. M. Wordie
1954–1958	General Sir James Marshall-Cornwall
1958–1961	Lord Nathan
1961–1963	Sir Raymond Priestley
1963–1966	Prof. L. Dudley Stamp
1966–1969	Sir Gilbert Laithwaite
1969–1971	Rear Admiral Sir Edmund Irving
1971–1974	Lord Shackleton
1974–1976	Sir Duncan Cumming
1976–1980	Lord Hunt

Lord Hunt of Llanfair Waterdine, C.B.E., D.S.O., K.G., the Society's president today

Secretaries of the Society

Prior to 1864 the Society had a number of honorary, part-time and assistant secretaries. It was Bates who by his devoted work and attractive personality endowed the position with the importance and permanence it has since maintained.

1864–1892	H. W. Bates
1892–1915	Dr. J. Scott Keltie
1915–1945	A. R. Hinks
1945–1975	Sir Laurence Kirwan
1975–	J. H. Hemming

Appendix II

Medals and Awards Presented by the Society

The Gold Medal (Founder's and Patron's Medals)

These originated in an annual gift of fifty guineas from King William IV, first made in 1831, "to constitute a premium for the encouragement and promotion of geographical science and discovery". In 1839 the Society decided that "this sum should be converted into two gold medals of equal value, to be designated the Founder's Medal and the Patron's Medal". Recipients have been:—

1832   Richard Lander: "for important services in determining the course and termination of the Niger".

1833   John Biscoe: "for his discovery of Graham's Land and Enderby's Land in the Antarctic".

1834   Captain Sir John Ross: "for his discovery of Boothia Felix and King William Land and for his famous sojourn of four winters in the Arctic".

1835   Sir Alexander Burns: "for his remarkable and important journeys through Persia".

1836   Captain Sir George Back: "for his recent discoveries in the Arctic, and his memorable journey down the Great Fish River".

1837   Captain Robert Fitzroy: "for his survey of the coasts of South America, from the Rio de la Plata to Guayaquil in Peru".

1838   Colonel Francis Rawdon Chesney: "for valuable materials in comparative and physical geography . . . in Syria, Mesopotamia and the delta of the Susiana".

1839   Thomas Simpson: "for tracing the hitherto unexplored coast of North America".
     Dr. Edward Rüppell: "for his travels and researches in Nubia, Arabia and Abyssinia".

1840   Major Henry Rawlinson: "for researches in Persian Guayana".
     Robert H. Schomburgk: "for his perseverance and success in exploring the territory and investigating the resources of British Guyana".

1841   Lieutenant H. Raper: "for excellent work on Practical Navigation and Nautical Astronomy".
     Lieutenant John Wood: "for his journey to the source of the Oxus and for valuable labours on the Indus".

1842   Captain Sir James Clark Ross: "for his brilliant achievement at the South Pole, to within less than 12° of which he safely navigated his vessels, discovering a great Antarctic continent".
     Rev. Dr. E. Robinson: "for his valuable work *Biblical Researches in Palestine, Mount Sinai and Arabia*".

1843   Edward John Eyre: "for his enterprising and extensive explorations in Australia, under circumstances of peculiar difficulty".
     Lieut. J. F. A. Symonds: "for his triangulation over Palestine and for his

Three of the Society's earliest Gold Medallists: (above) Richard Lemon Lander (1804–1834), (centre) Admiral Sir Robert Fitzroy (1805–1865) and (below) Carl Ritter (1779–1859)

determination of the difference between the level of the Mediterranean and the Dead Sea".

1844   W. J. Hamilton: "for valuable researches in Asia Minor".
Professor Adolph Erman: "for important geographical labours in Siberia and Kamstchatka".

1845   Dr. Charles Beke: "for his exploration in Abyssinia".
Professor Carl Ritter: "for his important geographical labours".

1846   Count P. E. de Strzelecki: "for exploration in the south-eastern portion of Australia".
Professor A. Middendorff: "for explorations in Northern and Eastern Siberia".

1847   Captain Charles Sturt: "for explorations in Australia, and especially for his journey fixing the limit of Lake Torrens and penetrating into the heart of the continent to lat. 24° 30'S, long. 138° 0'E".
Dr. Ludwig Leichhardt: "for explorations in Australia, especially for his journey from Moreton Bay to Port Essington".

1848   Sir James Brooke: "for his expedition to Borneo, and the zeal he has shown in promoting geographical discovery".
Captain Charles Wilkes, USN: "for the talent and perseverance he displayed in a voyage in the Antarctic regions . . . and for splendid scientific work".

1849   Austen Henry Layard: "for important contributions to Asiatic geography, interesting researches in Mesopotamia, and for his discovery of the remains of Nineveh".
Baron Charles von Hugel: "for his enterprising exploration of Cashmere".

1850   John Charles Frémont of the U.S. Topographical Engineers: "for his important geographical labours in the far West of the American Continent". [Patron's Medal]
Rev. David Livingston,* the enterprising missionary: "for his journey to the great lake of Ngami". [Chronometer Watch]

1851   Dr. George Wallin: "for his interesting and important travels in Arabia".
Thomas Brunner: "for meritorious labours in exploring the Middle Island of New Zealand".

1852   Dr. John Rae: "for his survey of Boothia under most severe privations . . . and for his very important contributions to the Geography of the Arctic".
Captain Henry Strachey: "for extensive explorations and surveys in Western Tibet".

1853   Francis Galton: "for fitting out and conducting an Expedition to explore the centre of Southern Africa".
Commander E. A. Inglefield: "for his enterprising Survey of the coasts of Baffin Bay, Smith Sound and Lancaster Sound".

1854   Admiral William Smyth: "for his valuable Maritime Surveys in the Mediterranean".
Captain Robert McClure: "for his remarkable exertions . . . in navigating his ship through the ice of the Polar Seas, and for his discovery of the North West Passage".

1855   Rev. David Livingstone: "for his recent explorations in Africa".
Charles Andersson: "for travels in South Western Africa".

1856   Elisha Kent Kane: "for services and discoveries in the Polar Regions during the American Expeditions in search of Sir John Franklin".
Heinrich Barth: "for his extensive explorations in Central Africa, his excursions about Lake Chad and his perilous journey to Timbuctu".

1857   Augustus C. Gregory: "for extensive and important explorations in Western and Northern Australia".
Colonel Andrew Scott Waugh: "for geodetical operations, as remarkable for their extent as for their accuracy, whereby [India] has been covered by triangulation".

*The omission of the 'e' from Livingstone was not an oversight; this was how he originally spelt his name.

Gold Medallists who received their award for very different achievements: (above) Captain Charles Wilkes, U.S.N (1798–1877) *for Antarctic exploration;* (centre) John Arrowsmith (1790–1873) *for his pre-eminence as a cartographer;* (below) Peter Egerton Warburton (1813–1869) *for his crossing of the Gibson desert, Australia, by camel*

1858   Captain Richard Collinson: "for discoveries in the Arctic Regions".
     Professor Alexander Bache: "for extensive and accurate surveys of America".

1859   Captain Richard F. Burton: "for his various exploratory enterprises, and especially for his perilous expedition with Captain J. H. Speke to the great lakes in Eastern Africa".
     Captain John Palliser: "for the valuable results of his explorations in the Rocky Mountains of North America".

1860   Lady Franklin: "for self-sacrificing perseverance in sending out expeditions to ascertain the fate of her husband".
     Captain Sir F. L. McClintock: "for the skill and fortitude displayed by him and his companions in their search for records of the lost [Franklin] expedition, and for valuable coast surveys".

1861   Captain John Hanning Speke: "for his eminent geographical discoveries in Africa, and especially for his discovery of the great lake Victoria Nyanza".
     John McDouall Stuart: "for very remarkable explorations in the interior of Australia".

1862   Richard O'Hara Burke: "in remembrance of that gallant explorer who with his companion Wills, perished after having traversed the continent of Australia".
     Captain Thomas Blakiston: "for his survey of the Yang-tsze-Kiang".

1863   Frank T. Gregory: "for successful explorations in Western Australia".
     John Arrowsmith: "for the very important services [in cartography] he has rendered to geographical science".

1864   Captain J. A. Grant: "for his journey across Eastern Equatorial Africa with Captain Speke".
     Baron C. von der Decken: "for his Geographical Surveys of the lofty mountains of Kilima-ndjaro".

1865   Captain T. G. Montgomerie: "for his great trigonometrical journey from the plains of the Panjab to the Karakoram Range".
     Samuel Baker: "for his vigorous explorations in the interior of Africa".

1866   Dr. Thomas Thomson: "for his researches in the Western Himalayas and Thibet".
     W. Chandless: "for his Survey of the River Purus [South America]".

1867   Admiral Alexis Boutakoff: "for being first to launch and navigate ships in the Sea of Aral . . . and for his survey of the mouths of the Oxus".
     Dr. Isaac Hayes: "for his expedition towards the open Polar Sea".

1868   Dr. Augustus Petermann: "for his important services as a Writer and Cartographer".
     Gerhard Rohlfs: "for his extensive travels in the interior of Northern Africa . . . and especially for his traverse of the continent from Tripoli to Lagos".

1869   Professor A. E. Nordenskiöld: "for designing and carrying out the Swedish expeditions to Spitzbergen . . . whereby great additions have been made to our acquaintance with zoology, botany, geology and meteorology".
     Mrs. Mary Somerville: "who throughout her very long life has been eminently distinguished by her proficiency in those branches of science which form the basis of Physical Geography".

1870   George W. Hayward: "for his journey into Eastern Turkistan, and for reaching the Pamir Steppe".
     Lieutenant Francis Garnier: "for his extensive surveys . . . from Cambodia to the Yang-tsze-Kiang . . . and for bringing his expedition to safety after the death of his chief".

1871   Sir Roderick Murchison: "who for 40 years watched over the Society with more than paternal solicitude, and has at length placed it among the foremost of our scientific Societies".
     A. Keith Johnson: "for distinguished services in the promotion of Physical Geography".

1872   Colonel Henry Yule: "for eminent services to Geography".
     Robert B. Shaw: "for Journeys in Eastern Turkistan, and for his extensive

astronomical and hypsometrical observations".

1873 Ney Elias: "for his enterprise and ability in surveying the course of the Yellow River, and for his journey through Western Mongolia".

Henry Morton Stanley: "for his Relief of Livingstone, and for bringing his valuable journal and papers to England".

1874 Dr. Georg Schweinfurth: "for his explorations in Africa".

Colonel P. Egerton Warburton: "for his successful journey across the previously unknown western interior of Australia".

1875 Lieutenant Karl Weyprecht: "for his enterprise and ability in command of expeditions to Spitzbergen and Nova Zembla".

Lieutenant Julius Payer: "for explorations and discoveries in the Arctic regions".

1876 Lieutenant Verney Lovett Cameron: "for his journey across Africa from Zanzibar to Benguela, and his survey of Lake Tanganyika".

John Forrest: "for his numerous successful explorations in Western Australia".

1877 Captain Sir George Nares: "for having commanded the Arctic Expedition of 1875/6, during which ships and sledge parties reached a higher Northern latitude than had previously been attained".

The Pundit Nain Singh: "for his great journeys and surveys in Tibet and along the Upper Brahmaputra, during which he determined the position of Lhasa and added largely to our knowlwdge of the map of Asia".

1878 Baron F. von Richthofen: "for his extensive travels and scientific explorations in China".

Captain Henry Trotter: "for services to geography . . . which resulted in the connection of the Trigonometrical Survey of India with Russian Surveys from Siberia".

1879 Colonel N. Prejevalsky: "for successive expeditions and route-surveys in Mongolia and the high plateau of Northern Tibet".

Captain W. J. Gill: "for important work along the Northern frontier of Persia".

1880 Lieutenant A. Louis Palander: "for his services in connection with the Swedish Arctic Expeditions in the *Vega*".

Ernest Giles: "for his explorations and surveys in Australia".

1881 Major Serpa Pinto: "for his journey across Africa . . . during which he explored 500 miles of new country".

Benjamin Leigh Smith: "for important discoveries along the coast of Franz-Josef Land".

1882 Dr. Gustav Nachtigal: "for his journeys through the Eastern Sahara".

Sir John Kirk: "for unremitting services to geography, as a naturalist, as second-in-command to Dr. Livingstone, and as H.M. Consul-General at Zanzibar".

1883 Sir Joseph Hooker: "for eminent services to scientific geography".

E. Colborne Baber: "for scientific works during his many exploratory journeys in the interior of China".

1884 A. R. Colquhoun: "for his journey from Canton to the Irawadi".

Dr. Julius von Haast: "for his extensive explorations in the Southern Island of New Zealand".

1885 Joseph Thomson: "for his zeal, promptitude and success during two expeditions into East Central Africa".

H. E. O'Neill: "for his 13 journeys of exploration along the coast and into the interior of Mozambique".

1886 Major A. W. Greely: "for having so considerably added to our knowledge of the shores of the Polar Sea and the interior of Grinnell Land".

Guido Cora: "for important services as a writer and cartographer".

1887 Lieutenant-Colonel T. H. Holdich: "for zeal and devotion in carrying out surveys of Afghanistan".

Rev. G. Grenfell: "for extensive explorations in the Cameroons and Congo".

1888 Clements R. Markham: "in acknowledgment of the value of his numerous contributions to geographical literature . . . on his retirement from the Secretaryship of the Society after 25 years' service".

Lieutenant H. Wissmann: "in recognition of his great achievements as an explorer in Central Africa".

1889 A. D. Carey: "for his remarkable journey in Central Asia during which he travelled 4,750 miles through regions never visited by an Englishman".

Dr. G. Radde: "for a life devoted to the promotion of Scientific Geography".

1890 Emin Pasha: "for the great services he rendered to Geography during his twelve years' administration of the Equatorial Province of Egypt".

Lieutenant F. E. Younghusband: "for his journey from Manchuria and Pekin to Kashmir, and especially for his route-surveys and topographical notes".

1891 Sir James Hector: "for investigations pursued as Naturalist to the Palliser expedition".

Dr. Fridtjof Nansen: "for having been first to cross the inland ice of Greenland . . . as well as for his qualities as a scientific geographer".

1892 Alfred Russel Wallace, "the well-known naturalist and traveller and co-discoverer with Charles Darwin of the theory of natural selection, in recognition of the high geographical value of his great works".

Edward Whymper: "for his route-map and detailed survey among the Great Andes of the Equator".

1893 Frederick Selous: "in recognition of twenty years' exploration and surveys in South Africa".

W. Woodville Rockhill: "for his travels and explorations in Western China and Tibet".

1894 Captain H. Bower: "for his remarkable journey across Tibet, from west to east".

Elisée Reclus: "for eminent services rendered to geography as the author of *Nouvelle Géographie Universelle*".

1895 Dr. John Murray: "for services to physical geography, especially oceanography, and for his work on board the *Challenger*".

The Hon. George Curzon: "for travels and researches in Persia, French Indo-China, the Hindu Kush, and Pamirs".

1896 Sir William MacGregor: "for services to geography in British New Guinea, in exploring, mapping and giving information on the natives".

St. George Littledale: "for important journeys in the Pamirs and Central Asia".

1897 P. Semenoff: "for his long-continued efforts in promoting Russian exploration in Central Asia".

Dr. George M. Dawson: "for exploration in the North West Territories and Alaska".

1898 Dr. Sven Hedin: "for important exploring work in Central Asia".

Lieutenant R. E. Peary, USN: "for explorations in Northern Greenland, and especially for discovering the northern termination of the Greenland ice".

1899 Captain G. L. Binger: "for valuable work within the great bend of the Niger".

Fernand Foureau: "for continuous exploration in the Sahara".

1900 Captain H. H. P. Deasy: "for exploring and survey work in Central Asia".

James McCarthy: "for great services to geographical science in exploring and mapping all parts of the kingdom of Siam".

1901 H.R.H. The Duke of the Abruzzi: "for his journey to the summit of Mount St. Elias, and for his Arctic voyage in the *Stella Polare*".

Dr. Donaldson Smith: "for memorable journeys across the unknown parts of Lake Rudolf and the Omo".

1902 General Sir Frederick Lugard: "for persistent attention to African geography".

Major Molesworth Sykes: "for journeys in Persia and for the support given by him to native explorers".

1903 Douglas Freshfield: "in recognition of his valuable contributions to our knowledge of the Caucasus".

Captain Otto Sverdrup: "for important discoveries in Jones Sound and for the important part he played as captain of the *Fram* during Dr. Nansen's famous expedition".

1904 Sir Harry Johnston: "for his many valuable services towards the exploration of Africa".

Commander Robert Scott: "for services as leader of the National Antarctic Expedition, and for his great sledge journey to 82° 17′S".

1905 Sir Martin Conway: "for explorations in the mountain regions of Spitsbergen".

Captain C. H. D. Ryder: "for his survey of Yunnan and his work in connection with the Tibet Mission".

1906 Alfred Grandidier: "the veteran French savant who for forty years has devoted himself to the exploration of Madagascar, and for his monumental work on the island in 52 large quarto volumes".

Dr. Robert Bell: "who during forty-five years of field work has mapped an immense area of Canada previously unknown".

1907 Dr. Francisco Moreno: "for extensive explorations in the Patagonian Andes".

Captain Roald Amundsen: "for his daring voyage for purposes of research in the region of the North Magnetic Pole, and for his first accomplishment by any vessel of the famous North-West Passage".

1908 Lieutenant Boyd Alexander: "for his three years' journey across Africa from the Niger to the Nile".

H.S.H. The Prince of Monaco: "for oceanographical studies off the coast of Spitsbergen".

1909 Dr. M. A. Stein: "for his extensive explorations in Central Asia, and in particular his archaeological work".

Colonel M. G. Talbot: "for the large amount of excellent survey-work done by him on the Afghan frontier and in the Sudan".

1910 Colonel H. H. Godwin-Austen: "for geographical discoveries and surveys along the North-eastern frontier of India, especially his pioneer exploring in the Karakoram".

Dr. William Speirs Bruce: "for explorations in the Arctic and Antarctic".

1911 Colonel P. K. Kozloff: "for explorations in the Gobi desert, Northern Tibet and Mongolia".

Dr. J. B. Charcot: "for his important expeditions to the Antarctic, during which he conducted investigations of high scientific value in geology, meteorology, magnetic conditions and biology".

1912 Charles M. Doughty: "for his remarkable exploration in Northern Arabia, and for his classic work in which the results were described".

Douglas Carruthers: "for important expeditions to Ruwenzori, Turkestan, Arabia and Mongolia".

1913 The Founder's Medal was not awarded, but an inscribed casket was presented to Lady Scott containing the Patron's Medal and the Special Antarctic Medal awarded to her late husband.

The late Dr. E. A. Wilson: "for his excellent work in the study of the zoology of the Antarctic . . . and for his skill as an artist".

1914 Professor Albrecht Penck: "for his advancement of almost every branch of scientific geography, and in particular his idea of an International map of the world on the millionth scale".

Dr. Hamilton Rice: "for his meritorious work on the head waters of the Orinoco and the Northern tributaries of the Amazon".

1915 Sir Douglas Mawson: "for his conduct of the Australian Antarctic Expedition which achieved highly important scientific results".

Dr. Filippo de Filippi: "for his great expedition to the Karakoram and Eastern Turkestan".

1916 Colonel P. H. Fawcett: "for his contributions to the mapping of South America".

Captain F. M. Bailey: "for explorations on the border of India and Tibet . . . and especially for tracing the course of the Tsang-po-Brahmaputra".

Gold Medallists who won awards for their work in the Arctic and Antarctic: (above) Sir Douglas Mawson (1882–1958); (centre) Dr. Knud Rasmussan (1879–1934) and (below) Sir Vivian Fuchs (1908–)

1917   Commander D. G. Hogarth: "for explorations in Asiatic Turkey".
    Brigadier-General C. G. Rawling: "for explorations in Western Tibet and New Guinea".

1918   Gertrude Bell: "for her important explorations and travels in Asia Minor, Syria, Arabia and on the Euphrates".
    Commandant J. Tilho: "for his long-continued surveys and explorations in Northern Africa".

1919   Colonel E. M. Jack: "for his geographical work on the Western Front".
    Professor William Davis: "for his eminence in the development of Physical Geography".

1920   H. St. John B. Philby: "for his two journeys in South-Central Arabia".
    Professor Jovan Cvijic: "for his distinguished studies of the geography of the Balkan Peninsula".

1921   Vilhjalmur Stefansson: "for his distinguished services in the exploration of the Arctic Ocean".
    General R. Bourgeois: "for long and eminent services to geography and geodesy".

1922   Colonel C. K. Howard-Bury: "for his distinguished services in command of the Mount Everest Expedition".
    E. de Kovan Leffingwell: "for surveys and investigations on the coast of Northern Alaska".

1923   Dr. Knud Rasmussen: "for exploration and research in the Arctic regions".
    The Hon. Miles Cater Smith: "for explorations in the unknown interior of Papua".

1924   Ahmed Hassanein Bey: "for his journey to Kutara and Darfur".
    Commander Frank Wild: "for his long services to Antarctic exploration".

1925   Brigadier-General C. G. Bruce: "for lifelong geographical work in the exploration of the Himalaya . . . and his leadership of the Mount Everest Expedition of 1922".
    A. F. R. Wollaston: "for his journeys in Central Africa and Dutch New Guinea".

1926   Colonel E. F. Norton: "for his distinguished leadership of the Mount Everest Expedition, 1924, and his ascent to 28,100 feet".
    Sir Edgeworth David: "for his work on the Funafuti atoll and for his leadership of the first ascent of Mount Erebus".

1927   Major Kenneth Mason: "for his connection between the surveys of India and Russian Turkestan, and his leadership of the Shakshagam Expedition".
    Dr. Lauge Koch: "for his very remarkable six years' exploration of Northern Greenland".

1928   Dr. Tom Longstaff: "for long-continued geographical work in the Himalaya".
    Captain G. H. Wilkins: "for his many years' systematic work in Polar Regions, culminating in his remarkable flight from Point Barrow to Spitsbergen".

1929   Francis Rennell Rodd: "for his journeys in the Sahara and his studies of the Tuareg people".
    C. H. Karius: "for his crossing in Papua from the Fly River to the Sepik".

1930   F. Kingdom Ward: "for geographical exploration, and work on botanical distribution in China and Tibet".
    Carsten E. Borchgrevink: "for his pioneer Antarctic Expedition, which was the first to winter in the Antarctic, to travel on the Ross Barrier and to obtain proof of its recession".

1931   Bertram Thomas: "for geographical work in Arabia and his successful crossing of the Rub al Khali".
    Rear Admiral Richard E. Byrd, USN: "for his expedition to the Antarctic . . . and for his flights over both North and South Poles".

1932   Henry George Watkins: "for his work in the Arctic Regions, especially as leader of the British Arctic Air Route Expedition".
    H.R.H. the Duke of Spoleto: "for work in the Himalaya".

1933   J. M. Wordie: "for work in Polar exploration".
      Professor Erich von Drygalski: "for researches in glaciology in the Arctic and Antarctic".

1934   Hugh Ruttledge: "for his journeys in the Himalayas and his leadership of the Mount Everest Expedition, 1933".
      Captain Ejnar Mikkelsen: "for exploration in the Arctic and his work in Eskimo resettlement in Greenland".

1935   Major R. A. Bagnold: "for journeys in the Libyan Desert".
      W. Rickmer Rickmers: "for long-continued travels in the Caucasus, culminating in his leadership of the Alai-Pamir Russo-German Expedition of 1928".

1936   G. W. Murray: "for explorations and surveys in the deserts of Sinai and Eastern Egypt, and his studies of the Badawin tribes".
      Major R. E. Cheesman: "for explorations and surveys of the Blue Nile and Lake Tana".

1937   Colonel C. G. Lewis: "for surveys in Iraq, Syria and the Irrawaddy Delta, and for his work on the Afghan and Turco-Iraq Boundary Commissions".
      Lincoln Ellsworth: "for his work in developing the technique of aerial navigation in the Polar regions, culminating in his successful flight across the Antarctic".

1938   John Rymill: "for the valuable scientific work of his British Graham Land Expedition".
      Eric Shipton: "for his most distinguished record of mountain climbing".

1939   Arthur M. Champion: "for his surveys of the Turkana Province [Kenya] and the volcanoes south of Lake Rudolf".
      Professor Hans Ahlmann: "for exploration and glaciological studies in the Arctic".

1940   Mr. and Mrs. Harold Ingrams: "for exploration and studies in the Hadhramaut".
      Lieutenant Alexander Glen: "for his expeditions in Spitsbergen and North-East Land".

1941   Captain P. A. Clayton: "for his surveys in the Libyan desert, and his application of his experience to desert warfare".
      Dr. Isaiah Bowman: "for his travels in South America and for his great services to the science of Geography".

1942   Freya Stark: "for her travels in the East and her account of them".
      Owen Lattimore: "for his travels and studies in Central Asia".

1943   No medals awarded.

1944   No medals awarded.

1945   Dr. Charles Camsell: "for his contributions to the geology of the Canadian North".
      Sir Halford J. Mackinder: "for his long and distinguished service in the advancement of the science of geography".

1946   Brigadier Edward A. Glennie: "for his work on geodesy in India and his contributions to mapping in the Far East".
      Inspector Henry A. Larsen, RCMP: "for his achievement of the North West Passage from both west to east and east to west".

1947   Brigadier M. Hotine: "for research work in Air Survey . . . and for his cartographic work".
      Colonel Daniel van der Meulen: "for exploratory journeys in the Hadhramaut, and his contributions to the geography of Southern Arabia".

1948   Wilfred Thesiger: "for contributions to the geography of Southern Arabia and for his crossing of the Rub al Khali desert".
      Thomas H. Manning: "for exploration and survey work in the Canadian Arctic".

1949   Professor L. Dudley Stamp: "for his work in organising the Land Utilisation Survey of Great Britain and his application of geography to National planning".
      Professor Hans Pettersson: "for his leadership of the recent oceanographical cruise in the *Albatross*".

Great explorers of the desert: Gold Medallists Wilfred Thesiger and Dame Freya Stark

Two great explorers of mountains: Gold Medallists (above) Eric Shipton; (below) Sir Edmund Hillary

(On the facing page) *Some of the Society's Gold and Special Medals*

1950   George F. Walpole: "for contributions to the mapping of the Western Desert of Egypt".

Professor Harald Sverdrup: "for contributions to polar exploration and for oceanographical investigations".

1951   Dr. Vivian E. Fuchs: "for his contributions to Antarctic exploration and his research as leader of the Survey 1948–50".

Dr. Donald Thomson: "for geographical exploration and studies in Arnhem Land".

1952   H. W. Tilman: "for exploratory work among the mountains of East Africa and Central Asia".

Paul-Emile Victor: "for contributions to Polar exploration and for his geophysical investigations of the Greenland Icecap".

1953   P. D. Baird: "for explorations in the Canadian Arctic".

Count Eigil Knuth: "for explorations in Northern Greenland . . . and for his contributions to Eskimo archaeology".

1954   Brigadier Sir John Hunt: "Leader of the British Mount Everest Expedition".

Dr. N. A. Mackintosh: "for research and exploration in the Southern Ocean".

1955   Dr. John K. Wright: "for services in the development of geographical research and exploration".

Commander C. J. W. Simpson: "leader of the British Expedition to North Greenland".

1956   John Giaever: "leader of the Norwegian–British–Swedish Antarctic Expedition, for contributions to Polar exploration".

Charles Evans: "for contributions to Himalayan exploration".

1957   Professor Ardito Desio: "for geographical exploration and surveys in the Himalayas".

Sir George Binney: "for contributions to Arctic exploration . . . the pioneer use of air survey technique . . . and to the development of the university exploring expedition".

1958   Dr. Paul A. Siple: "for contributions to Antarctic exploration and research".

Sir Edmund Hillary: "for Antarctic and Himalayan exploration".

1959   Commander W. R. Anderson, USN: "for the first trans-Polar submarine voyage in command of USS *Nautilus*".

Sir Raymond Priestly: "for services to Antarctic exploration".

1960   Professor Theodore Monod: "for geographical exploration and research in the Sahara".

Phillip G. Law: "for Antarctic exploration and research".

1961   Dr. Mikhail M. Somov: "for Polar exploration and research".

Dr. John Bartholomew: "Editor *The Times Atlas of the World*, for contributions to cartography".

1962   Captain Erwin McDonald, USN: "for coastal explorations in the Bellingshausen Sea [Antarctica]".

Tom Harrisson: "Government Ethnologist and Curator Sarawak Museum, for explorations in Central Borneo".

1963   Captaine Jacques-Yves Cousteau: "for underwater exploration and research".

Dr. Albert P. Crary: "for Antarctic research and exploration".

1964   Dr. L. S. B. Leakey: "for palaeographical exploration and discoveries in East Africa".

1965   Dr. E. F. Rootes: "for Polar exploration and research, with special reference to the Canadian Arctic".

Professor Lester C. King: "for geomorphological exploration in the Southern Hemisphere".

1966   Professor E. J. H. Corner: "for botanical exploration in North Borneo and the Solomon Islands".

Dr. G. Hattersley-Smith: "for glaciological investigations in the Canadian Arctic".

1967   Claudio and Orlando Vilas Boas: "for contributions to exploration and

development in the Mato Grosso".
    Professor Eduard Imhof: "for contributions to cartography".

1968 Dr. W. Brian Harland: "for Arctic exploration and research".
    Professor Augusto Gansser: "for geological exploration and mapping in the Himalaya".

1969 Rear Admiral Rodolfo N. M. Panzarini: "for services to Antarctic exploration and research and to international co-operation in Antarctic science".
    Drs. R. Thorsteinsson and E. T. Tozer: "for contributions to exploration and economic development in the Canadian Arctic".

1970 Walter William Herbert: "for Arctic and Antarctic exploration and surveys".
    Dr. Haroun Tazieff: "for volcanological research and exploration".

1971 Sir George Deacon: "for oceanographical research and exploration".
    Dr. Charles Swithinbank: "for glaciological research and exploration".

1972 Rear Admiral G. S. Ritchie: "for hydrographical charting and oceanographical exploration".
    Dr. M. D. Gwynne: "leader, the RGS's South Turkana [Kenya] Expedition".

1973 N. L. Falcon: "leader, the RGS's Musandam [North Oman] Expedition. For contributions to the geographical history of the Persian Gulf region".
    Professor E. H. Thompson: "professor of photogrammetry and surveying, University College London".

1974 Christian J. S. Bonington: "for mountain explorations".
    Gordon de Q. Robin: "for polar research and exploration".

1975 Sir Laurence Kirwan: "for contributions to the geographical history of the Nubian Nile valley and Eastern Africa, and for services to exploration".
    Dr. J. P. Kuettner: "for explorations of the Earth's atmosphere and oceans".

1976 Dr. Brian B. Roberts: "for Polar exploration, and for contributions to Antarctic research and political negotiation".
    Rear Admiral Sir Edmund Irving: "for services as Hydrographer of the Navy and for his encouragement of exploration".

1977 Professor Michael Wise: "for economic geography, and for his contributions to international understanding in geographical teaching".
    Professor Kenneth Hare: "for discoveries in Arctic geography".

1978 Major-General R. Brown: "for services to the science of map making".
    Professor Miezyslaw Klimaszewski: "for his contributions to geomorphology and international understanding in geography".

1979 Dr. David Stoddart: "for contributions to geomorphology, the study of coral reefs and the history of academic geography".
    Robin Hanbury-Tenison: "for leadership of scientific expeditions, including the Mulu Expedition, and for his work on behalf of primitive peoples".

(On the facing page)
The old way of travelling –
Wally Herbert's "rough
sledging over polar ice".
And the new – Jeremy
Sutton-Pratt's "Hercules
aircraft at McMurdo Sound
about to take off for the
Pole"

The Victoria Medal

This originated in 1902, "in memory of the late Queen, when the Council decided that a medal be awarded from time to time for research in the various departments of geography, but only when a candidate of sufficiently high standard is available." This is the only one of the Society's medals to be given specifically for scientific research, and it is not unusual for the award to be made biannually. Recipients have been:

1902	E. G. Ravenstein	1950	Prof. Emmanuel de Martonne
1903	Dr. Sven Hedin	1951	Dr. C. A. Cotton
1905	John George Bartholomew	1953	Prof. Sir John Myres
1906	Prof. W. M. Ramsay	1955	Sir John Russell
1909	Prof. Alexander Agassiz	1957	Prof. S. W. Wooldridge
1911	Capt. H. G. Lyons	1958	Prof. Roberto Almagia
1912	Sir George H. Darwin	1959	Mr. Gerald Seligman
1913	Colonel S. G. Burrard	1960	Dr. Armando Cortesao and
1915	Dr. Hugh Robert Mill		Prof. J. A. Steers
1917	Dr. John Scott Keltie	1961	Prof. W. William-Olsson
1919	Prof. J. W. Gregory	1962	Prof. Carl Troll
1920	Lt.-Col. H. S. L. Winterbotham	1963	Prof. H. C. Darby
1922	J. F. Baddeley	1964	J. N. L. Baker
1924	J. F. Hayford	1965	Prof. Henri Marcel Gaussen
1926	Dr. John Ball	1966	G. R. Crone
1927	Col. Sir Charles F. Close	1967	C. W. Phillips
1928	E. A. Reeves	1968	Dr. Walter Christaller
1930	Emmanuel de Margerie	1969	Prof. M. Aurousseau
1932	Prof. A. P. Coleman	1970	Dr. R. A. Skelton
1934·	Edward Heawood	1971	Prof. O. H. K. Spate
1935	E. J. Wayland	1972	Prof. G. H. J. Daysh
1936	Dr. Stanley Kemp	1973	Prof. E. Estyn Evans
1938	Arthur R. Hinks	1974	Prof. C. A. Fisher
1940	O. G. S. Crawford	1975	Prof. Carl. O. Sauer
1942	Dr. Harold Jeffreys	1976	Prof. J. N. Jennings
1946	Prof. H. J. Fleure	1977	Prof. Emrys Jones
1947	Prof. E. G. R. Taylor	1978	Dr. T. E. Armstrong
1948	Prof. Frank Debenham	1979	Prof. T. Hägerstrand

Special Medals

1890　H. M. Stanley. Special Gold Medal – "for his journey across Africa for the relief of Emin Pasha, and for the geographical results obtained."

1897　Dr. Fridtjof Nansen. Special Gold Medal – "for his expedition across the North

1968   Sir Francis Chichester. Special Gold Medal – "for sailing single-handed round the world, and for the encouragement his historic exploit has given to the pioneering spirit among young people."

1970   Neil Armstrong. Special Gold Medal – "leader of the Apollo 11 Expedition, and the first man to stand on the surface of the moon . . . for space exploration."

Appendix III

Principal Expeditions Aided by the Society

If the word "aid" is used in its broadest sense then the Society has aided well over a thousand expeditions, and the explorers and scientists it has supported have added to our knowledge of almost every country on earth. It is not practicable to list all these expeditions. The following selection includes only those projects to which the Society contributed money or equipment, and which carried out important new exploration or research.

Back's expedition crossing Lake Aylmer in the Canadian Arctic, 1833

1832	Back's Arctic Land Expedition: discovery of Great Fish River and key section of North West Passage.
1833	Biscoe's Antarctic Voyage in the *Tula*: early sighting of Graham Land, discovery of Enderby Land.
1834–1839	Schomburgk's Guiana Expeditions: first detailed survey of topography, botany and geology of British Guiana.
1836–1838	Alexander's South African Expedition: safari through Cape Province and Namibia.
1837	Grey's Australian Expedition: abortive attempts to survey Hanover and Shark Bays.
1838–1840	Ainsworth's Kurdistan Expedition: travels on the Turkish-Iranian border to contact Nestorian Christians.
1842	Beke's Abyssinian Expedition: research work in Shoa, and exploration of Blue Nile.
1843	Symond's Palestinian Survey: level of Dead Sea ascertained.
1847–1855	The Society helped to launch many expeditions during the search for Franklin: especially important were the land journeys of Richardson and Rae, and the voyages of Ross (*Enterprise*), Collinson (*Enterprise*), McClure (*Investigator*), Austin (*Intrepid*), and McClintock (*Fox*).
1851	Brunner's New Zealand Expedition: first survey of Southern Alps.
1852	Wallin's Arabian Expedition: first crossing of the Arabian desert.
1853	Livingstone's African Expedition: first crossing of the continent. The world awakened to the evils of the slave trade.
1855	Barth's North African Expedition: first crossing of the North Sahara; detailed study of topography and history of the area around Lake Chad.
1856	Burton's Search for the Source of the Nile: discovery of Lake Tanganyika, and Speke's first sighting of Lake Victoria.
1856	Gregory's North Australian Expedition: a 6,500-mile survey of the hinterland of North Australia.

The Discovery *in her winter quarters. Nares' Arctic Expedition, 1876*

Stanley watching a phalanx dance by Mazambodi's warriors, 1888

1860–1861	Speke's Search for the Source of the Nile: first sighting of primary source at Ripon Falls, and the first expedition to follow the river – albeit intermittently – from source to mouth.
1863	Baker's Search for the Source of the Nile: discovery of Lake Albert as a secondary feeder of the White Nile.
1865	Livingstone's Search for the Source of the Nile: extensive travels around Lake Tanganyika and the headwaters of the Congo.
1866	Chandless's South American Expedition: exploration of River Purus and first mapping of the South Amazon basin.
1866–1872	Livingstone Relief Expedition: extensive travels in central Africa by Young, Stanley, Grady and Cameron. Stanley's magnificent exploits as an explorer tarnished by his massacre of the natives.
1869	Hayward's East Turkestan Expedition: journeys to the semi-legendary cities of Kashgar and Yarkand on the Chinese-Tibetan border.
1870	Wilson and Palmer survey the Sinai Peninsula.
1872	Mauch's South African Expedition: discovery of the Zimbabwe goldfields.
1873	Elias's Chinese Expedition: traces course of Yellow River.
1874	Trotter's Pamír Expedition: discovery of source of Oxus (Amu) River; work of Indian and Russian Surveys connected.
1876	Nares's Arctic Expedition: attainment of Markham's "farthest north".
1877–1880	Johnston and Thomson survey of the drainage system of Lakes Nyasa and Tanganyika: a little-known highly-successful expedition, very different from Stanley's in that its leader was "never once obliged to fire a gun".
1882	*Eira* Relief Expedition: rescue of Leigh-Smith and his crew after loss of their vessel off Franz Josef Land.
1883	Thomson's East African Expedition: first geological survey of the Great Rift Valley.
1885	Forbes's New Guinea Expedition: the Society's first venture to an island where it was to do much valuable work.
1887–1888	Emin Bey Relief Expedition: Stanley's epic west-east journey across the continent leads to the final mapping of equatorial Africa and the River Nile. Presentation of the Society's first Special Medal.
1888–1898	Asia Minor Exploration Fund provided numerous grants to Ramsay, Maunsell, Hogarth, Paton, Green, Bent, Wilson and others, for geological survey work.
1889	Freshfield's Caucasus Expedition: first recognition of mountaineering as an adjunct of geographical research.
1891	Conway's Karakoram Expedition: the Society's first major mountaineering venture in the Himalaya.
1892	Bruce's Antarctic whaling voyage in the *Balaena* and *Active* heralds a revival of interest in the Antarctic.
1893	Nansen's Polar Expedition: in spite of misgivings, the Society makes a small contribution to the proposed drift of the *Fram* across the Arctic Ocean. The outstanding success of this expedition led in 1896 to the presentation of the Society's second Special Medal.
1895–1897	Conway's Spitsbergen Expeditions: first use of the sub-Arctic islands as a training ground for young explorers; first crossing of the island.
1897	Forbes's Expedition to Socotra: first attempt to classify the island's *flora* and *fauna*.
1899–1902	British National Antarctic Expedition. In the face of government apathy, Markham raises nearly £50,000 to build and equip the *Discovery*. Scott

spends three years in Antarctica in charge of a team of explorer-scientists. Perhaps the most important and successful expedition ever launched by the Society – the scientific data brought back contains as much material as the *Encyclopaedia Britannica*. Scott awarded the Society's third Special Medal.

1906–1907   Mikkelsen's Arctic Expeditions: extensive journeys in Canadian Arctic and North Greenland.

1908–1909   Shackleton's Farthest South: the *Nimrod* Expedition: determined attempt to reach the South Pole. In one of the greatest journeys ever made, Shackleton fails by less than 100 miles to reach his goal: is awarded the fourth of the Society's Special Medals.

1910–1912   Scott's *Terra Nova* Expedition: a privately organized expedition to which the Society donated £850, but had no part in organizing. Scott's divided objective – part scientific and part exploratory – and his dislike of using dogs, leads to the tragedy of his and his companions' death on their return from the Pole.

1912–1913   Mawson's Australian Expedition: accurate location of South Magnetic Pole and extensive scientific programme.

1913–1915   De Filippi's Himalayan Expedition: traced course of Yarland River, connected work of Indian and Russian-Turkestan surveys.

1914–1916   Shackleton's Trans-Antarctic Expedition: the first abortive attempt to cross the continent. Loss of the *Endurance* leads to Shackleton's famous voyage from Elephant Island to South Georgia to rescue his crew, probably the greatest small-boat journey ever made.

During the years 1916–24 the Society sponsored only a couple of Everest expeditions. This was partly because of the war, and partly because, in 1920, one of the Society's accounts clerks absconded with a large part of its funds!

Shackleton's dogs watch the Endurance *breaking up in the Antarctic pack-ice, 1915*

1921   Howard-Bury's reconnaissance of Mount Everest. Successful pioneering of the most practicable route up the north face of the mountain via the Rongbuk Glacier). Height attained 23,000 feet. Accurate and valuable survey of surrounding peaks.

1922   Bruce's first full-scale assault on the summit. Height attained 27,300 feet. The formidable nature of the mountain, especially its last 2,000 feet, now made apparent.

1924   Norton's "near-success" on Everest. He and Somerville achieve 28,000 feet, and Mallory and Irvine probably a few hundred feet higher before falling to their death.

1924   Fawcett's Expedition to Brazil. The Society agrees to sponsor Fawcett in spite of misgivings over his aims – misgivings vindicated by the explorer's subsequent disappearance and death.

1924   Oxford University Exploration Club Expedition to Spitsbergen: first scientific study of the Svalbard Archipelago.

1926   Mason's Expedition to Shaksgam: first detailed survey of the Karakoram on the borders of India and China.

1928   Steers and Spender explore the Great Barrier Reef: first major study of coral formations.

1930–1931   Watkins and Courtauld survey Greenland and the Canadian Arctic for the proposed Arctic Air Route. Courtauld spends seven months manning a polar meteorological station alone.

1933   Thesiger crosses the Danakil Desert in Abyssinia: one of the last great solo journeys of discovery and self-discovery.

1933   Ruttledge's Expedition to Everest. Harris and Wager and Shipton and

	Smythe reach 28,100 feet, but are defeated by bad weather and the technical difficulties of the final 1,000 feet of the summit ridge.
1934	Rymill's Antarctic Expedition: the establishment of scientific posts for permanent study; first detailed survey of Graham Land.
1935	Kingdon Ward's botanical survey of the little-known area on the borders of Assam and Tibet.
1935	Shipton's reconnaissance of Everest to investigate the possibility of new routes and a monsoon or post-monsoon assault. Useful work on the mountain, and the climbing of 26 peaks all over 20,000 feet.
1936	Ruttledge's second Expedition to Everest: a large-scale assault thwarted at 23,000 feet by exceptionally bad weather.
1937	Freya Stark's travels in Hadhramaut: an arduous and dangerous journey through a little-known part of the Arabian Desert.
1938	Tilman's Expedition to Everest: a small informal group of dedicated climbers reach 27,200 feet in spite of appalling weather. Shipton and Smythe's assault on the summit defeated by impossible snow conditions.
1938	Kennedy Shaw's topographical survey of Libyan desert routes and oasis. Pioneer use of mechanized transport in desert travel.
1949–1950	Tilman's two expeditions to Nepal. Extensive botanical collection by Oleg Polunin, and valuable reconnaissance of the Southern approaches to Everest.
1950–1951	John Giaever's joint Norwegian/British/Swedish expedition to Queen Maud Land, Antarctica: detailed ice studies: extensive use of aerial reconnaissance.
1952–1954	British North Greenland Expedition (Commander C. J. W. Simpson). First detailed scientific study of North Greenland. Extensive use of air and land mechanized transport. Largest British Polar expedition for 40 years.
1954	Duncan Carse's study of South Georgia: amendments to existing maps. John Heaney's survey of Gough Island: establishment of weather station; scientific programme, including study of seal population.
1956	Wilfred Thesiger's exploration of the little-known Hindu Kush: valuable surveying and botanical collecting.
1957–1958	Commonwealth Trans-Antarctic Expedition. First crossing of Antarctica by Fuchs and Hillary. Extensive use of mechanized transport: valuable scientific research. An expedition initiated, organized, administered and financed almost entirely by the Society.
1961	John Tyson's mapping of the Kanjiroba Himal, the least-known mountain group in the Nepal Himalaya.
1967–1969	Wally Herbert's Trans-Arctic Expedition: first crossing on foot of Arctic Ocean: "one of the most skilful and physically-demanding journeys ever made".
1967–1969	Royal Society/RGS Mato Grosso Expedition (Dr. Iain Bishop); detailed analysis of an ecology about to be obliterated: exhaustive biological, anthropological and medical studies.
1968–1970	South Turkana (Kenya) Expedition: detailed studies of the pastoral economy of Turkana, and the unique fish and crocodile population of Lake Rudolf.
1971	Norman Falcon's Musandam (North Oman) Expedition: geological and hydrographical studies.
1974–1976	Douglas Shearman's Iranian-Makran expedition: detailed study of the area's rock structure.

1977–1978   RGS Mulu (Sarawak) Expedition (Robin Hanbury-Tenison): extensive science programme. Management plan formulated for the forest's conservation. The Society's largest-ever expedition.

Bibliography

The basic material for the story of the Society is in:-
The Minutes and Annual Reports of the Council
The Proceedings of the Royal Geographical Society
The Geographical Journal
The latter is especially valuable as a primary source for research.
The bibliography for almost every chapter could run to many pages. I have listed only those books and articles which I read and found especially useful.

1. The Founding of the Society
Books
The Fifty Years' Work of the R.G.S.: Sir Clements Markham: London 1880
The Record of the R.G.S.: H. R. Mill: London 1930

2. The Search for a North West Passage
Books
Narrative of a Voyage by Capt. Ross, 1829–33: Sir John Ross: London 1835
Narrative of the Arctic Land Expedition to the Mouth of the Great Fish River: Sir George Back: London 1836
Narrative of an Expedition in H.M.S. Terror: Sir George Back: London 1838
Arctic Exploration in Search of Sir John Franklin: E. K. Kane: New York 1877
The North West Passage: Roald Amundsen: London 1908
North-west to Fortune: Vihjalmur Stefansson: New York 1958
In Quest of the North West Passage: Leslie H. Neatby: London 1958
The Search for Franklin: Leslie H. Neatby: London 1970
The North West Passage: George Malcolm Thomson: London 1975
The Fate of Franklin: Ruderic Owen: London 1978

Articles
Voyages Through the North West Passage: *Polar Record*, 1944
The British Search for a Northwest Passage in the Eighteenth Century: *Imperial Studies*, 1962
Early Geographical Concepts of a Northwest Passage: *Cartographer* (Toronto), 1965
The Last Voyage of H.M.S. Investigator 1850/53: *Polar Record*, 1967

3. The Crossing of the Australian Deserts
Books
The Exploration of Australia, 1844–1896: A. F. Calvert: London 1896
Thomas Baines of King's Lynn, Artist and Explorer, 1820/75: J. P. R. Wallis: London 1941
The Sixth Continent: Arthur Scholes: London 1958
Australia, the Quiet Continent: Douglas Pike: London 1962
Cooper's Creek: Alan Moorehead: London 1963
The Inland Sea and the Great River: J. H. L. Cumpson: Australia 1964
Explorations in Australia (reprint): John Forrest: Australia 1969
The Discovery and Exploration of Australia (a fine book with valuable maps): E. H. J. Feeken and O. H. K. Spate: London 1971

A Continent Takes Shape: E. and E. Kunz: London 1972
To the Desert with Sturt: D. G. Brooke: Australia 1975
Thomas Baines: His Life and Explorations, 1820/75: J. P. R. Wallis: Cape Town 1976

Articles
The Gregory Brothers: *Queensland G. J.,* 1943
The Story of John Macdouall Stuart: *Walkabout,* 1957
The Victorian Exploring Expedition and Relieving Expeditions, 1860/61: *Victorian Hist. Mag.,* 1959
In the Steps of Burke and Wills: *Walkabout,* 1960
Sturt's Expedition of 1844–46: *R.G.S. Australia (S. Aust. br.)* 1963
The Enigma of Leichhardt: *Walkabout,* 1963

4. The Quest for the Sources of the Nile

Books

Missionary Travels and Researches in South Africa: David Livingstone: London 1857
The Lake Regions of Central Africa: Sir Richard Burton: London 1860
Journal of the Discovery of the Source of the Nile: J. H. Speke: London 1863
The Albert Nyanza: great basin of the Nile: Sir Samuel Baker: London 1866
The Last Journals of David Livingstone in Central Africa: ed. H. Waller: London 1874
Through the Dark Continent: Sir H. M. Stanley: London 1878
In Darkest Africa: Sir H. M. Stanley: London 1890
The Nile Quest: Sir Harry Johnston: London 1903
The Nile: Emil Ludwig: London 1936
The Nile Basin, showing Tanganyika to be Ptolemy's western lake reservoir, by Richard F. Burton. And Captain Speke's discovery of the Source of the Nile, by James Macqueen: original edition 1864, new edited edition 1967
The Long Walks: Frederick Bradnum: London 1969
The White Nile: Alan Moorehead: London 1971
Morning Star: Anne Baker: London 1972

Articles
The Discovery of the Victoria N'yanza (Speke): *Blackwoods Magazine,* 1859
Slavery and the Slave Trade: *Harper's Magazine,* 1893
Sir Richard Burton and the Nile Sources: *Eng. Hist. Review,* 1944
Notes on the exploration of the Sources of the Nile: *Tanganyika Notes Rec,* 1957
The Search for the Nile Sources by Dorothy Middleton: London 1972

5. The Conquest of the North Pole

Books

Narrative of a Voyage to the Polar Sea during 1875/76 in H.M. Ships Alert and Discovery: Sir George Nares: London 1878
The Voyage of the Vega: A. E. Nordenskjold: London 1881
Handbook of Arctic Discoveries: A. W. Greely: New York 1896
Farthest North: Fridtjof Nansen: London 1897
Nearest the Pole: Robert E. Peary: London 1907
The North Pole: Robert E. Peary: London 1910
My Attainment of the Pole: Frederick Cook: London 1911
The Lands of Silence: Sir Clements Markham: London 1921
Arctic and Antarctic: the Technique of Polar Travel: Colin Bertram: Cambridge 1939
The White Road: Sir Laurence Kirwan: London 1959
Man and the Conquest of the Poles: Paul-Emile Victor: London 1964
A History of Polar Exploration: David Mountfield: London 1974

Articles
How the North Pole Will be Reached: *Wide World Magazine,* 1898

Scurvy during some British Polar Expeditions, 1875–1917: *Polar Record*
Did Peary Reach the Pole? *J. Manchester G.S.*, 1924
John Rae's correspondence with the Hudson Bay Company on Arctic Exploration, 1844–1855: *The Hudson Bay Record Society*, 1953
Arctic Sledge Travelling by Officers of the Royal Navy (1819–1849): *Mariners' Mirror*, 1963

6. The Race for the South Pole

Books

A Voyage of Discovery and Research in the Southern and Antarctic Regions, 1839–1843: Sir James Clark Ross: London 1847
Antarktis: Dr. Karl Fricker: Berlin 1898
The Voyage of the Discovery: Robert Falcon Scott: London 1905
The Logs of S.S. Discovery: Robert Falcon Scott: unpublished MS
Through the First Antarctic Night: Frederick Cook: London 1905
The Heart of the Antarctic: Sir Ernest Shackleton: London 1910
The South Pole: Roald Amundsen: London 1912
Scott's Last Expedition: ed. Huxley: London 1913
South: Sir Ernest Shackleton: London 1919
The Great White South: H. G. Ponting: London 1922
Explorers of the Antarctic: W. H. Hobbs: New York 1941
The Crossing of Antarctica: Sir Vivian Fuchs and Sir Edmund Hillary: London 1958

Articles
Antarctic Research: *Nature*, 1898
Scientific Advantages of an Antarctic Expedition (contributors, Murray, Hooker, Nansen, Neumayer, Markham etc.): *Proceedings of the Royal Society*, 1889
The Antarctic Expedition: *Annual Report, Liverpool G.S.*, 1900
Antarctic Sledge Travelling by Sir Clements Markham
Recent Antarctic Exploration: *Quarterly Review*, 1906
Wilkes' Antarctic Discoveries: *Science*, 1911
Amundsen Answers his Critics: *The World's Work*, 1927
Antarctic Exploration: *J. Manchester G.S.*, 1938

7. The Discovery and Ascent of Everest

Books
The Historical Records of the Survey of India, Vols. I–V: R. H. Phillimore: Dehra Dun (India)
Himalayan Journals: Sir Joseph Hooker: London, 1854
A Memoir on the Indian Survey: Sir Clements Markham: London 1878
Climbing and Exploration in the Karakoram Himalayas: W. M. Conway: London 1894
The Heart of a Continent: Sir Francis Younghusband: London 1896
Mount Everest: the Reconnaissance: Lt. Col. G. K. Howard-Bury: London 1922
The Assault on Mount Everest: Brig. C. G. Bruce: London 1923
The Fight for Everest: Col. E. F. Norton: London 1925
Everest 1933 and *Everest: the Unfinished Adventure:* H. Ruttledge: London 1934, 1937
Everest: The Challenge: Sir Francis Younghusband
Mount Everest, 1938: H. W. Tilman: London 1939
Upon that Mountain, The Mount Everest Reconnaissance Expedition, 1951 and *That Untravelled World:* Eric Shipton: London 1943, 1952 and 1969
Abode of Snow: Kenneth Mason: London 1955
High Adventure: Sir Edmund Hillary: London 1955
The Ascent of Everest and *Life's Meeting:* Lord Hunt of Llanfair Waterdine, 1955 and 1978

Memorandum on the Everest Leadership for 1953; compiled from Notes made at the Various Committee Meetings by T. S. Blakeney, Assistant Sec. of the Alpine Club

8. The Educational Role of the Society

Books

Cosmos: A. von Humboldt: Berlin 1848
The Earth of Man: A Guyot: Paris 1862
Report of the Proceedings of the Society in Reference to the Improvement of Geographical Education: J. Scott Keltie: London 1886
Geography in Education and Citizenship: W. H. Baker: London 1927
Hints to Travellers: various editions, the latest London 1938
Scope and Methods of Geography and the Geographical Pivot of History: Sir Halford MacKinder: London 1951
A Hundred Years of Geography: T. W. Freeman: London 1961
A Traveller's Guide to Health: Col. J. M. Adam: London 1966
Geography for the Teacher: J. H. Wise: Brisbane (Australia) 1966
Modern Geographers: G. R. Crone: London 1970

Articles

Geographical Education – Report to the Council of the R.G.S.: *Supp. Papers R.G.S.,* 1886
Modern Geography: German and English: *G.J.,* 1895
The Oxford Report on Geography (MacKinder): *G.J.,* 1893, 1894, 1895, 1896 and 1898
The Progress of Geography in the Field and in the Study: *G.J.,* 1935
History, Geography and Social Studies (a summary of school programmes in 53 countries): *Unesco* (Paris) 1953
Geography and Technical Education: *Memo Prepared by the Education Committee of the R.G.S.,* 1958
Education and the New Geography: *Geography* (Sheffield), 1970

9. "Something more than scientific investigation"

Books

Across the River of Death: Jorgen Bisch: London 1958
The Heart of the Forest: Adrian Cowell: London 1960
Mato Grosso: Last Virgin Land: Anthony Smith: London 1971
Caves of Mulu: D. B. Brock and A. C. Waltham: London 1978

Articles
The Pantanal: *Unesco Courier* (Paris), 1970
Mato Grosso, R.G.S.'s Expedition: a symposium: *G.J.,* 1970
Science in Central Brazil: *G.J.,* 1972
The Musandam Peninsula and its People the Shihuh: *J. Cent. Asian Soc.,* 1929
Expedition to Unknown Musandam: *G. Mag.,* 1972
R.G.S. Expedition to Musandam, report on a marine geophysical survey: *Hunting Geology and Geophysics Ltd.,* 1972
The Musandam Expedition: *G.J.,* 1973
The Musandam Expedition, Scientific Results, parts I and II: *G.J.,* 1973 and 1974
Virgin Rain Forest of Sarawak: *G. Mag.,* 1978
The R.G.S. Expedition to Borneo: *Expedition,* 1978
Operation Rain Forest: *Illustrated London News,* 1979
R.G.S.'s Symposium on Gunung Mulu National Park: *Borneo Res. B.,* 1979
Caves in the Mulu Hills: *G. Mag.,* 1979
It Always Rains in Gunung Mulu: *G. Mag.,* 1979

Index

References in *italic* numerals are to illustrations.